The Complete Mediterranean Diet Cookbook for Beginners

1800 Days of Delicious & Healthy Mediterranean Recipes to Change Your Eating Lifestyle, 90-Day Meal Plan to Help You Build Healthy Habits

Rachel Cooper

TABLE OF CONTENTS

Brief History of Mediterranean Diet

The Mediterranean is outlined during the time spent central area float when Africa runs into Eurasia. The ensuing sea is of a size and a shape great to improve improvement. Over 10,000 km of coastline, around a fairly peaceful sea, with extensive harbors and different islands as sorting out posts, give an ideal setting to puzzling instances of trade, development, and battling - all of which energize a perspective of creative energy in human organizations.

An enormous piece of the extreme shore on the northern shore is a problematic scene. So the certifiable ability of the area expects the presence of sea boats.

Egyptians and Phoenicians: 2000-250 BC

The Egyptians have been trading by sea since around 2000 BC. Their business accessories are the Minoans in Crete and later the Phoenicians.

The Phoenicians, more than a few other marine people, open up the Mediterranean, laying out dealer settlements along its entire length. In this, they are in a little while, followed by the Greeks. An illustration of rival Phoenician and Greek areas on the islands and shores of the Mediterranean is well established by the fifth century BC. The third uncommon power of the period isn't yet in the field. Exactly when Rome began to take an interest, in the third hundred years, the situation changed rapidly.

Rome's secret sea: first century BC - 6th century AD

The opening between the underpinning of Rome's most essential region outside the focal area of Italy (Sicily in 241 BC) and Roman control of the entire Mediterranean is negligible for more than two centuries. With the expansion of Egypt in 30 BC, the Mediterranean turns out to be strangely one political unit - a tremendous lake inside a lone domain.

This current situation happened for quite a while until Germanic tribes moved around the western Mediterranean in the fifth century AD. This by and large important of seas will continue to expect a central part in humankind's arrangement of encounters, but at positively no point later on under bound together control. Genealogical strain from the north has been little by little fostering all through the prime of Rome.
Around the completion of the fifth hundred years, southern France and Spain are under the ownership of Visigoths. Lowlifes are spread out along the coastline of northwest Africa. For sure, even the eastern bank of Italy is regulated by Ostrogoth.
For quite a while, under Justinian in the 6th 100 years, the Roman domain reasserts control over Italy and North Africa. Regardless, the impression of a re-appearance of a bound-together Mediterranean shows duplicity. An unequivocal change occurs in the seventh 100 years, bringing to most of the Mediterranean shore one more culture that will win starting there until our own time - that of Islam.
An expanse of two religions: seventh - sixteenth 100 years
The discharge of the Arabs into world history in the seventh hundred years, with their dynamic new religion, changes the Mediterranean scene in a shockingly short period. Antioch in the upper east tumbles to the Muslims in 645; they are in Toledo, in the west, by 711.
The exceptional sea is, as of now, consistently split between Christianity and Islam. Anatolia on one side and Spain on the other become the division focuses along which, again and again, the two religions fight for an area. They, in like manner, look for the islands of the Mediterranean. Cyprus, Crete, and Sicily have become standard tourist spots.

From the twelfth 100 years, a fortune for quite a while slants toward the Christians. The crusaders spread out the Latin domain of Jerusalem. Barcelona, Genoa, Venice, and Constantinople manufacture wide trading domains in the Mediterranean, notwithstanding consistent risks from Muslim privateers.
Anyway, the Christians, partitioned, over the long haul, hurt their tendencies - most strikingly in the sack of Constantinople in 1204. Additionally, the incapacitated Byzantine area logically confronted one more Muslim risk from the Turks.
The Turks make reliable advances into A Christian region in the heartland of the Byzantine space. They won Anatolia and, a short time later, the Balkans previously, finally getting the honor of Constantinople itself in 1453.
During the following 100 years, the improvement of the Turks in and around the Mediterranean seems, by all accounts, to be steadfast. In 1516-17 Turkish military steered the Mameluke line of Egypt, bringing the entire eastern Mediterranean (the banks of Syria, Palestine, and Egypt) into the Ottoman domain. Some places were within reach, somewhere in the range between 1512 and 1574. Muslim privateers, with Ottoman assistance, secure the rest of North Africa for the rapidly creating domain.
The amazing islands lying off Turkey are, in like manner, brought into the Ottoman wrinkle. Rhodes was taken exactly on schedule in 1523, yet the Turkish assault on Cyprus in 1570 prompted a vivacious Christian response. A joint Spanish and Venetian task force beat the Turks unequivocally at Lepanto in 1571. It shows an unfilled victory. Only two years sometime later, in 1573, Venice gave the island over to Turkey. In any case, practically a century passed before the Turks,

in 1669, finally expelled the Venetians from another uncommon honor, Crete.

Of the island orchestrating presents on the east, so carefully accumulated by Venice, simply the Ionian get-together (counting Corfu, Cephalonia, and Zante) moves away from Turkish encroachment.

On the off chance that the Mediterranean gives off an impression of being a somewhat more settled sea after the clash of Lepanto in 1571, this is most of the way since it has lost a lot of its importance. For quite a while, this has been both the central expanse of western human progress and the trade associated with the abundance of the east; by and by, in the sixteenth hundred years, the point of convergence of gravity developments to the Atlantic coastline of Europe. America is the wellspring of untold new overflow from the west, and Portuguese aides have opened up a safer course through sea eastward.

The Mediterranean can never be a backwater. In any case, not until the send-off of the Suez channel will it recuperate its full and authentic status in the world.

What is Mediterranean Diet?

A Mediterranean eating routine is an approach to handling food that underlines plant-based food sources, including normal things, vegetables, entire grains, and nuts. It is low in red meat and high in fiber. It additionally contains moderate measures of fat from olive oil, rapeseed oil, and nuts.

The Mediterranean eating regimen has been related to a diminished gamble of coronary illness, type 2 diabetes, and weight. A few assessments have likewise demonstrated the way that it can add to mental prosperity by decreasing paces of melancholy and tension.

Main Benefits of the Mediterranean Diet

The Mediterranean eating regimen has been related to various medical advantages. Here is a portion of the fundamental ones:
Diminished hazard of coronary illness and stroke: The eating routine is low in immersed fat, which has been connected to coronary illness. It likewise contains a ton of fiber and cell reinforcements, the two of which assist with diminishing irritation in the body and further develop the bloodstream.
Further developed mindset and emotional wellness: Research shows that individuals who follow the Mediterranean eating routine will quite often have preferable psychological well-being results over the people who don't. The fundamental reasons are both the low measure of immersed fat in the eating routine (which is connected to wretchedness) as well as its elevated degrees of cell reinforcements, which assist with further developing a state of mind by diminishing irritation in the cerebrum.
More slow weight reduction: When individuals cut back on carbs and supplant them with protein-rich food varieties like fish, poultry, and eggs, they will generally get in shape more leisurely than on different sorts of diets (like Atkins). One investigation discovered that individuals who followed this kind of diet were 44% more outlandish than individuals following other famous eating regimens like Atkins or Weight Watchers to be overweight toward the finish of a half year!

Prevents Cardiovascular Diseases

Mediterranean weight control plans are related to a decreased gamble of coronary illness and stroke, as per

a review distributed in the Journal of the American Medical Association (JAMA).
Specialists found that more established grown-ups who stuck to a Mediterranean eating regimen (decreased fat admission, expanded fiber consumption, and frequently consumed fish) were 22% less inclined to be determined to have a coronary illness or stroke than the individuals who didn't stick to this dietary example. The investigation likewise discovered that more seasoned grown-ups who consumed more organic products, vegetables, and entire grains had a lower hazard of these circumstances; the individuals who consumed more red meat had an expanded gamble.
The specialists presumed that Mediterranean weight control plans are significant for forestalling cardiovascular infection.

Prevents Alzheimer's disease

A Mediterranean eating routine has been connected to a decreased gamble of Alzheimer's illness.
The review, led by the University of Eastern Finland and distributed in the Journal of Neurology, Neurosurgery, and Psychiatry, tried the impacts of a Mediterranean eating routine on individuals with gentle mental impedance.
The exploration group found that members who followed this sort of eating design had altogether lower levels of irritation and different markers of maturing than the people who didn't. A Mediterranean eating routine comprises mostly natural products, vegetables, vegetables, and seeds — all food sources that are high in cancer prevention agents that help safeguard against cell harm brought about by free extremists. The specialists likewise found that the people who ate a Mediterranean eating routine scored higher on tests

estimating their memory and figuring abilities than the individuals who didn't follow such an example.

Manage Type 2 Diabetes

The Mediterranean eating routine is an eating routine that has been used to direct kind two diabetes for a significant length of time. It was at first developed during the 1950s by a get-together of scientists who were managing approaches to hindering coronary sickness. They saw that people who lived on the Mediterranean coast had a lower speed of coronary sickness, and they found that it might be credited to their dietary examples.

The Mediterranean eating routine relies upon eating food assortments that are affluent in plant-based food assortments, like the results of the dirt. It moreover enables eating moderate proportions of fish and low-fat dairy things, which are seen as strong fats; this helps with weight decrease because these food assortments are high in protein and fiber.

The method for advancing with this diet is to guarantee you're getting adequate protein from your meals so your body can work suitably. You should, in like manner, endeavor to avoid dealing with food sources — you needn't bother with those replacing strong trimmings like nuts or beans!

Burn Fat

The Mediterranean diet is a solid, tailored method of eating that has proven to be effective in helping you shed pounds. It emphasizes organic produce, vegetables, whole grains, and fish as the basis of your diet.

While this may seem prohibitive, it is not. The key is to choose good sources of each type of nutrition - and make sure you incorporate them frequently!

Natural products: Berries like strawberries, blueberries, and blackberries are excellent decisions. They are rich in fiber and supplements like L-ascorbic acid and cell reinforcements. Bananas are also an excellent decision because of their high potassium content, a mineral that helps control blood pressure levels and improve digestion.
Vegetables: Vegetables are rich in fiber and nutrients A and C, which can help prevent oxidation in your body and reduce irritation. Choose beautiful natural products or vegetables to further strengthen your cells!
Whole grains: Whole grains contain more nutrients and minerals than refined grains - so choose whole grains over white bread if possible! They also contain fewer calories than a similar amount of refined carbohydrates like white bread. One cup of brown rice has only 150 calories, compared to 450 for white rice!
Fish: Salmon is a

Consume seafood

The Mediterranean eating routine is portrayed by the intense usage of dairy items, products of the soil, entire grains, and vegetables. Fish is a vital piece of this eating routine, and that implies you ought to consume it consistently.
One serving of fish or shellfish each week gives the suggested measure of omega-3 unsaturated fats (EPA and DHA) while additionally giving different supplements like protein, selenium, and zinc. Fish are an astounding wellspring of vitamin B12, which supports red platelet creation and upkeep.
Notwithstanding these advantages, fish is low in soaked fat and cholesterol, settling on them an amazing decision for individuals with coronary illness or who are in danger of creating it.
Different sorts of fish that you can integrate into your eating routine include:

Salmon: contains omega-3 unsaturated fats, which assist with managing your body's chemicals. It additionally contains nutrients B12 and D, which back cerebrum capability and state of mind balance separately. Salmon is additionally high in protein which assists keep you fulling longer than other meat sources like chicken or hamburger; it additionally contains zinc which upholds safe framework capability; iron which upholds hemoglobin creation; calcium which helps construct sound bones.

Consume red meat (monthly)

A serving of red meat contains around five servings of vegetables or potentially natural products. This is comparable to generally 1.5-2 ounces of red meat each day. If you have any desire to consume more than that, basically add more veggies or natural products! We suggest consuming no less than two servings each day for ideal medical advantages.

Eating Healthy Fats

Practicing good eating habits and fats is an extraordinary method for benefiting from your Mediterranean eating regimen.

The Mediterranean eating regimen, which depends on eating new, natural food varieties with a lot of products from the soil, makes it simple to integrate solid fats into your eating regimen. You can begin by adding olive oil or avocado to your plates of mixed greens or sandwiches or sprinkling some extra-virgin olive oil over simmered vegetables.

You can likewise have a go at utilizing nut oils like almond, hazelnut, and peanut butter in cooking rather than margarine. You could involve nut portions of margarine instead of mayonnaise for sandwiches! Assuming you're searching for a much more tasty dish,

have a go at mixing nuts with flavors like cumin, stew powder, and paprika.
With regards to snacks, keep nuts and seeds available so you can appreciate them depending on the situation over the day. While picking nuts and seeds for nibbling, search for ones that are high in protein but low in sodium, like almonds and pecans (as well as cashews). Have a go at blending almonds in with dried natural products, for example, cranberries and dried apricots, for a heavenly granola bar that will keep you feeling full long after noon has traveled every which way!

Make Your Body Work

The Mediterranean eating routine is a technique for making your body work for you instead of permitting it to kill you.
The Mediterranean eating routine was made by Dr. Aseem Malhotra in 2009 and has been focused broadly from there on out. It revolves around pursuing great eating routines fats, natural items, vegetables, whole grains, and dairy things. The goal of this diet is to cut down your bet of coronary ailment and Type 2 diabetes by helping you with getting more fit and cut down your circulatory strain.
While doubtlessly that the Mediterranean eating routine influences prosperity, certain people choose not to follow it since they feel off-kilter with explicit food assortments like beans or red wine. On the off chance that this sounds like you, maybe this present time is the best opportunity to change your point of view set about what appears to be OK for you personally!

Enjoy it with Friends and Family

The Mediterranean eating routine is one of the most well-known eating plans out there. The way into its fame? It depends on the possibility that an eating

regimen wealthy in vegetables and foods are grown from the ground can assist with forestalling coronary illness and other constant sicknesses.
It's not just about practicing good eating habits. It's tied in with eating with your loved ones. In any case, do you have any idea that when you eat with others, it can be more charming than eating alone? This is because social help assists us with remaining propelled to adhere to our solid ways of behaving — and makes us bound to pursue better choices over the long run. So remember to incorporate social help as a feature of your solid way of life!

Meal Planning

The Mediterranean eating regimen is tied in with preparing for your dinners and tidbits. This incorporates planning good dinners, eating no less than one serving of natural product or vegetables every day, and drinking somewhere around one glass of water before each feast.
To prepare, you ought to attempt to integrate these sound propensities into your routine by booking time for eating every day. On the off chance that you eat out frequently or have under seven hours between when you awaken and when you hit the hay, take a stab at saving a period every day to plan food. You can likewise set up a couple of days of feasts without a moment's delay, so you don't need to shop habitually.
Here are a few hints for feast arranging:
•Continuously prepare! You can't practice good eating habits on the off chance that you don't have any idea what you will eat. Plan your feasts and snacks all week long so that you're not left scrambling without a second to spare.
•Adhere to the Mediterranean eating routine! This diet depends on natural products, vegetables, entire grains,

fish, and low-fat dairy items. Ensure that you're eating various food sources over time.

•Have a nibble previously or after every dinner. Something special before sleep time can hold you back from getting ravenous while you rest, and having a tidbit before lunch will assist with forestalling hunger during the morning hours.

Meal Planning Techniques and Shopping list

The Mediterranean eating regimen is intended to assist you with practicing good eating habits and feeling perfect. To benefit from this eating plan, you ought to follow some feast arranging strategies.

To start with, make a staple rundown before you go out to shop. You will want to find food in stores that are simple for you to get, and the costs will not be as high as they would assume if you went to a supermarket ill-equipped.

Second, prepare time by working out each of the dinners you'll eat during the week (or month). You can purchase whatever is as of now ready or cook everything yourself if conceivable. This will make it more straightforward for you to stay with your eating regimen plan and cut back on burning cash at cafés or inexpensive food places.

Third, don't stress over making every dinner without any preparation! You needn't bother with those new fixings since it's conventional Mediterranean cooking; all things being equal, center around planning things like rice or pasta so that when it's the ideal opportunity for supper later in the day, you will not experience any difficulty getting imaginative with your fixings by utilizing something like pesto sauce rather than real pesto greens for instance!

What is the Mediterranean diet food pyramid?

"The Mediterranean Diet Pyramid tends toward the standard elements of the food routine and lifestyle of nations that border the Mediterranean Sea and can be deciphered, if all else fails, to follow a Mediterranean food routine," Knudsen checks.

It was made in 1993 by Oldways, a great objective related to food and words, with the help of the Harvard School of Public Health and the World Health Organization.

The base of the pyramid revolves around collections of food assortments that you should consume regularly and coordinate in every dinner. These assortments include regular produce, vegetables, whole grains, olive oil, vegetables, nuts and seeds, and olive oil.

A more important level is the range of food assortments that you should preferably eat twice a week, including endless fish products.

Next are the food assortment groups that should be consumed for certain restrictions. These include poultry, eggs, cheddar cheese, yogurt, and a rare glass of red wine.

Finally, the smallest piece of the Mediterranean food routine (usually for uncommon events) includes red meat, reduced fat, and a few cakes.

FAQ

How to Buy the Right Ingredients for Your Meals

While you're purchasing elements for your feasts, it means a lot to know what to search for.

The Mediterranean eating regimen is perhaps the best out there, and it's not difficult to follow. However, if you're curious about the fixings in this eating regimen, you may be in for a shock about looking for food. Many sorts of food fall under the Mediterranean umbrella: fish, olive oil, vegetables (beans), organic products

(counting olives), vegetables (counting lettuce), nuts, and seeds are undeniably included.
Yet, the main thing while purchasing fixings is realizing how they'll work in your feasts. Here are a few hints on the most proficient method to purchase Mediterranean-accommodating food sources:
-Ensure you get a lot of new produce — it doesn't need to be natural or neighborhood, yet don't skip purchasing veggies like tomatoes or cucumbers since they're in season!
-Purchase various leafy foods from various regions of the planet — this incorporates a few colorful ones like eggplants from India or fennel seeds from Italy — because there are so many various sorts that can be utilized in cook!
Hunger or appetite?
You might ponder, "Yearning or craving?"
How about we start with the food varieties you eat the first thing? Do you eat something that makes your stomach snarl, or do you get a piece of products from the soil daily? On the off chance that it's the last option, you're doing good. Yet, if it's the previous, you have an issue.
A great many people don't experience difficulty having breakfast — however, they truly make experience difficulty eating enough. Furthermore, that is because they haven't figured out how to meet their yearning needs with good food. The Mediterranean Diet assists you with doing exactly that.
The Mediterranean Diet is more than just "eating bunches of vegetables" or "continually eating olive oil." It's additionally about ensuring that your dinners are adjusted regarding proteins and fats, that they come from entire grains, organic products, vegetables, vegetables, nuts, and seeds, and that they incorporate moderate measures of dairy items (milk and cheeses).

These things assist with guaranteeing that your glucose stays stable over the day, so you don't get eager between feasts – thus that there are an adequate number of supplements in your food to keep you feeling full longer.

The #1 Secret to Weight Loss

There are numerous ways of getting thinner and keeping it off; however, you can't do it without a sound eating regimen. The Mediterranean eating routine is one of the most mind-blowing ways of achieving this objective.

A Mediterranean eating routine is an approach to eating those underscores plant-based food sources and entire grains while restricting red meat, desserts, and immersed fat. The explanation's so successful at assisting individuals with getting more fit (and keeping it off) is because it decreases irritation in your body, which makes your digestion increment and assists you with feeling full when you eat less food. This implies that you'll have the option to eat less food than you would on a regular eating routine arrangement – but since your body feels full in the wake of eating low-calorie dinners, you won't be eager over the day!

Assuming you're attempting to get more fit or keep up with your weight reduction, adding this sort of eating plan into your way of life could be exactly what you want:

SAUCES, DIP, AND DRESSING

Garlic and Onion Dip Recipe

Prep Time: 5 mins, Servings: 6

INGREDIENT

- 1/8 little onion
- 1 little clove of garlic
- 1 tbsp parsley (slashed)
- 120 g acrid cream
- 60 g mayonnaise
- 1 tsp lemon juice
- Pepper and salt
- ½ tsp sugar

PREPARATION

- To begin with, mesh or squash the onion and garlic. Cleave the parsley and put every one of the fixings in a bowl.
- 1/8 little onion,1 little clove garlic,1 tbsp parsley,120 g acrid cream,60 g mayonnaise,1 tsp lemon juice

- Blend until very much joined. Then, at that point, cover and leave in the cooler for an hour for the flavors to imbue.
- Taste, and if essential, season with salt and pepper. On the off chance that you find the plunge excessively acidic, mix after all other options have been exhausted of sugar to adjust it.

  NUTRITION FACTS
  Pepper and salt, ½ tsp sugar
  Fat 11g17%
  Saturated Fat 3g19%
  Trans Fat 0.02g
  Polyunsaturated Fat 5g
  Monounsaturated Fat 3g
  Cholesterol 16mg5%
  Sodium 70mg3%
  Potassium 36mg1%
  Carbohydrates 2g1%
  Fiber 0.1g0%
  Sugar 1g1%
  Protein 1g2%
  Vitamin A 187IU4%
  Vitamin C 2mg2%
  Calcium 23mg2%
  Iron 0.1mg1%

Sour Cream and Chive Dip Recipe

Prep Time: 5 mins, Servings: 6

INGREDIENT

- 120 g harsh cream
- 60 g mayonnaise
- 3 tbsp chives (slashed)
- 1 tsp lemon juice
- ½ tsp garlic powder (discretionary)

PREPARATION

- Set up every one of the fixings in a bowl.
- 120 g harsh cream,60 g mayonnaise,3 tbsp chives,1 tsp lemon juice,½ tsp garlic powder
- Blend until very much consolidated. Do this with a spoon or fork. Try not to utilize a blender, as this damages the surface.
- Leave in the ice chest for basically 60 minutes. The flavors will inject, and the plunge will thicken somewhat.

NUTRITION FACTS

Calories 109 Calories from Fat 99

Fat 11g17%

Saturated Fat 3g19%

Trans Fat 0.02g
Polyunsaturated Fat 5g
Monounsaturated Fat 3g
Cholesterol 16mg5%
Sodium 70mg3%
Potassium 35mg1%
Carbohydrates 1g0%
Fiber 0.1g0%
Sugar 1g1%
Protein 1g2%
Vitamin A 196IU4%
Vitamin C 1mg1%
Calcium 23mg2%
Iron 0.1mg1%

Easy Bang Bang Sauce Recipe

Prep Time: 2 mins, Servings: 6

INGREDIENT

- 120 ml mayonnaise
- 2 tbsp sweet stew sauce
- 1 tbsp sriracha stew sauce
- 2 tsp. honey (runny)
- Discretionary
- 1 tsp. lemon squeeze (or lime)
- Embellish - cut chilies, cut spring onion, sesame seeds, and squashed peanuts (completely discretionary yet pleasant for engaging)

PREPARATION

- Add every one of the fixings to a bowl and blend.
- 120 ml mayonnaise, 2 tbsp sweet bean stew sauce, 1 tbsp sriracha bean stew sauce, 2 tsp. honey, 1 tsp. lemon juice
- Take a look at the taste - add more stew sauce or sriracha to ramp up the intensity whenever wanted.
- Store in a fixed container in the refrigerator for as long as seven days. Serve embellished as you like.

- Embellish - cut chilies, cut spring onion, sesame seeds, squashed peanuts
  NUTRITION FACTS
  Calories 148Calories from Fat 126
  Fat 14g22%
  Saturated Fat 2g13%
  Trans Fat 0.03g
  Polyunsaturated Fat 8g
  Monounsaturated Fat 3g
  Cholesterol 8mg3%
  Sodium 177mg8%
  Potassium 6mg0%
  Carbohydrates 5g2%
  Fiber 0.04g0%
  Sugar 5g6%
  Protein 0.2g0%
  Vitamin A 12IU0%
  Vitamin C 0.3mg0%
  Calcium 2mg0%
  Iron 0.05mg0%

Traditional English Parsley Sauce

Prep Time: 5 mins, Cook Time: 10 mins, Total Time: 15 mins,
Servings: 4

INGREDIENTS

- Modest bunch of new parsley (around 15g)
- 25 g margarine
- 25 g flour
- 250 ml milk
- Salt and pepper

OPTIONAL

- 1 tsp. mustard
- 1 tbsp twofold cream
- 2 tsp. lemon juice

PREPARATION

- Eliminate a large portion of the stalks, and afterward, finely slash your parsley.
- Modest bunch of new parsley

- Liquefy the margarine in a medium pan over a mid to low intensity. When the spread is dissolved, add the flour.

- 25 g butter,25 g flour
- Mix the flour in until you have a thick glue or roux. Then, at that point, cook for a couple of moments, blending constantly. Cook the roux completely. If not, the sauce might taste like flour.

- Progressively begin to add the milk, a little at once, in well to make a smooth glue after every option. As the glue goes to a sauce, you can add more milk each time.
- 250 ml milk

- Bring to a stew for a couple of moments, so the sauce thickens. Continue to mix constantly. Ensure you scratch the sides and lower part of the dish where the sauce will thicken quicker to guarantee an even consistency and abstain from consuming.

- Mix in the newly slashed parsley and season with pepper and salt to taste. On the off chance that you are utilizing mustard, lemon or cream, add these at this stage.

- small bunch of new parsley, salt, and pepper

- The sauce will save warm in the prospect 20 minutes. On the off chance that you want to leave it for longer, place a circle of buttered material or greaseproof paper on the top to stop skin shaping.
  NUTRITION FACTS
  Calories 107Calories from Fat 63
  Fat 7g11%
  Saturated Fat 4g25%

Tran's Fat 1g
Polyunsaturated Fat 1g
Monounsaturated Fat 2g
Cholesterol 20mg7%
Sodium 74mg3%
Potassium 111mg3%
Carbohydrates 8g3%
Fiber 1g4%
Sugar 3g3%
Protein 3g6%
Vitamin A 573IU11%
Vitamin C 5mg6%
Calcium 78mg8%
Iron 1mg6%

Easy BBQ Sauce

Prep Time: 5 mins, Cook Time: 10 mins, Total Time: 15 mins
Servings: 16

INGREDIENTS

- 240 g ketchup
- 3 tbsp dull earthy colored sugar
- 2 tbsp honey or maple syrup
- 3 tbsp white wine or apple juice vinegar
- 1 tsp. smoked paprika
- ½ tsp. garlic granules
- 1 tsp. English mustard
- 2 tsp. Worcestershire Sauce
- Optional
- Run stew sauce (to taste)
- ½ tsp. fluid smoke

PREPARATION

- Toss every one of the fixings into a pot. Then, at that point, give it a decent mix.
- Bring to a stew on the most reduced heat, blending constantly. As you mix, take care to scrape the sides

and lower part of the container, so it doesn't catch and consume.

- Your BBQ sauce is prepared whenever it has diminished down to about a similar volume and thickness to the ketchup you began with. It will be lustrous and coat the rear of a spoon.

NUTRITION FACTS
Calories 27Calories from Fat 9
Fat 1g2%
Saturated Fat 1g6%
Polyunsaturated Fat 1g
Monounsaturated Fat 1g
Sodium 145mg6%
Potassium 60mg2%
Carbohydrates 6g2%
Fiber 1g4%
Sugar 6g7%
Protein 1g2%
Vitamin A 139IU3%
Vitamin C 1mg1%
Calcium 5mg1%
Iron 1mg6%

Sweet chilli dressing

Prep Time: 10 mins, Total Time: 10 mins, **Servings:** 180

INGREDIENT

- 3 tbsp olive oil
- 1 tbsp sesame oil
- 3 tbsp apple cider vinegar
- 3 tbsp sweet chili sauce
- 2 tbsp honey
- 2 tbsp soy sauce
- 1 tsp mustard
- Salt and pepper

PREPARATION

- Measure all ingredients into a jam jar. Shake well just before dressing salad.

NUTRITION FACTS
Calories 4Calories from Fat 9 %
Fat 1g2%

Saturated Fat 1g6%
Polyunsaturated Fat 1g
Monounsaturated Fat 1g
Sodium 14mg1%
Potassium 1mg0%
Carbohydrates 1g0%
Fiber 1g4%
Sugar 1g1%
Protein 1g2%
Vitamin A 1IU0%
Vitamin C 1mg1%
Calcium 1mg0%
Iron 1mg6%

Easy Homemade Sandwich Spread

Cook Time: 10 mins, Servings: 8

INGREDIENTS

•Sandwich Spread Sauce
•3 tbsp mayonnaise (full fat)
•3 tbsp salad cream
•2 tsp pickle vinegar
•1 tsp English mustard (or other smooth mustard to taste)

Vegetables (About one liberal cup altogether once slashed)

•1 stick celery
•6 little gherkins
•1 little carrot
•½ ringer pepper
•1 tbsp escapades
•2 spring onions
•Other crunchy, non-watery vegetables of decision

PREPARATION

•Put the mayonnaise, salad cream, and mustard into a medium blending bowl, alongside 2 teaspoons of vinegar from the container of gherkins or pickles, and blend well.

•Set up the vegetable by stripping, cutting it into a slight rod, and afterward dicing finely.

•They should be little but not so fine they have no surface.

•Add the diced vegetables to the mayonnaise blend, season with pepper and salt, and blend well.

•Store in a container in the cooler and use in 3 days or less.

Easy Salad Cream Recipe

Prep Time: 10 mins, Cook Time: 0 mins, Servings: 15

INGREDIENT

•2 hardboiled egg yolks
•2 tsp. mustard
•juice of a portion of a lemon
•3 tbsp white wine vinegar (or juice vinegar)
•1 sparse tbsp sugar
•150 ml twofold cream
•salt and pepper
•milk

PREPARATION

•Strip and divide the eggs, eliminate the yolks, and set the whites aside. Juice the half lemon. Put the egg yolks, mustard, sugar, and white wine vinegar into a small-scale blender or high-sided bowl.

•Mix to make a smooth fluid. (You can likewise utilize a stick blender or electric blender)

•Add around 50% of the cream. Mix gradually, adding more cream as you go. On account of the acridity and speed of the blender, the plate of mixed greens cream will, out of nowhere, thicken. Beat delicately, a little at a time, until you have the ideal consistency.

•Taste and blend in a little pepper and salt to prepare. If the serving of mixed greens cream is excessively thick, momentarily whizz in a sprinkle of milk to thin it. It is better if it is somewhat excessively thick at this stage than excessively slim.

•Move the newly made salad cream to a serving bowl or container. On the off chance that it is essential, mix in a further little sprinkle of milk by hand to thin it to the ideal consistency.

NUTRITION FACTS
Calories 44Calories from Fat 36
Fat 4g6%
Saturated Fat 3g19%
Cholesterol 40mg13%
Sodium 13mg1%
Potassium 10mg0%
Carbohydrates 1g0%
Fiber 1g4%
Sugar 1g1%
Protein 1g2%
Vitamin A 182IU4%
Vitamin C 1mg1%
Calcium 10mg1%
Iron 1mg6%

Easy Homemade Raito

Prep Time: 5 mins, Servings: 4

INGREDIENT

- •½ cucumber
- •1 cup normal yogurt (240b, full fat)
- •1 tbsp new mint
- •squeeze salt

Optional

- •¼ tsp ground cumin
- •1 tbsp new coriander leaf (cilantro)
- •½ hot green bean stew (finely hacked)

PREPARATION

- •Slice the cucumber down the middle the long way, scoop out the seeds with a teaspoon and dispose of it. If you need to, you can likewise strip the cucumber.
- •Grind the cucumber.
- •Give the ground cucumber a delicate crush, either in your grasp or by enveloping it in a piece of muslin fabric.

•Take the mint leaves from the stalks, hold a couple for decorating, and finely hack.
•Blend the ground cucumber, mint, yogurt, and salt. Permit to represent something like 20 minutes, 2-3 hours if conceivable.
•Mix, embellish with the saved mint leaves and serve at room temperature.

NUTRITION FACTS
Calories 43Calories from Fat 18
Fat 2g3%
Saturated Fat 1g6%
Cholesterol 8mg3%
Sodium 29mg1%
Potassium 146mg4%
Carbohydrates 4g1%
Fiber 1g4%
Sugar 3g3%
Protein 2g4%
Vitamin A 105IU2%
Vitamin C 2mg2%
Calcium 79mg8%
Iron 1mg6%

Sticky onion marmalade

Prep Time: 10 mins, Cook Time: 1 hr 30 mins, **Servings:** 20

INGREDIENT

- 1 kg onions (white, red prior to a combination)
- 75 g margarine (preclude the spread and utilize additional olive oil to keep away from dairy)
- 2 tbsp olive oil (additional virgin)
- 2 cloves garlic (stripped and finely hacked)
- 70 g sugar (delicate brown is great)
- 2 tbsp balsamic vinegar
- 75 ml juice vinegar

Optional

- 1 tsp Dijon mustard (smooth)
- ½ tsp dried spices (oregano or thyme)

PREPARATION

- Strip and cut the onions into half-moons, about ½ cm (¼ inch) thick.
- Put the margarine and oil in a major weighty skillet (I utilize a weighty cast iron goulash dish) and soften over

a low intensity. Mix in the onion to cover it completely with the oil and dissolve the spread.

•Sauté the onions at a low intensity, occasionally blending until they are tacky and delicate. The key here is to gradually go. You need to relax as opposed to sear them.

•Try not to be enticed to turn the intensity up and rush this stage, which requires something like 20-30 minutes. Utilizing a decent strong dish will truly assist with forestalling problem areas, so the onions cook uniformly.

•Add the other fixings and mix in. At this stage, you might think there is an excess of fluid; however, relax. It will all cook down to make an exquisite tacky last jelly.

•Turn the intensity directly down and pass on it to do its thing. Mix every once in a while, swiping the spoon all around the lower part of the dish to make sure that nothing has stuck. Once more, don't rush this stage, which can require as long as 60 minutes.

•The onion preserves are prepared once the onion is a rich dim brown, sparkling and tacky with no fluid in the dish. You can test it by drawing a spoon across the lower part of the skillet, where it will leave an unmistakable path for a few seconds.

•Eliminate the intensity and move to clean, sanitized containers and seal. When cool, keep in the refrigerator and eat within 2 to 3 weeks.

NUTRITION FACTS

Calories 76Calories from Fat 45

Fat 5g8%

Saturated Fat 2g13%

Cholesterol 8mg3%

Sodium 32mg1%

Potassium 78mg2%

Carbohydrates 9g3%

Fiber 1g4%
Sugar 6g7%
Protein 1g2%
Vitamin A 94IU2%
Vitamin C 4mg5%
Calcium 13mg1%
Iron 1mg6%

FRUIT SALAD WITH MINT

Easy Fruit Salad Recipe

Prep: 20 mins, **Cook:** 0 mins, **Total:** 20 mins, **Servings:** 8

INGREDIENTS

For the Fruit

•3 cups hulled, cut strawberries

•2 cups blueberries

•2 cups seedless grapes

•2 cups pineapple lumps, new or canned

•2 medium navel oranges, stripped and cut into reduced down pieces

•1 cup cut kiwi

•For the Dressing

•1/4 cup honey

•2 tablespoons newly crushed squeezed orange

•2 tablespoons newly crushed lime juice

•2 teaspoons finely ground lime zing

PREPARATION
•Assemble the fixings.
•Throw the organic product together in a huge serving bowl.
•Join the honey, orange, and lime squeeze, and lime zing, speed to mix.
•Pour honey-lime dressing over the organic product.
•Throw to cover and serve right away.

NUTRITION FACT
Calories 124
Total Fat 0g 1%
Saturated Fat 0g 0%
Cholesterol 0mg 0%
Sodium 3mg 0%
Total Carbohydrate 32g 12%
Dietary Fiber 4g 13%
Total Sugars 25g
Protein 1g
Vitamin C 86mg 432%
Calcium 37mg 3%
Iron 1mg 4%
Potassium 314mg 7%

Buko Salad (Filipino Fruit Salad)

Prep: 10 mins, **Cook:** 0 mins, **Total:** 10 mins, **Servings:** 6

INGREDIENTS

- 2 cups canned natural product mixed drink, very much depleted, chilled
- 2 cups diced canned peaches, all around depleted, chilled
- 1/2 cup cream, all-around chilled
- 1/4 cup improved consolidated milk, very much chilled

PREPARATION

- Accumulate the fixings.
- Consolidate the organic product mixed drink and peaches in a bowl and mix.
- Utilizing a whisk, whip the cream and improve consolidated milk in an estimated cup or bowl until marginally thickened, around 2 minutes.

- Pour the cream and dense milk over the natural product mixed drink and peaches. Mix well. Keep chilled until prepared to serve.

NUTRITION FACT
Calories 154
Total Fat 6g 8%
Saturated Fat 4g 20%
Cholesterol 20mg 7%
Sodium 22mg 1%
Total Carbohydrate 25g 9%
Dietary Fiber 1g 5%
Total Sugars 23g
Protein 2g
Vitamin C 4mg 19%
Calcium 44mg 3%
Iron 0mg 2%
Potassium 184mg 4%

Ambrosia Fruit Salad with Sour Cream Dressing

Prep: 30 mins, **Cook:** 0 mins, **Total:** 30 mins, **Servings:** 6

INGREDIENTS

- 1 cup blended natural product lumps, or organic product mixed drink, depleted
- 1/2 cup mandarin orange segments
- 1/2 cup pineapple goodies
- 1/4 cup maraschino cherries, divided
- 1/4 cup red seedless grapes
- 1/2 cup smaller than expected marshmallows
- 3/4 cup harsh cream, or as wanted
- 1/4 cup chopped coconut, for decorating
- 6 leaves lettuce or blended greens

PREPARATION

- Assemble the fixings.
- Join the depleted organic products, marshmallows, harsh cream, and coconut, blending tenderly yet completely in a medium bowl.

- Cover and refrigerate the organic product salad until completely chilled.
- Serve the serving of mixed greens on lettuce leaves or blended greens.

NUTRITION FACT
Calories 167
Total Fat 7g 9%
Saturated Fat 4g 19%
Cholesterol 17mg 6%
Sodium 57mg 2%
Total Carbohydrate 27g 10%
Dietary Fiber 3g 11%
Total Sugars 21g
Protein 3g
Vitamin C 27mg 137%
Calcium 82mg 6%
Iron 1mg 7%
Potassium 382mg 8%

Thai Banana-Lychee Dessert in Coconut Milk

Prep: 5 mins, **Cook:** 5 mins, **Total:** 10 mins, **Servings:** 2

INGREDIENTS

•2 little ready bananas

•1 might coconut at any point milk, standard or light

•1/4 to 1/3 cup earthy-colored sugar

•1 squeeze of salt

•8 to 10 lychees, new or canned

PREPARATION

•Assemble the fixings.

•Strip the bananas, then cut them in half longwise. Cut these lengths into more modest segments, approximately 2 inches long.

•Empty the coconut milk into a pan or pot and spot it over medium-high intensity.

•Add the sugar and salt, blending to break up (around 30 seconds to 1 moment). Begin by adding 1/4 cup sugar and taste-testing for pleasantness. On the off chance that you'd like it better, add somewhat more.

•Add the bananas and lychees. Keep blending until the bananas and lychees are warmed through (1 to 2 minutes).

•Serve warm or chill, and serve cold.

NUTRITION FACT
Calories 814
Total Fat 31g 40%
Saturated Fat 26g 128%
Cholesterol 0mg 0%
Sodium 74mg 3%
Total Carbohydrate 143g 52%
Dietary Fiber 10g 36%
Total Sugars 124g
Protein 9g
Vitamin C 460mg 2,300%
Calcium 75mg 6%
Iron 7mg 37%
Potassium 1641mg 35%

Mexican Christmas Eve Fruit Salad (Ensalada de Nochebuena)

Prep: 40 mins, **Cook:** 35 mins, **Total:** 75 mins, **Servings:** 6

INGREDIENTS

For the Dressing:

•2 cups/1/2 L of water

•2 cups white sugar

•3 tablespoons new crushed lime juice

•3 tablespoons apple or wine vinegar

For the Salad:

•2 medium-sized red beets (or 2 jars of cut beets)

•1/2 head romaine lettuce

•1/2 medium jicama

•2 red or green apples (or one of each tone)

•1/2 little to medium new pineapple (or 6 rings of canned pineapple)

•1 lime (cut into equal parts)

•1 huge orange
•1/3 cup pomegranate seeds
•1/3 cup peanuts (shelled and toasted)
•Cilantro leaves

PREPARATION

•Make the Dressing
•Assemble the fixings.
•Place the water and sugar together in a medium-sized skillet. Heat, blending continually until you have a light, straightforward syrup.
•Empty syrup into a glass container and add the three tablespoons of lime juice and vinegar. Put the cover on the container and shake it well.
•Empty the dressing into a little serving pitcher or beautiful container and refrigerate.
•Set up the ingredients
•Accumulate the fixings.
•On the off chance that you are utilizing new beets, wash them well and bubble them in enough water to cover them for 30 to 40 minutes until a fork embedded as far as possible in the middle goes in without any problem. Remove the beets from the water, strip them, and cut them into cuts of around 1/3 to 1/2 inch each. Assuming you are utilizing canned beets, channel them.
•Keeping them entire, wash and dry the romaine lettuce leaves. Leave the more modest leaves in one piece; cut the bigger ones down the middle.
•Strip the jicama and cut it into cuts similar width as the beets.
•On the off chance that you have new pineapple, strip and center it, cut into cuts. On the off chance that your pineapple cuts are canned, channel them.
•Leave the apple strip on for variety, or strip the apples assuming you lean toward that. Slice them into 6 to 8

wedges for every apple, disposing of the stem, center, and seeds. Press the lime parts over the apples, then, at that point, throw them, so the juice covers all uncovered apple surfaces and keeps them from becoming brown.

- Strip the orange, taking off as large part of the white part between segments as possible. Separate the orange into wedges.
- Open up the pomegranate and eliminate the seeds, disposing of the strip and extreme white layers.
- Pick the cilantro leaves off of the stems.

Assemble the Salad

- On an enormous plate or individual serving of mixed greens plates, place the natural products as a whole and vegetables in an appealing plan. For instance, begin with the lettuce on the base, then form layers of the other fixings in differentiating tones.
- Sprinkle the pomegranate seeds, peanuts, and cilantro leaves over the top.
- Deliver the pitcher of dressing once again from the refrigerator with the goal that every cafe can pour a tad bit of it onto their plate of mixed greens whenever it is served.

NUTRITION FACT
Calories 324
Total Fat 4g 5%
Saturated Fat 0g 2%
Cholesterol 0mg 0%
Sodium 25mg 1%
Total Carbohydrate 74g 27%
Dietary Fiber 6g 21%
Protein 4g
Calcium 61mg 5%

Apple Salad with Pecans and Raisins

Prep: 10 mins, **Cook:** 0 mins, **Total:** 10 mins, **Servings:** 6

INGREDIENTS

•5 medium Red Delicious apples

•1 medium lemon, squeezed, around 3 tablespoons

•1/2 cup meagerly cut celery

•1/2 cup coarsely slashed walnuts

•1/2 cup raisins

•1/3 to 1/2 cup mayonnaise

•Lettuce leaves for serving

PREPARATION

•Assemble the fixings.

•Wash the apples; however, don't strip them. Center and cut them into 1/2-inch blocks.

•Sprinkle with lemon juice to forestall staining.

•Join apples with celery, walnuts, raisins, and 1/3 cup mayonnaise in a huge bowl and afterward delicately blend. Add more mayonnaise whenever wanted.

•Serve scoops of apple salad on lettuce leaves.

NUTRITION FACT
Calories 313
Total Fat 21g 26%
Saturated Fat 3g 14%
Cholesterol 8mg 3%
Sodium 127mg 6%
Total Carbohydrate 35g 13%
Dietary Fiber 6g 20%
Total Sugars 25g
Protein 2g
Vitamin C 18mg 91%
Calcium 32mg 2%
Iron 1mg 5%
Potassium 356mg 8%

Old-Fashioned Frozen Fruit Salad Recipe

Prep: 10 mins, **Cook:** 0 mins, **Total:** 10 mins, **Servings:** 8

INGREDIENTS
•1 cup weighty cream, or whipping cream, chilled
•2 (3-ounce) bundles of cream cheddar, relaxed
•1 cup mayonnaise
•1/2 cup red maraschino cherries, quartered
•1/2 cup green maraschino cherries, quartered
•1 (16-or 20-ounce) can natural product mixed drink, depleted
•2 1/2 cups marshmallows, diced (around 24 marshmallows)
PREPARATION
•Assemble the fixings.
•In a little bowl with an electric blender, beat the weighty chilled cream to firm pinnacles.

•In an enormous blending bowl with an electric blender, beat together the cream cheddar and mayonnaise.
•Overlap in the whipped cream, cherries, depleted organic product mixed drink, and marshmallows.
•Transform the combination into a 1-quart cooler holder or portion skillet.
•Decorate with extra maraschino cherries or walnut parts.
•Freeze the plate of mixed greens until firm. Turn out of the compartment and cut to serve.
•Appreciate.

NUTRITION FACT
Calories 497
Total Fat 39g 50%
Saturated Fat 14g 72%
Cholesterol 67mg 22%
Sodium 267mg 12%
Total Carbohydrate 37g 13%
Dietary Fiber 1g 5%
Total Sugars 31g
Protein 3g
Vitamin C 2mg 8%
Calcium 58mg 4%
Iron 0mg 2%
Potassium 129mg 3%

Strawberry Pretzel Salad

Prep: 20 mins, **Cook:** 10 mins, **Total:** 30 mins, **Servings:** 10

INGREDIENTS

•2 cups (around 6 ounces) finely squashed pretzels

•3/4 cup (6 ounces) spread, dissolved

•3 tablespoons granulated sugar

•1 (6-ounce) bundle of strawberry gelatin

•2 cups bubbling water

•20 to 24 ounces cut frozen strawberries, unthawed, or a 15-ounce tub of frozen strawberries in syrup

•1/2 cup freezing water, if utilizing cut frozen strawberries

•8 ounces cream cheddar, mellowed

•2 cups whipped cream or whipped besting

•1 cup granulated sugar

•New cut strawberries, for discretionary trimming

PREPARATION

•Accumulate the fixings.

•Preheat the stove to 400 F. In a bowl, consolidate the squashed pretzels, dissolved margarine, and 3 tablespoons of sugar.

•Press into a 9-by-13-by-2-inch baking dish. Prepare in the preheated broiler for 8 to 10 minutes. Allow the hull to cool totally.

•In a bowl with an electric blender, beat the cream cheddar with 1 cup of sugar.

•Overlay in the whipped besting.

•Spread the cream cheddar blend over the cooled pretzel layer. Cover and refrigerate for 15 to 20 minutes

•In a huge bowl, consolidate the strawberry gelatin with the bubbling water; mix until disintegrated. Add the frozen cut strawberries and cold water. Blend and refrigerate for a couple of moments to gel just somewhat, or until it is about the consistency of egg white.

•Spoon the set, cold gelatin, and strawberry blend over the chilled cream cheddar combination.

•Cover the dish with saran wrap and chill completely.

•Embellish with new strawberries or more whipped cream whenever wanted.

NUTRITION FACT
Calories 402
Total Fat 19g 24%
Saturated Fat 11g 56%
Cholesterol 50mg 17%
Sodium 211mg 9%
Total Carbohydrate 61g 22%
Dietary Fiber 8g 28%
Total Sugars 41g
Protein 3g
Vitamin C 152mg 759%
Calcium 83mg 6%
Iron 3mg 16%
Potassium 580mg 12%

Thai Grapefruit Salad

Prep: 20 mins, **Cook:** 5 mins, **Total:** 25 mins, **Servings:** 6

INGREDIENTS

For the Salad Dressing:

•1/3 cup newly crushed lime juice, from 2 to 3 medium limes

•3 tablespoons fish sauce

•1 tablespoon soy sauce

•2 1/2 to 3 tablespoons earthy colored sugar, to taste

•1 to 2 teaspoons Thai bean stew sauce, to taste

For the Salad:

•12 to 16 medium shrimp, stripped, deveined
•2 tablespoons destroyed coconut, unsweetened or improved
•1 pomelo, or 2 pink grapefruit
•1 cup cucumber, diced
•1 red pepper, diced
•1/4 cup finely slashed shallots
•1/4 cup slashed new basil
•1/4 cup slashed new cilantro
•1 red bean stew pepper, minced, discretionary
•1/4 cup dry-simmered unsalted cashews
•Modest bunch of salad greens, discretionary, for serving

PREPARATION

•Join all dressing fixings together in a cup, blending great to disintegrate the sugar.

•Set a pot of water to bubble in the oven. Add shrimp and bubble for only a couple of moments until the shrimp become pink and full and firm to the touch. Channel and put away to cool.

•Place destroyed coconut in a dry griddle or wok over medium-high intensity and mix until the coconut becomes light brilliant brown and fragrant. Place coconut in a little bowl to cool and save.

•Set up your grapefruit, eliminating however much of the white strip as could be expected from the natural product. Break into scaled-down pieces, 3 to 4 cups is a decent sum. Set arranged natural product in a plate of mixed greens bowl.

•Add to the bowl the cucumber, red pepper, shallots, basil, cilantro, and new stew, if utilized.

•To assemble the serving of mixed greens, add shrimp to the serving of mixed greens bowl, then, at that point, pour over the dressing. Throw well to consolidate. Add the majority of the toasted coconut and cashews, holding a little for embellishing, then, at that point, throw once more.

•Trial the serving of mixed greens for an equilibrium of sweet/harsh/fiery/pungent. Conform however you would prefer, adding more sugar if excessively sharp. Your plate of mixed greens is presently prepared to serve, or on the other hand, on the off chance that ideal, plan individual plates with a bed of greens and top with liberal parts of the pomelo salad. Sprinkle with held coconut and cashews.

NUTRITION FACT

Calories 160

Total Fat 4g 5%

Saturated Fat 2g 8%

Cholesterol 28mg 9%

Sodium 1011mg 44%

Total Carbohydrate 27g 10%

Dietary Fiber 3g 10%

Total Sugars 11g

Protein 6g

Vitamin C 113mg 563%

Calcium 48mg 4%

Iron 1mg 6%

Potassium 510mg 11%

Fruit Salad with Vanilla Pudding

Prep: 10 mins, **Cook:** 0 mins, **Total:** 10 mins, **Servings:** 10

INGREDIENTS

•1 (20-ounce) can of pineapple lumps in juice
•1 cup standard or low-fat sharp cream
•1 (3-to 4-ounce) box vanilla moment pudding blend
•2 1/2 cups cut red seedless grapes
•2 cups cut new strawberries
•1 cup new blueberries
•1 (10-ounce) can of mandarin oranges, depleted

PREPARATION

•Channel the pineapple lumps, saving the juice in a 1-cup estimating cup. You will require 3/4 cup of the pineapple juice; dispose of (or drink!) any extra. If you need more pineapple juice, add sufficient water to the juice to make 3/4 cup.
•Blend the pineapple juice, harsh cream, and moment vanilla pudding in a little bowl. Cover and refrigerate for 60 minutes.
•In the meantime, additionally, refrigerate the pineapple lumps.
•Throw the grapes, strawberries, blueberries, mandarin oranges, and pineapple lumps together. Place the natural product salad in a tall glass, precious stone serving bowl, or glass serving dishes.
•Spoon the chilled pudding blend over the organic product salad - - if you like your fixing a piece fluffier, you can beat it with an electric hand blender briefly before spooning it over the organic product.
NUTRITION FACT
Calories 132
Total Fat 4g 5%
Saturated Fat 2g 10%
Cholesterol 8mg 3%
Sodium 19mg 1%
Total Carbohydrate 25g 9%
Dietary Fiber 2g 8%
Total Sugars 20g
Protein 3g
Vitamin C 38mg 191%
Calcium 54mg 4%
Iron 1mg 3%
Potassium 293mg 6%

BREAKFAST RECIPES

PEANUT BUTTER BANANA SMOOTHIE

Prep Time: 5 mins, Total Time: 5 mins, Servings: 1

INGREDIENTS

•1 frozen banana, cut
•2 Tbsp peanut butter
•1 tsp earthy-colored sugar
•1/4 tsp vanilla concentrate
•1 cup of milk

PREPARATION

•Add the cut banana, peanut butter, earthy-colored sugar, vanilla concentrate, and milk to a blender.

•Mix the fixings until smooth. Assuming the smoothie is excessively thick, add more milk. Assuming the smoothie is excessively flimsy, add more frozen bananas. Taste and change the pleasantness as you would prefer.

NUTRITION
Serving: 1 smoothie · Calories: 461 kcal · Carbohydrates: 49 g · Protein: 16 g · Fat: 25 g · Sodium: 232 mg · Fiber: 5 g

MENEMEN (TURKISH SCRAMBLED EGGS WITH TOMATOES)

Prep Time: 10 mins, **Cook Time:** 10 mins, **Total Time:** 20 mins,
Servings: 4

INGREDIENTS
•2 Tbsp olive oil
•1 yellow onion
•1 chime pepper (any tone)
•1/2 tsp dried oregano
•1/4 tsp squashed red pepper (or Aleppo pepper)
•1 15oz. can diced tomatoes
•1 tsp salt
•1/4 tsp newly broken dark pepper
•4 huge eggs, daintily beaten
•1/4 cup packed parsley
•1 cup disintegrated feta
PREPARATION

•Heat olive oil in a 10-inch skillet over medium intensity. Include onion, pepper, dried oregano, and red pepper chips. Cook, blending as often as possible until vegetables are mellowed for around 7-8 minutes.
•Mix in the tomatoes (with their juices), salt, and pepper. Sauté for 2-3 minutes or until tomatoes are warmed through.
•Tenderly empty the delicately beaten eggs into the skillet and cook, blending habitually, until eggs are set at this point still delicate, around 2-3 minutes, only by a hair.
•Quickly sprinkle it with cleaved parsley and disintegrated feta cheddar, if utilized. Present with dry bread as an afterthought.

NUTRITION
Serving: 1 serving · Calories: 255 kcal · Carbohydrates: 7 g · Protein: 12 g · Fat: 20 g · Sodium: 1086 mg · Fiber: 1 g

BREAKFAST NACHOS

Prep Time: 20 mins, Cook Time: 12 mins, Total Time: 32 mins,
Servings: 4

INGREDIENTS

- 1 Roma tomato
- 1/4 red onion
- 1 jalapeño
- 1 15oz. can dark beans, washed and depleted
- 4 oz. cheddar, destroyed
- 6 huge eggs
- 1/4 tsp salt
- 1/4 tsp pepper
- 2 Tbsp spread
- 1 15oz. sack tortilla chips
- 1/2 cup acrid cream

PREPARATION

- Dice the tomato and red onion. Cut the jalapeño. Wash and channel the dark beans. Shred the cheddar.

•Preheat the stove to 350°F. Whisk together the eggs, salt, and pepper in a huge bowl.
•Liquefy the spread in a huge non-stick skillet over medium intensity. Once hot, add the whisked eggs and tenderly mix and overlay until the eggs are, for the most part set, yet somewhat wet (they'll complete the process of cooking on the stove).
•Line a huge baking sheet with material paper for simple cleanup. A spread portion of the tortilla chips over the outer layer of the baking sheet, then, at that point, top with half of the eggs, a big part of the dark beans, and a big part of the destroyed cheddar.
•Rehash with the second layer of chips, eggs, beans, and cheddar.
•Prepare the nachos on the pre-heated stove for 5-7 minutes or until the cheddar is softened.
•Eliminate the nachos from the broiler and top with the leftover new fixings: tomato, onion, jalapeño, and sharp cream. Serve hot.

NUTRITION
Serving: 0.25 batch · Calories: 933 kcal · Carbohydrates: 93 g · Protein: 31 g · Fat: 50 g · Sodium: 1249 mg · Fiber: 13 g

HOMEMADE BLUEBERRY MUFFINS

Prep Time: 15 mins, Cook Time: 35 mins, Total Time: 50 mins,
Servings: 8

INGREDIENTS

- •1.5 cups regular flour
- •2 tsp. baking powder
- •3/4 tsp. salt
- •1/4 tsp. cinnamon
- •1/8 tsp. nutmeg
- •1 cup plain yogurt
- •1/2 cup granulated sugar
- •4 Tbsp dissolved spread
- •2 Tbsp cooking oil
- •1 huge egg
- •1.5 tsp vanilla concentrate
- •1 cup blueberries

Disintegrate TOPPING (OPTIONAL)

- 1 Tbsp dissolved spread
- 2 Tbsp granulated sugar
- 1/8 tsp cinnamon
- 2 Tbsp regular flour

PREPARATION

- If utilizing the disintegrate besting, set up that first. Mix the liquefied spread, sugar, and cinnamon, then, at that point, include the flour and mix until it looks like sodden sand. Put the fixing away.
- Preheat the stove to 375°F. Whisk together the dry fixings (flour, baking powder, salt, cinnamon, and nutmeg) in a huge bowl until very much joined.
- In a different bowl, whisk together the yogurt, sugar, liquefied spread, oil, egg, and vanilla concentrate.
- Empty the wet fixings into the bowl of dry fixings and mix until they're around 75% consolidated (there ought to, in any case, be pockets of dry flour all through).
- In the case of utilizing frozen blueberries, dust them with around 1/2 tsp flour first. Add the blueberries to the hitter and complete the process of collapsing until the blueberries are equitably consolidated, and there are not any drier pockets of dry flour in the player. It's all right on the off chance that it's knotty; simply try to abstain from over-blending.
- Split the hitter between eight wells of a lubed or lined biscuit tin. Top the unbaked biscuits with the disintegrated beating.
- Prepare the biscuits for around 35 minutes, or until brilliant brown on top. Permit the biscuits to cool for around 5 minutes in the biscuit tin, then, at that point, slacken the edges with a blade and move them to a wire rack to complete the process of cooling.

NUTRITION Serving: 1 muffin · Calories: 287 kcal · Carbohydrates: 39 g · Protein: 5 g · Fat: 13 g · Sodium: 404 mg · Fiber: 1 g

HOW TO FRY AN EGG

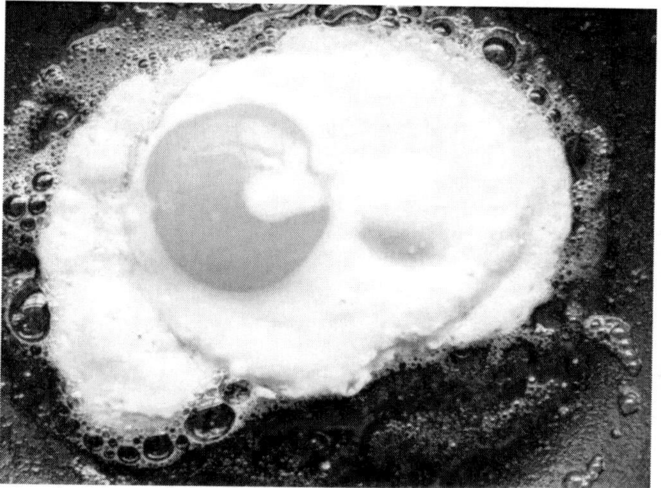

Cook Time: 8 mins, Total Time: 8 mins, Servings: 1

INGREDIENTS

•1/2 tsp. margarine

•1 enormous egg

PREPARATION

•Heat a skillet over medium-low, permitting it to completely pre-heat (3-5 minutes).

•Add the margarine (or fat of the decision) and twirl to cover the outer layer of the skillet.

•Break the egg into the griddle and cook until the whites are set, and the yolk is as yet fluid (just right).

•For done on both sides, done on both sides, or done on both sides, cook the egg until the whites are 50-75% set; then, at that point, flip the egg and keep cooking on the second side until the yolk is cooked to your ideal doneness.

•Move the egg to a plate and season with salt and pepper. Appreciate!

NUTRITION Serving: 1 serving · Calories: 89 kcal · Carbohydrates: 1 g · Protein: 6 g · Fat: 7 g · Sodium: 87 mg

MUESLI

Prep Time: 5 mins, Total Time: 5 mins, Servings: 8

INGREDIENTS

- 3 cups dry antiquated oats
- 1/2 cup hacked pecans
- 1/2 cup dried cranberries
- 1/4 cup sunflower seeds
- 2 Tbsp earthy colored sugar (discretionary)
- 1/2 tsp cinnamon

PREPARATION

- Consolidate the oats, cranberries, pecans, earthy-colored sugar, and cinnamon in a bowl. Mix until equally blended. Store blend in an impermeable holder in a cool, dry spot until prepared to eat.
- To set up the muesli, consolidate 1/2 cup muesli with 1/2 cup of cold milk. Let drench for 5 minutes, or as long as four days, in the fridge.

NUTRITION Serving: 1 Serving · Calories: 222 kcal · Carbohydrates: 32 g · Protein: 6 g · Fat: 9 g · Sodium: 4 mg · Fiber: 4 g

FLUFFY HOMEMADE PANCAKES

Prep Time: 10 mins, Cook Time: 20 mins, Total Time: 30 mins,
Servings: 4

INGREDIENTS

- 1 cup of regular flour
- 1.5 tsp baking powder
- 1/2 tsp salt
- ¾ cup +2 Tbsp warm milk
- 2 Tbsp liquefied margarine
- 1 huge egg
- 2 Tbsp sugar
- 1/2 tsp vanilla concentrate
- 4 tsp cooking oil

PREPARATION

- Whisk together the flour, baking powder, and salt in a bowl.
- In a different bowl, whisk together the milk, egg, liquefied margarine, sugar, and vanilla concentrate.

•Pour the bowl of wet fixings into the bowl of dry fixings and mix just until joined. The combination ought to be thick yet pourable and somewhat uneven. Allow the player to rest for 15 minutes.

•Heat an enormous skillet or frying pan on both sides; when hot, add sufficient cooking oil to cover the surface (I use about ½ tsp per flapjack). Add the flapjack player to the hot iron, ¼ cup at a time. Utilize the rear of the estimating cup to spread the hitter into a 4.5-inch width circle.

•Cook the hotcakes until bubbles structure over the surface and start to pop, the edges of the flapjacks look dry, and the base is brilliant brown (around 60 seconds). Flip the hotcakes and cook on the second side until brilliant brown (around 30 seconds).

•Rehash with the leftover player, adding more oil to the skillet between groups or on a case-by-case basis until the flapjacks have been all cooked. Keep the hotcakes warm on a plate under a towel or in a warm broiler until the flapjacks have been all cooked. Serve warm with your number one fixings!

NUTRITION

Serving: 2 pancakes · Calories: 279 kcal · Carbohydrates: 33 g · Protein: 7 g · Fat: 13 g · Sodium: 536 mg · Fiber: 1 g

APPLE PIE OVERNIGHT OATS

Prep Time: 8 hrs. Total Time: 8 hrs. Servings: 4

INGREDIENTS

- 1 1/3 cups antiquated moved oats
- 1/2 tsp cinnamon
- 1/4 tsp ground ginger
- 1/4 tsp ground cloves
- 1/2 cup hacked pecans
- 1/4 cup dried cranberries
- 1 1/3 cups unsweetened fruit purée
- 1 1/3 cups milk

PREPARATION

- Add ⅓ cup oats each to four resealable compartments. Likewise, add ⅛ tsp cinnamon, a spot of ginger, and a touch of cloves to every compartment.
- Add 2 Tbsp hacked pecans and 1 Tbsp dried cranberries to every compartment.

•At last, add ⅓ cup fruit purée and ⅓ cup milk to every compartment.
•Close the compartments and refrigerate for the time being or as long as four days. Mix the items in the compartment before eating.

NUTRITION
Serving: 1 Serving · Calories: 306 kcal · Carbohydrates: 40 g · Protein: 9 g · Fat: 14 g · Sodium: 35 mg · Fiber: 5 g

EASY HOMEMADE CREPES

Prep Time: 10 mins, Cook Time: 15 mins, Total Time: 25 mins,
Servings: 6

INGREDIENTS

- 1 cup of regular flour
- 1/2 tsp salt
- 2 huge eggs, room temperature
- 1 cup milk, warmed
- 3 Tbsp dissolved margarine
- 1/4 cup water
- 2 Tbsp cooking oil for the skillet

PREPARATION

- Add the flour, salt, eggs, milk, dissolved margarine, and water together in a huge bowl until it shapes a smooth and somewhat thick hitter.
- Allow the hitter to rest at room temperature for 30 minutes, or cover and refrigerate for as long as two days.

•At the point when prepared to make your crepes, heat a 10-inch skillet over medium intensity. Once hot, brush with about ½ tsp oil.
•Pour about ⅓ cup of the hitter into the skillet and start to shift the skillet in a round movement to permit the player to cover the outer layer of the skillet equally.
•Permit the player to cook until generally set, then flip and cook until brilliant brown on the subsequent side. The all-out cook time for each side will fluctuate contingent upon your skillet and burner. You might have to change the intensity up or down as you go.
•Rehash with the remainder of the hitter, adding more oil between crepes, depending on the situation. As you cook the crepes, stack them on a perfect plate and cover them with a towel to keep warm. When the crepes are all cooked, fill, crease, or roll the crepes, then, at that point, serve.

NUTRITION
Serving: 1 crepe · Calories: 216 kcal · Carbohydrates: 18 g · Protein: 6 g · Fat: 13 g · Sodium: 279 mg · Fiber: 1 g

MINI BROCCOLI CHEDDAR QUICHES

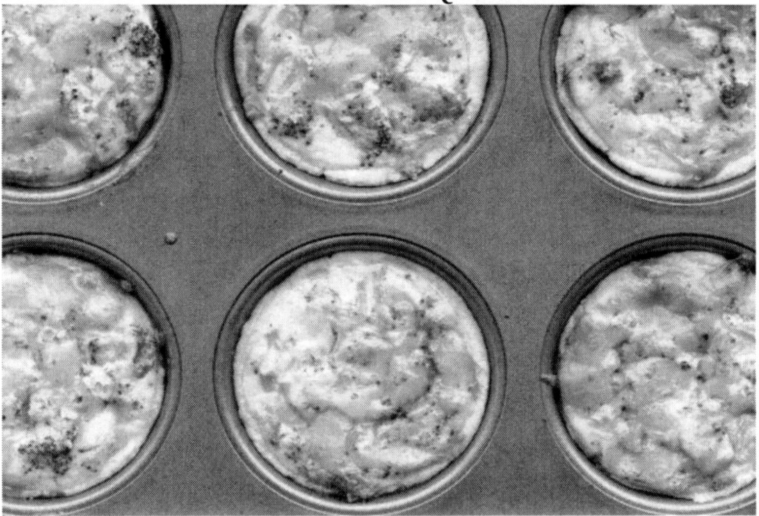

Prep Time: 30 mins, **Cook Time:** 35 mins, **Total Time:** 1 hr 5 mins,
Servings: 2

INGREDIENTS
CRUST
•8 Tbsp spread, room temperature
•4 oz. cream cheddar, room temperature
•1 cup + 2 Tbsp regular flour
FILLING
•2 huge eggs
•1/2 cup milk
•1/4 cup ground Parmesan
•1/4 tsp garlic powder
•1/4 tsp newly broken pepper
•1/4 tsp salt
•1/2 lb. frozen broccoli florets, defrosted
•4 oz. cheddar, destroyed
PREPARATION

•Preheat the stove to 350°F. Add the room temperature spread and room temperature cream cheddar to a bowl. Utilize a blender to whip them together until uniformly consolidated.
•Start mixing in the flour, about ¼ cup at a time, until a battered structure. The mixture ought to be delicate yet, at the same, not tacky.
•Partition the mixture into 12 equivalent bits (start by isolating it into four pieces, then partition each quarter into three equivalent estimated pieces). Fold each piece of batter into a ball, then drop everyone into the well of a biscuit tin. Utilize your fingers to press the batter down into the middle and up the sides of the wells (see bit-by-bit photographs underneath for more assistance).
•Whisk together the eggs, milk, Parmesan, garlic powder, pepper, and salt in a bowl.
•Finely slash the defrosted broccoli florets (around 1.5 cups once hacked). Shred the cheddar (around 1 cup destroyed). Add the broccoli and cheddar to the egg combination and mix to consolidate.
•Split the broccoli cheddar combination between the twelve smaller-than-usual pie coverings. The fluid egg blend won't completely lower the broccoli and cheddar in the coverings, yet it will puff up and fill the outside layer once prepared.
•Heat the smaller-than-normal quiches in the preheated broiler for 35 minutes or until puffed in the middle and brilliant brown around the edges.
•Cautiously move the heated quiches to a wire rack to cool. Serve warm or at room temperature for no less than two hours of baking.

NUTRITION Serving: 1 mini quiche · Calories: 213 kcal · Carbohydrates: 11 g · Protein: 7 g · Fat: 16 g · Sodium: 259 mg · Fiber: 1 g

DOUBLE CHOCOLATE OVERNIGHT OATS

Prep Time: 1 d 10 mins, Total Time: 1 d 10 mins, Servings: 4

INGREDIENTS

•1 1/3 cup outdated moved oats

•2 Tbsp chia seeds (discretionary)

•2 Tbsp unsweetened cocoa powder

•2 Tbsp earthy-colored sugar

•1/4 cup scaled-down chocolate chips

•1/4 tsp salt

•1 1/3 cup milk

•1/2 tsp vanilla concentrate

PREPARATION

•Join the oats, chia seeds, cocoa powder, earthy-colored sugar, chocolate chips, and salt in a bowl.

•Add the milk and vanilla concentrate, then, at that point, mix to join. Permit the combination to sit for around five minutes.

•Split the oat combination between four resealable holders. Close the compartments and refrigerate for the time being or as long as five days.
•Mix the oats not long before appreciating. Gobble cold or warm it up in the microwave.

NUTRITION
Serving: 0.75 cup · Calories: 268 kcal · Carbohydrates: 40 g · Protein: 8 g · Fat: 9 g · Sodium: 193 mg · Fiber: 6 g

BEST EGG RECIPES

Prep Time: 5 mins, Cook Time: 25 mins, Total Time: 30 mins,
Servings: 2

INGREDIENTS

•1/2 Tbsp olive oil
•1 8" flour tortilla
•1 cup of new spinach
•4 huge eggs
•1/8 tsp salt
•1/8 tsp newly broken dark pepper
•1/2 cup grape tomatoes
•1/4 cup destroyed cheddar
•1/8 tsp squashed red pepper (Optional)

PREPARATION

•Preheat the stove to 350°F. Brush within a cycle a 7-inch measurement stove-safe dish* with olive oil. Press the tortilla down into the dish, so the edges of the

tortilla are collapsed up the sides of the dish (see bit-by-bit photographs underneath).
•Generally, hack the spinach, then add it to the lower part of the tortilla. Break the four eggs into the tortilla on top of the spinach. Add a touch of salt and pepper on top of the eggs.
•Cut the grape tomatoes down the middle, then sprinkle them over the eggs. At last, top with destroyed cheddar.
•Prepare the egg-filled tortilla on the stove for 20-25 minutes or until the whites are set and the yolks are still jammy. You can shake the dish to check whether the whites wiggle or, on the other hand, assume that they are set. Baking time might change depending upon the size of your tortilla and the number of eggs utilized.
•Eliminate the tortilla heated eggs from the broiler and slide them out of the dish. Cut into four pieces, then, at that point, serve!

NUTRITION
Serving: 0.5 recipe · Calories: 320.55 kcal · Carbohydrates: 15.55 g · Protein: 18.6 g · Fat: 20.35 g · Sodium: 618.95 mg · Fiber: 2.45 g

SALSA POACHED EGGS

Prep Time: 5 mins, Cook Time: 20 mins, Total Time: 25 mins,
Servings: 4

INGREDIENTS

•1 yellow onion
•2 cloves garlic
•2 Tbsp olive oil
•1 15oz. can fire-cooked diced tomatoes
•1 4oz. can dice green chiles
•2 Tbsp tomato glue
•1/2 tsp cumin
•1/8 tsp cayenne
•1/2 tsp salt
•1/4 tsp newly broken dark pepper
•1/2 cup water
•4 enormous eggs
•2 green onions, cut

•2 Tbsp cleaved cilantro (optional)

PREPARATION

•Dice the onion and mince the garlic. Add both to a profound skillet with the olive oil and sauté over medium intensity until the onions are delicate.

•Add the diced tomatoes (with juices), green chiles (with juices), tomato glue, cumin, cayenne, salt, pepper, and water. Mix to join.

•Permit the salsa too, at times, come up to a stew, mixing. Allow the salsa to stew for around ten minutes or until it is somewhat thickened.

•Utilize the rear of a spoon to make four spaces in the sauce. Break one egg into every space.

•Put a top on the skillet, turn the intensity down to medium-low, and let the eggs stew in the sauce for 7-10 minutes, or until they arrive at your ideal doneness (less time for runny yolks, additional opportunity for strong yolks).

•When the eggs are cooked, decorate with cut green onion and slashed cilantro, then present with tortilla chips or over a bowl of corn meal.

NUTRITION

Serving: 1 serving · Calories: 187 kcal · Carbohydrates: 12 g · Protein: 8 g · Fat: 12 g · Sodium: 706 mg · Fiber: 2 g

WHITE CHOCOLATE STRAWBERRY SCONES

Prep Time: 20 mins, Cook Time: 15 mins, Total Time: 35 mins,
Servings: 8

INGREDIENTS

•2 cups of regular flour
•2 Tbsp granulated sugar
•2 tsp baking powder
•1/2 tsp salt
•6 Tbsp cold spread
•1 cup cut strawberries
•1/2 cup white chocolate chips
•2 huge eggs
•1/4 cup milk
•1/2 tsp vanilla concentrate
•Coat
•1/2 cup powdered sugar
•1/4 tsp vanilla concentrate
•1 Tbsp milk

PREPARATION

- Preheat the stove to 425°F. In a huge bowl, mix the flour, granulated sugar, baking powder, and salt.
- Grind the virus spread (or cut into little lumps) and add it to the flour blend. Utilize your hands or a cake shaper to work the spread into the flour until a couple of little pieces remain.
- Add the cut strawberries and white chocolate chips to the flour blend and mix to join.
- In a different bowl, whisk together the eggs, milk, and vanilla concentrate.
- Empty the whisked wet fixings into the bowl with the flour blend. Mix until a bundle of batter structures and no dry flour stays on the lower part of the bowl. The batter might be marginally brittle right away, yet it will start to keep intact better as the dampness from the strawberries starts to retain.
- Shape the batter into a level circle, around 8-crawls in measurement. Cut the circle into eight wedge-molded pieces. Move the cut scones to a material-lined baking sheet.
- Prepare the scones for around 15 minutes or until brilliant brown. Move the prepared scones to a wire rack to cool.
- While the scones are cooling, set up the coating, mix the powdered sugar, vanilla, and milk in a bowl until it frames a thick coating.
- Shower the coating over the cooled scones, then serve.

NUTRITION

Serving: 1 scone · Calories: 321 kcal · Carbohydrates: 43 g · Protein: 6 g · Fat: 14 g · Sodium: 359 mg · Fiber: 1 g

EASY EGG SALAD

Prep Time: 10 mins, Cook Time: 15 mins, Total Time: 25 mins,
Servings: 2

INGREDIENTS

- 4 enormous eggs
- 3 Tbsp mayonnaise
- 1 Tbsp dill relish
- 1 tsp Dijon mustard
- 1/4 tsp lemon juice
- 1/8 tsp salt
- 1/8 tsp pepper

PREPARATION

- Add the eggs to a saucepot and cover with water. Put a top on the pot and turn the intensity on to high. Bring the water up to a full bubble. When it arrives at a bubble, switch the intensity off and allow the eggs to sit in hot water (top on) for 12 minutes.

•Following 12 minutes in hot water, move the eggs to an ice shower or run under chilly water until cool. Strip the eggs, then hack them into ½-inch pieces.
•Add the hacked egg to a bowl alongside the mayonnaise, Dijon, relish, lemon squeeze, salt, and pepper. Mix to consolidate, squashing a portion of the egg yolk into the dressing as you mix.
•Taste the egg salad and change the fixings however you would prefer. Serve right away or refrigerate until prepared to eat.

NUTRITION
Serving: 0.75 cups · Calories: 295 kcal · Carbohydrates: 3 g · Protein: 13 g · Fat: 25 g · Sodium: 531 mg · Fiber: 1 g

SAUSAGE BREAKFAST CASSEROLE

Prep Time: 10 mins, Cook Time: 50 mins, Total Time: 1 hr,
Servings: 6

INGREDIENTS
•1 lb. country sausage
•12 oz. frozen peppers and onions
•10 huge eggs
•1/2 cup milk
•1/4 tsp pepper
•1/2 lb. tortilla chips
•8 oz. cheddar, destroyed
•1 Tbsp spread

PREPARATION
•Preheat the stove to 350°F. Assuming your frozen peppers are in strips, cleave them into little pieces.
•Brown the hotdog in an enormous skillet over medium intensity. Once seared, add the frozen peppers and onions and keep on cooking over medium intensity until warmed through. Eliminate the wiener and peppers from the intensity and put them away.

•Whisk together the eggs, milk, and pepper.
•Utilize the margarine to lube within a 3-quart meal dish. Place the tortilla contributes to the lower part of the meal dish and press them down, marginally smashing them until they lay genuinely level.
•Utilize an opened spoon to move the wiener and peppers to the goulash dish on top of the tortilla chips, abandoning any fluid in the container.
•Add ¾ of the destroyed cheddar on top of the wiener and peppers. Mix marginally to consolidate the tortilla chips, hotdog and peppers, and cheddar.
•Pour the egg blend over the fixings in the goulash dish, then top with the leftover destroyed cheddar. The fixings won't be completely lowered in the egg blend, and that is not a problem. The eggs will puff somewhat as they prepare.
•Prepare the morning meal goulash for around 40 minutes, or until the inner temperature arrives at 160°F and the external edges are softly cooked.
•Allow the dish to cool for around five minutes, then, at that point, cut it into six or eight pieces and serve.

NUTRITION
Serving: 1 serving · Calories: 752 kcal · Carbohydrates: 35 g · Protein: 37 g · Fat: 52 g · Sodium: 1045 mg · Fiber: 4 g

LEFTOVER STUFFING MUFFINS

Prep Time: 15 mins, Cook Time: 25 mins, Total Time: 40 mins,
Servings: 12

INGREDIENTS

- •2 tsp margarine (for lubing the biscuit tin)
- •3 cups arranged stuffing or dressing
- •1 cup slashed turkey or ham
- •1/4 lb. frozen spinach, defrosted and crushed
- •6 enormous eggs
- •2 Tbsp milk
- •1/4 tsp salt
- •1/4 tsp Freshly broken pepper

PREPARATION

•Preheat the broiler to 375 degrees. Oil a biscuit tin with margarine, oil, or a non-stick shower. Defrost and crush the spinach dry.

•Add the stuffing, turkey, and spinach to a bowl, then mix delicately to consolidate without separating the stuffing excessively.

•Split the stuffing combination between every one of the 12 wells of the biscuit tin. Leave the stuffing approximately pressed in the cups with the goal that the egg blend can fill in around the stuffing.
•In a medium bowl, whisk together the eggs, milk, salt, and pepper. Split the egg blend between the 12 wells, beginning with 2 Tbsp per biscuit and afterward adding somewhat more until the egg combination has been all utilized. The egg won't completely cover the stuffing; it will puff up as it heats.
•Heat the biscuits for 25-30 minutes or until brilliant brown and fresh on top. Permit the biscuits to cool somewhat, then, at that point, run a blade around the edges to slacken and eliminate every biscuit. Serve warm.

NUTRITION
Serving: 1 muffin · Calories: 143 kcal · Carbohydrates: 12 g · Protein: 7 g · Fat: 7 g · Sodium: 347 mg · Fiber: 2 g

SPINACH AND MUSHROOM CRUSTLESS QUICHE

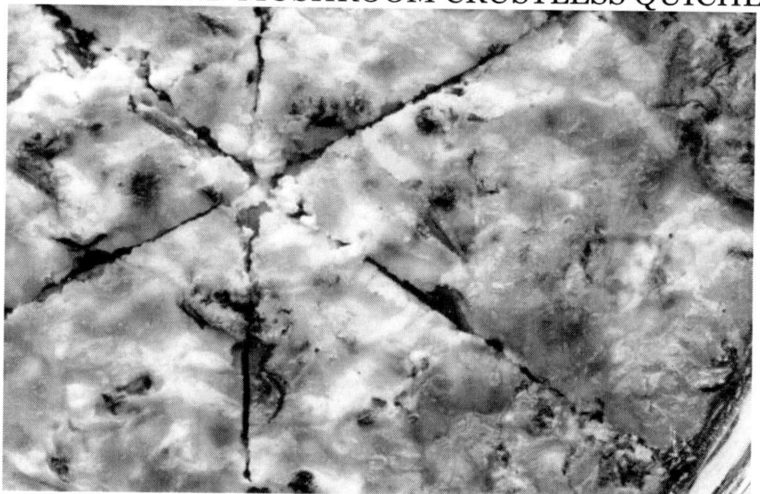

Prep Time: 15 mins, **Cook Time:** 50 mins, **Total Time:** 1 hr 5 mins,
Servings: 6

INGREDIENTS
•1 10oz. box frozen slashed spinach
•8 oz. mushrooms
•1 clove of garlic, minced
•1/8 tsp Salt
•1 Tbsp cooking oil, isolated
•2 oz. feta cheddar
•4 enormous eggs
•1/4 cup ground Parmesan
•1/4 tsp pepper
•1 cup milk
•1/2 cup destroyed mozzarella
PREPARATION
•Preheat the broiler to 350°F. Defrost and crush however much dampness out of the spinach as could reasonably be expected. Flush any soil or trash from the mushrooms, then cut daintily. Mince the garlic.

•Cut the mushrooms and mince the garlic. Add the mushrooms, garlic, salt, and ½ Tbsp cooking oil to a skillet. Sauté the mushrooms over medium intensity until they have delivered the entirety of their dampness and it has dissipated from the skillet. No water ought to stay in the skillet.
•Brush the other ½ Tbsp cooking oil inside a 9-inch pie plate. Layer the mushrooms, spinach, and disintegrated feta into the pie plate.
•In a huge bowl, whisk together the eggs, Parmesan, pepper, and milk.
•Empty the egg blend into the pie plate over the spinach, mushrooms, and feta. Top with the destroyed mozzarella.
•Prepare the crustless quiche in the preheated 350°F broiler for around 50 minutes, or until it is brilliant brown on top and the inside temperature comes to 160°F. Cut and appreciate!

NUTRITION
Serving: 1 slice · Calories: 187 kcal · Carbohydrates: 6 g · Protein: 13 g · Fat: 13 g · Sodium: 378 mg · Fiber: 2 g

HOW TO MAKE HARD-BOILED EGGS

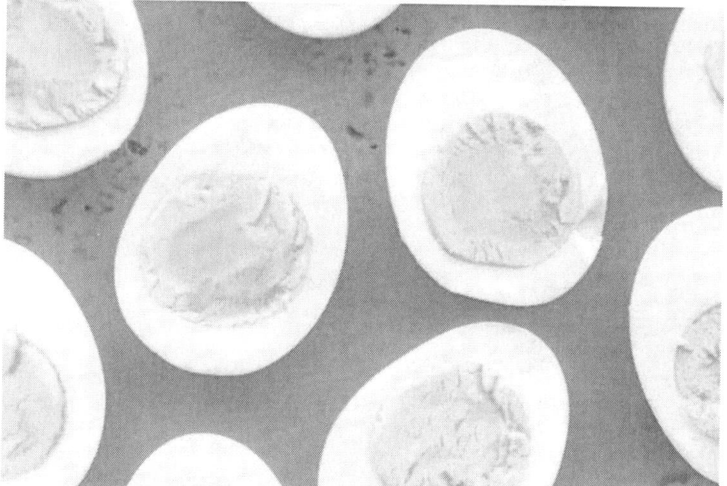

Prep Time: 5 mins, Cook Time: 15 mins, Total Time: 20 mins,
Servings: 4

INGREDIENTS

•4 large eggs

PREPARATION

•Add cold eggs to a saucepot. Add sufficient water to the pot to cover the eggs by one inch.

•Put a top on the pot and turn the intensity on to high. Permit the water to come up to a bubble.

•When the water arrives at a full moving bubble, switch the intensity off and leave the pot on the burner (with the top on) for around 12 minutes.*

•Following 12 minutes, move the eggs to a bowl of ice water. Cool the eggs in the ice water for around five minutes. Strip and appreciate.

NUTRITION

Serving: 1 egg · Calories: 72 kcal · Carbohydrates: 1 g · Protein: 6 g · Fat: 5 g · Sodium: 71 mg

PUMPKIN SMOOTHIE

Prep Time: 5 mins, Total Time: 5 mins, Servings: 1

INGREDIENTS

- 1/3 cup pumpkin purée
- 1 frozen banana
- 1 Tbsp ground flaxseed
- 1/4 tsp pumpkin pie zest
- 1 cup milk
- 1/4 tsp. vanilla concentrate
- 1 tsp. earthy colored sugar

PREPARATION

- Add the pumpkin, frozen banana, flaxseed, pumpkin pie zest, milk, and vanilla to a blender. Mix until smooth.
- Add the earthy-colored sugar (or sugar of decision) and mix once more. Taste and change the pleasantness however you would prefer. Appreciate cold.

NUTRITION

Serving: 1 smoothie · Calories: 339 kcal · Carbohydrates: 52 g · Protein: 11 g · Fat: 12 g · Sodium: 114 mg · Fiber: 7 g

Fish and Seafood

Teriyaki Pineapple Salmon

PREP TIME: 5 mins, COOK TIME: 20 mins, TOTAL TIME: 25 mins,
SERVINGS: 2

INGREDIENTS

•2 tablespoon vegetable oil
•½ teaspoon salt
•½ teaspoon newly ground pepper
•2 salmon filets skin on
•⅓ cup teriyaki sauce
•½ teaspoon ginger powder
•¼ cup pineapple juice
•4 pineapples cuts

PREPARATION

•Heat vegetable oil in a dish. Sprinkle salt and pepper on the two sides of salmon filets.
•When the dish is hot, place the filets in the skillet, skin side down, and singe for 5 minutes until the skin is

fresh. Turn the fillets and cook for another 5 - 8 minutes until the fish is completely cooked.

•Blend teriyaki sauce, ginger, and pineapple juice in a little sauce dish and bring to a bubble. Stew for 3-4 minutes.

•Pour the sauce on the salmon filets (Save one tbsp) and cook for an additional two minutes.

•Singe pineapple cuts in the excess sauce until caramelized.

•Present with white rice and top with caramelized pineapple.

NUTRITION
Calories: 486kcal
Carbohydrates: 29g
Protein: 37g
Fat: 24g
Saturated Fat: 13g
Cholesterol: 94mg
Sodium: 2498mg
Potassium: 1121mg
Fiber: 1g
Sugar: 26g
Vitamin A: 125IU
Vitamin C: 14mg
Calcium: 51mg
Iron: 3mg

Mediterranean Style Shrimp Recipe

PREP TIME: 5 mins, COOK TIME: 20 mins, TOTAL TIME: 25 mins,
SERVINGS: 4

INGREDIENTS

- 2 lbs huge shrimp stripped and deveined
- ½ teaspoon Kosher salt
- ¼ teaspoon dark pepper
- ½ teaspoon allspice
- 1 tsp oregano
- 1 lemon juice of
- 3 tablespoon olive oil
- 1 white onion cut
- 8 smaller than normal peppers cut
- 5 cloves garlic minced
- ½ tsp cumin
- ½ teaspoon coriander
- ½ teaspoon nutmeg
- 2 huge tomatoes cut into lumps
- ⅓ cup water

PREPARATION

- Place the shrimp in a bowl. Include the salt, pepper, allspice, oregano, lemon juice, and 1 tablespoon of olive oil. Blend and allow it to sit as you set up the other fixings.
- Heat the leftover 2 tablespoons of olive oil in a cast iron skillet over medium intensity. Sauté the onion in the olive oil until it's gently brilliant, 5 to 8 minutes.
- Include the cut pepper and garlic. Add the cumin, coriander, and nutmeg. Sauté to mellow the peppers; this would require around 5 minutes.
- Include the shrimp and the tomatoes, followed by the water (you could require not exactly ⅓ cup of water, assuming your tomatoes are succulent). Bring down the intensity to medium-low. Cook until the shrimp is pink and the tomatoes are delicate.
- Serve warm with your number one side dish.

NUTRITION
Calories: 156kcal
Carbohydrates: 14g
Protein: 2g
Fat: 11g
Saturated Fat: 2g
Polyunsaturated Fat: 1g
Monounsaturated Fat: 8g
Sodium: 302mg
Potassium: 443mg
Fiber: 4g
Sugar: 7g
Vitamin A: 2533IU
Vitamin C: 102mg
Calcium: 47mg
Iron: 1mg

Best Garlic Lemon Shrimp Recipe

PREP TIME: 5 mins, COOK TIME: 15 mins, SERVINGS: 4

INGREDIENTS

•2 tablespoon olive oil

•4 cloves garlic

•1 lb shrimp stripped and deveined

•¼ teaspoon salt

•½ teaspoon paprika

•¼ teaspoon cumin

•2 tablespoons lemon juice

•2 tablespoon parsley

PREPARATION

•Heat olive oil in a skillet over medium intensity.

•Cut the garlic and add it to the skillet and sauté briefly.

•Include shrimp and cook briefly.

•Add paprika, cumin, and salt.

•Pour in the lemon squeeze and sauté for one more moment until the shrimp is pink and cooked.

•Top with hacked parsley and present with bread.

NUTRITION

Calories: 230kcal

Mediterranean Grilled Branzino Recipe

PREP TIME: 15 mins, COOK TIME: 15 mins, SERVINGS: 8

INGREDIENTS

•4 Branzinos cleaned and destroyed
•4 tablespoon olive oil
•3 shallots cut
•8 cloves garlic minced
•1 ½ cup new parsley hacked
•1 cup new dill hacked
•½ teaspoon legitimate salt
•1 teaspoon Aleppo pepper discretionary
•3 lemons juice two of them and cut the other one into dainty half-moons.
•Tomato spice relish
•2 enormous tomatoes slashed finely
•1 jalapeno deseeded and cleaved finely
•1 cup new cilantro cleaved
•¾ cup parsley cleaved
•½ red onion diced finely
•1 lemon juice of
•2 tablespoon olive oil
•½ teaspoon genuine salt

•1/4 teaspoon dark pepper
•1 tsp sumac
PREPARATION
•Cut 3 cuts on the branzino utilizing a sharp blade; you don't have to carve the entire way through.
•In a medium measuring bowl, blend the olive oil with shallots, mince garlic, parsley, dill, Aleppo pepper, salt, and lemon juice. Spoon a portion of this blend inside the branzino. Place the lemon cuts in the hole of the branzino and seal it utilizing two or three toothpicks. Put the branzino on a baking sheet and spoon the remainder of the lemon spice blend on top.
•While the fish is being marinated, set up the barbecue to high; you can utilize charcoal or gas barbecue. Rub half of a potato on the meshes to keep away from the fish staying.
•Put the branzino on the meshes and barbecue for around 8 minutes on each side. Flip just a single time. It's OK if the skin adheres to the meshes. Barbecue the branzino until the skin is brown and firm and the fish is cooked totally.
•Make the tomato spice relish. In a medium estimated bowl, blend the tomatoes with the jalapeno, cilantro, parsley, red onion, lemon juice, olive oil, salt, pepper, and sumac.
•Put the barbecued branzino on the platter and top with the tomato spice relish. Serve right away.

NUTRITION
Calories: 572kcal
Carbohydrates: 11g
Protein: 82g
Fat: 21g
Saturated Fat: 4g
Polyunsaturated Fat: 5g
Monounsaturated Fat: 11g

Cholesterol: 360mg
Sodium: 624mg
Potassium: 1502mg
Fiber: 3g
Sugar: 3g
Vitamin A: 2777IU
Vitamin C: 64mg
Calcium: 130mg
Iron: 6mg

Garlic Lemon Tilapia Recipe

PREP TIME: 5 mins, COOK TIME: 20 mins, TOTAL TIME: 25 mins,
SERVINGS: 4
INGREDIENTS
•4 tilapia filets boneless
•¼ cup additional virgin olive oil
•1 lemon juice of
•4 cloves garlic minced
•½ tsp salt
•tsp dark pepper
•1 tsp Aleppo pepper
•½ teaspoon cumin
•½ teaspoon coriander
•½ teaspoon allspice
•1 cup regular baking flour
•2 tablespoon unsalted margarine
•Decorate
•1 lemon cut
•½ cup parsley slashed
PREPARATION
•Wipe off the tilapia filets and put them away.
•In a shallow bowl, blend olive oil, lemon juice, garlic, salt, dark pepper, Aleppo pepper, cumin, coriander, and allspice.

- Place the flour in another shallow bowl or a plate.
- Soften the spread in an enormous nonstick dish over medium-low intensity.
- Plunge the fish filets in the olive oil combination, and afterward, dig in the flour. Shake to dispose of abundance flour and spot the filet in the skillet. Rehash with the leftover filets.
- Cook the filets for around 4 minutes on each side until they are brilliant.
- Pour the excess olive oil and lemon juice combination into the dish and turn the intensity to medium. On the off chance that anything has adhered to the container, tenderly scratch it utilizing a spatula. Cook for another 5-8 minutes until the sauce has thickened a little and the fish is cooked totally.
- Plate and sprinkle some sauce on top. Get done with lemon cuts and hacked parsley.

NUTRITION
Calories: 473kcal
Carbohydrates: 31g
Protein: 39g
Fat: 23g
Saturated Fat: 7g
Polyunsaturated Fat: 3g
Monounsaturated Fat: 12g
Trans Fat: 1g
Cholesterol: 100mg
Sodium: 395mg
Potassium: 697mg
Fiber: 3g
Sugar: 2g
Vitamin A: 974IU
Vitamin C: 40mg
Calcium: 60mg
Iron: 4mg

Persian Style Shrimp and Rice (Meygoo Polo)

PREP TIME: 10 mins, COOK TIME: 30 mins, TOTAL TIME: 40 mins,
SERVINGS: 4
INGREDIENTS
•2 cups Basmati rice
•3 ½ cups of water
•1 teaspoon salt
•2 tablespoon vegetable oil partitioned
•2 yellow onions finely cleaved
•6 cloves garlic minced
•1 cup new cilantro cleaved
•1-inch new ginger ground
•1 teaspoon tomato glue
•½ teaspoon turmeric
•½ teaspoon salt more if necessary
•¼ teaspoon cayenne pepper see notes
•1 lb shrimp stripped and deveined
PREPARATION
•Set up the rice
•In a sauce container, add the rice, water, one tablespoon of vegetable oil, and salt.
•Bring to stew and cook until the water is practically dissipated.

•Put the top on and cook the rice for an additional 5 minutes on low intensity.
•Switch the intensity off and leave the rice covered and immaculate for 10 minutes.
•Following 10 minutes, gently cushion the rice utilizing a fork.
•Set up the shrimp
•Heat one tablespoon vegetable oil in a container and saute onion until brilliant brown.
•Mix in garlic and cook briefly.
•Mix in ginger. Cook for around 2 minutes.
•Include tomato glue, turmeric, salt, and cayenne pepper. Mix well to blend the fixings.
•Include the shrimp and cook for a couple of additional minutes until the shrimp is pink and completely cooked.
•On a platter, add a layer of rice and top with the shrimp and onion blend. Rehash until all the shrimp and rice is on the platter. (You can likewise add the rice to the shrimp and onion - as displayed in the video - and blend in the dish on the off chance that the container is sufficiently huge)
•Utilizing two forks, blend the rice and shrimp daintily.
•Serve right away.
NUTRITION
Serving: 4servings
Calories: 329kcal
Carbohydrates: 31g
Protein: 29g
Fat: 9g
Saturated Fat: 1g
Polyunsaturated Fat: 7g
Cholesterol: 239mg
Sodium: 1960mg
Fiber: 1g
Sugar: 3g

Baked Mahi Mahi Recipe Greek Style

PREP TIME: 10 mins, COOK TIME: 40 mins, TOTAL TIME: 50 mins,
SERVINGS: 2

INGREDIENTS
•16 ounces Mahi filets around 2
•4 tablespoon olive oil
•5 cloves of garlic are generally hacked
•1 teaspoon dried oregano
•¼ teaspoon newly ground dark pepper
•1 teaspoon dried rosemary
•1 lemon juice of
•½ teaspoon Kosher salt
•½ teaspoon cumin
•½ teaspoon Aleppo pepper or pul biber
•3 cups cherry tomatoes
PREPARATION
•Place the Mahi in a bowl and put it away.
•In a little bowl, blend 2 tablespoons of olive oil with cleaved garlic, oregano, dark pepper, rosemary, lemon

juice, salt, cumin, and Aleppo pepper. Shower over the Mahi and ensure all pieces of the filets are covered with the marinade.

•Cover and refrigerate for 20 minutes as long as 60 minutes.

•Preheat the stove to 400° F and coat a baking sheet with a cooking splash. You can likewise fix the baking sheet with aluminum foil first and coat it with a cooking shower to make cleaning more straightforward.

•Blend the cherry tomatoes in with the leftover 2 tablespoons of olive oil and a touch of salt and pepper. Orchestrate them on the baking sheet.

•Put the marinated Mahi on the baking sheet and Top with the garlic and flavors that were in the marinade.

•Prepare at 400° F for around 20 minutes until the fish is hazy and pieces effectively, and the tomatoes are broiled.

NUTRITION
Calories: 513kcal
Carbohydrates: 18g
Protein: 45g
Fat: 30g
Saturated Fat: 4g
Polyunsaturated Fat: 4g
Monounsaturated Fat: 21g
Cholesterol: 166mg
Sodium: 818mg
Potassium: 1567mg
Fiber: 4g
Sugar: 7g
Vitamin A: 1687IU
Vitamin C: 82mg
Calcium: 110mg
Iron: 6mg

20-minute Greek Shrimp Salad

PREP TIME: 14 mins, COOK TIME: 6 mins, TOTAL TIME: 20 mins,
SERVINGS: 4

INGREDIENTS

Garlic oregano dressing/marinade

•1 teaspoon dried oregano
•3 cloves garlic minced
•1 lemon juice of
•4 tablespoon olive oil
•½ tsp salt
•¼ teaspoon pepper
•½ teaspoon granulated sugar
•Greek shrimp salad
•1 lb huge shrimp defrosted
•2 Persian cucumbers
•1 cup kalamata olives
•1 Roma tomato
•1 green chime pepper
•½ red onion

PREPARATION

•In a bowl, blend oregano, mined garlic, lemon juice, olive oil, salt, pepper, and sugar.
•Put away 50% of the blend to use as dressing. Blend the other half in with defrosted, stripped shrimp and allow it to marinate for 10 minutes.
•In the meantime, cut the Persian cucumbers down the middle the long way and afterward cut every half into pieces. Add it to an enormous bowl.
•Dice the tomato and add it to the cucumbers.
•Cut the chime pepper and the onion, and add them to the bowl too. Throw the vegetables until they're joined.
•Heat a skillet over medium intensity and cook the shrimp for around 6 to 8 minutes until it's completely cooked.
•Add the cooked shrimp to the serving of mixed greens.
•Pour the held dressing over the plate of mixed greens and throw well.
•Serve right away.

NUTRITION
Calories: 319kcal
Carbohydrates: 10g
Protein: 25g
Fat: 21g
Saturated Fat: 3g
Polyunsaturated Fat: 3g
Monounsaturated Fat: 14g
Cholesterol: 286mg
Sodium: 1701mg
Potassium: 309mg
Fiber: 3g
Sugar: 4g
Vitamin A: 417IU
Vitamin C: 48mg
Calcium: 214mg
Iron: 3mg

Easy Parmesan Baked Cod Recipe

PREP TIME: 10 mins, COOK TIME: 15 mins, TOTAL TIME: 25 mins,
SERVINGS: 4

INGREDIENTS
•1 cup parmesan ground
•1 tsp paprika
•1 teaspoon dried oregano
•½ teaspoon salt
•¼ teaspoon dark pepper
•2 lb cod filet cut into little pieces
•1 tbsp olive oil

PREPARATION
•Preheat the broiler to 400 °F. Line a baking sheet with aluminum foil and coat it with a cooking shower.
•In a little bowl, blend parmesan in with paprika, dried oregano, salt, and pepper.
•Brush the cod filets with olive oil on all sides.
•Cover each filet with the parmesan combination, and ensure that the filets are covered well on all sides.

•Put the filets on the baking sheet. Prepare on the stove for 15 to 20 minutes, until the fish is cooked and chips without any problem.
•Present with earthy-colored rice or a side plate of mixed greens.

NUTRITION
Calories: 318kcal
Carbohydrates: 2g
Protein: 49g
Fat: 12g
Saturated Fat: 5g
Cholesterol: 115mg
Sodium: 814mg
Potassium: 971mg
Fiber: 1g
Sugar: 1g
Vitamin A: 532IU
Vitamin C: 2mg
Calcium: 340mg
Iron: 1mg

Healthy Mediterranean Tuna Salad Recipe

PREP TIME: 15 mins, TOTAL TIME: 15 mins, SERVINGS: 4

INGREDIENTS

- 2 jars of fish depleted
- 1 cup marinated artichoke hearts
- ½ cup Kalamata olives divided
- ½ red onion cleaved
- ⅓ cup cooked red pepper hacked
- 2 tablespoon escapades
- ⅓ cup new dill cleaved
- ⅓ cup mint cleaved
- ⅓ cup green onions cleaved
- Lemon Garlic Vinaigrette
- 1 lemon juice of
- 1 teaspoon dried oregano
- 4 cloves garlic minced
- ⅓ cup olive oil additional virgin
- ¼ teaspoon salt
- ⅛ teaspoon Aleppo pepper

PREPARATION

•Place the fish in an enormous bowl, and utilizing a fork, break the lumps into little pieces.

•Add artichokes, Kalamata olives, red onion, broiled red pepper, tricks, dill, mint, and green onions to the fish.

•Blend every one of the fixings well, utilizing an enormous spoon. Shower the lemon garlic vinaigrette over the fish salad and refrigerate for 30 minutes before serving.

•Lemon garlic vinaigrette

•Blend lemon juice, oregano, garlic, olive oil, salt, and pepper in a container or a bowl, then sprinkle it over the fish salad.

NUTRITION

Calories: 341kcal
Carbohydrates: 10g
Protein: 19g
Fat: 26g
Saturated Fat: 4g
Polyunsaturated Fat: 2g
Monounsaturated Fat: 15g
Trans Fat: 1g
Cholesterol: 31mg
Sodium: 1086mg
Potassium: 328mg
Fiber: 4g
Sugar: 2g
Vitamin A: 1259IU
Vitamin C: 38mg
Calcium: 87mg
Iron: 3mg

Salmon Croquette Recipe Mediterranean Style

PREP TIME: 15 mins, COOK TIME: 30 mins, SERVINGS: 6

INGREDIENTS

•4 chestnut potatoes were stripped and washed
•15 oz salmon canned or extras (see notes)
•2 enormous eggs
•3 green onions slashed
•½ teaspoon paprika
•1 teaspoon garlic powder
•¼ teaspoon salt
•1 tablespoon mustard
•⅓ cup breadcrumbs
•4 tablespoon olive oil

PREPARATION

•Carry a pot of water to bubble. Heat the potatoes until fork delicate.
•Channel and spot the potatoes in an enormous bowl and squash them utilizing a fork or a potato masher.
•Include cooked salmon and blend well.

•Include the eggs and mix.

•Add green onions, paprika, salt, garlic powder, mustard, and breadcrumbs. Blend well until every one of the fixings is consolidated.

•Cover the bowl and refrigerate for 60 minutes.

•Following 60 minutes, remove the bowl from the refrigerator and take around 2 tablespoons of the combination. Shape it into a chamber utilizing your hands. Rehash with the leftover combination.

•Heat 2 tablespoons olive oil in a dish over medium intensity and burn the croquettes on one side for 3 minutes. Flip and burn on different sides until brilliant brown. Add more oil to burn the following clump if necessary.

NUTRITION
Calories: 349kcal
Carbohydrates: 31g
Protein: 23g
Fat: 15g
Saturated Fat: 3g
Cholesterol: 129mg
Sodium: 475mg
Potassium: 889mg
Fiber: 2g
Sugar: 2g
Vitamin A: 290IU
Vitamin C: 9mg
Calcium: 245mg
Iron: 3mg

Spanish Garlic Shrimp Recipe (Gambas Al Ajillo)

PREP TIME: 5 mins, COOK TIME: 10 mins, TOTAL TIME: 15 mins,
SERVINGS: 4

INGREDIENTS
•¼ cup olive oil additional virgin
•1 teaspoon red pepper pieces
•10 cloves of garlic cut
•1 lb gigantic shrimp stripped and deveined
•½ teaspoon salt
•½ lemon juice of
•⅓ cup parsley cleaved
PREPARATION
•Heat olive oil in a container over medium intensity. Add the red pepper pieces and cut garlic. Saute until the garlic is fragrant.
•Throw shrimp with salt and add it to the garlic. Burn for a couple of moments until cooked and, as of now, not pink.
•Shower with lemon squeeze and sprinkle hacked parsley. Serve right away.

NUTRITION
Calories: 251kcal
Carbohydrates: 4g
Protein: 24g
Fat: 15g
Saturated Fat: 2g
Cholesterol: 286mg
Sodium: 1185mg
Potassium: 177mg
Fiber: 1g
Sugar: 1g
Vitamin A: 569IU
Vitamin C: 21mg
Calcium: 188mg
Iron: 3mg

Turkish Baked Cod Recipe

PREP TIME: 20 mins, COOK TIME: 30 mins, SERVINGS: 4

INGREDIENTS

•2 tablespoon olive oil
•onion slashed
•5 cloves garlic minced
•1 red ringer pepper cleaved
•1 green ringer pepper cleaved
•4 Roma tomatoes slashed
•½ teaspoon salt
•1 teaspoon oregano
•¼ teaspoon dark pepper
•2 lb cod filets
•2 lemons cut

PREPARATION

•Preheat the broiler to 375°F.
•Heat olive oil in a skillet over medium intensity.

•Saute onion and garlic until clear. Include slashed ringer pepper and tomatoes. Cook until the tomatoes are delicate.
•Include salt, pepper, and oregano. Mix well.
•Move the veggies into a broiler-safe dish.
•Sprinkle salt and pepper on the cod filets.
•Put the cod filets on top of the veggies and top the filets with lemon cuts.
•Heat in the broiler for 25 minutes until the fish is completely cooked.
•Present with your #1 side dish.

NUTRITION
Calories: 307kcal
Carbohydrates: 15g
Protein: 43g
Fat: 9g
Saturated Fat: 1g
Cholesterol: 98mg
Sodium: 421mg
Potassium: 1328mg
Fiber: 4g
Sugar: 6g
Vitamin A: 1649IU
Vitamin C: 104mg
Calcium: 77mg
Iron: 2mg

Grilled Alaska Halibut with Spicy Mango Salsa

PREP TIME: 15 mins, COOK TIME: 15 mins, TOTAL TIME: 30 mins,
SERVINGS: 2

INGREDIENTS

•1 lb. The Frozen North halibut skinless
•1 lemon juice of
•1/4 teaspoon dark pepper
•1/2 teaspoon bean stew pepper
•1/2 teaspoon cumin
•1/2 teaspoon salt
•3 tablespoon olive oil
•Zesty Mango Salsa
•1 mango finely diced
•1/2 red chime pepper diced
•1/2 red onion finely diced
•1/2 cup cilantro finely cleaved
•1/2 jalapeno seeds eliminated and finely diced
•1 lime juice of
•1/2 teaspoon salt

PREPARATION

•Blend lemon juice, dark pepper, bean stew pepper, cumin, salt, and olive oil in a bowl and pour it over Alaska halibut. Cover and refrigerate for 30 minutes.

•Heat the barbecue (or the barbecue container) over medium intensity. Once hot, put the marinated halibut filet on the endless barbecue for 5 minutes.

•Flip the fish and barbecue on the opposite side for an additional five minutes.

•Present with fiery mango salsa.

•Fiery mango salsa

•Blend diced mango, red ringer pepper, red onion, cilantro, and jalapeno in a bowl.

•Add lime squeeze and salt to the salsa and mix well.

•Refrigerate for 30 minutes before serving.

NUTRITION

Calories: 505kcal
Carbohydrates: 29g
Protein: 45g
Fat: 25g
Saturated Fat: 4g
Cholesterol: 111mg
Sodium: 1325mg
Potassium: 1393mg
Fiber: 5g
Sugar: 19g
Vitamin A: 2511IU
Vitamin C: 123mg
Calcium: 59mg
Iron: 2mg

Grilled Salmon Shish Kabobs

PREP TIME: 10 mins, COOK TIME: 10 mins, TOTAL TIME: 20 mins,
SERVINGS: 4

INGREDIENTS

- 1 lb salmon cut into strong shapes
- 1/4 cup olive oil extra virgin
- 1 lemon juice of
- 1 teaspoon cumin
- 1/2 teaspoon coriander
- 1 teaspoon paprika
- 1/2 teaspoon turmeric
- 1/2 teaspoon salt
- 1/2 teaspoon pepper
- onions and peppers to grill

PREPARATION

- Place the salmon's strong shapes in an enormous bowl.
- In another bowl, mix olive oil, lemon juice, cumin, coriander, paprika, turmeric, salt, and pepper.

•Shower over salmon pieces and blend well until totally mixed.
•Cover and marinate in the fridge for 30 minutes.
•Heat grill and start hanging the salmon and veggies on sticks.
•Grill over medium-extreme focus for 5 minutes on each side.

NUTRITION
Calories: 293kcal
Carbohydrates: 3g
Protein: 23g
Fat: 21g
Saturated Fat: 3g
Cholesterol: 62mg
Sodium: 343mg
Potassium: 613mg
Fiber: 1g
Sugar: 1g
Vitamin A: 292IU
Vitamin C: 14mg
Calcium: 25mg
Iron: 2mg

Sauteed Shrimp Mediterranean Style

PREP TIME: 10 mins, **COOK TIME:** 20 mins, TOTAL TIME: 30 mins,
SERVINGS: 4

INGREDIENTS
•1 lb shrimp stripped and deveined
•½ teaspoon salt
•1 ½ teaspoon dried oregano
•1 teaspoon paprika
•1 teaspoon cumin
•2 tablespoon olive oil, additional virgin
•1 yellow onion cut
•6 cloves garlic minced
•1 leek white and light green parts desolately cut
•1 yellow ringer pepper cut
•2 tremendous tomatoes diced
•1 tablespoon undertakings
•1 lemon juice of
To serve:

•2 cups Minute Ready to Serve Brown Rice

PREPARATION

•Place the shrimp in a gigantic bowl.

•Blend salt, oregano, paprika, and cumin. Blend half of the flavor, blend in with shrimp, and put away.

•Heat the olive oil in a gigantic dish. Saute onion until touchy.

•Add garlic, leek, and yellow ringer pepper to the onion. Add the flavors and saute until smooth.

•Integrate the tomatoes and cook for 5 minutes.

•Mix in the lemon press and misleads.

•Add the shrimp and cook for 3-5 minutes. Flip practically the entire way until pink on all sides.

•Present with Minute Ready to Serve Rice.

NUTRITION

Calories: 245kcal
Carbohydrates: 16g
Protein: 26g
Fat: 9g
Saturated Fat: 1g
Cholesterol: 286mg
Sodium: 1241mg
Potassium: 535mg
Fiber: 4g
Sugar: 5g
Vitamin A: 1447IU
Vitamin C: 92mg
Calcium: 228mg
Iron: 4mg

Alaska Cod Fish Curry

PREP TIME: 10 mins, COOK TIME: 30 mins, TOTAL TIME: 40 mins,
SERVINGS: 4

INGREDIENTS

- 1 tablespoon ghee or olive oil
- 1 enormous onion finely slashed
- 5 cloves garlic minced
- ½ tablespoon new ginger ground or minced
- 1 Serrano pepper seed eliminated and finely diced
- 2 tomatoes diced
- ½ teaspoon coriander powder
- ¼ teaspoon cardamom powder
- 1 tsp paprika
- ½ teaspoon turmeric
- 1 tablespoon garam masala
- 1 teaspoon salt
- ½ cup coconut milk
- ½ cup water
- 1 ½ lb Alaska cod cut into 1 ½ inch lumps

•To serve:
•Basmati rice
•Lime

PREPARATION

•Heat ghee in a skillet over medium intensity.
•Sauté onion. Garlic and new ginger until clear.
•Add in diced serrano pepper and cook briefly.
•Mix in diced tomatoes and add coriander powder, cardamom, paprika, turmeric, garam masala, and salt to the onion and tomato blend.
•Mix and cover the skillet to let the vegetables and flavors cook together for a couple of moments.
•Pour in water and coconut milk. Carry it to a sluggish stew.
•Include pieces of Alaska cod and settle them in the sauce.
•Allow the curry to stew and the cod to cook for around ten minutes until the fish is cooked totally.
•Serve warm with basmati rice, lime, and new tomatoes.

NUTRITION

Calories: 270kcal
Carbohydrates: 9g
Protein: 32g
Fat: 11g
Saturated Fat: 8g
Cholesterol: 83mg
Sodium: 685mg
Potassium: 992mg
Fiber: 2g
Sugar: 3g
Vitamin A: 841IU
Vitamin C: 15mg
Calcium: 54mg
Iron: 2mg

The Best Shrimp Avocado Salad

PREP TIME: 10 mins, COOK TIME: 10 mins, TOTAL TIME: 20 mins,
SERVINGS: 6
INGREDIENTS
•2 tablespoon vegetable oil
•20-25 enormous shrimp stripped and deveined
•4-6 cups spring blend
•½ cup pecans cleaved
•½ cup dried cranberries
•⅓ red onion cut
•2 avocados
•1 lemon
•½ cup green olives cut
•Dressing:
•1 teaspoon lemon pepper
•1 teaspoon spice de Provence
•½ teaspoon cumin
•½ teaspoon garlic powder
•½ teaspoon paprika
•2 tablespoons white vinegar
•¼ cup olive oil

•¼ cup water

PREPARATION

•Heat oil in a container over medium intensity. Sauté shrimps until light pink, around 2-3 minutes for every side.

•On an enormous platter, spread the spring blend and top with cooked shrimps, pecans, dried cranberries, and cut red onion.

•Slice the avocados down the middle, take the pit out and cut every half. Put the avocado on the platter with a serving of mixed greens.

•Cut the lemon into half-moons and add it to the plate of mixed greens.

•At long last, add cut pitted olives.

•Blend every one of the fixings in a bowl, and add salt to taste if necessary.

•Pour the dressing on the plate of mixed greens and serve.

NUTRITION

Calories: 379kcal
Carbohydrates: 22g
Protein: 7g
Fat: 32g
Saturated Fat: 7g
Polyunsaturated Fat: 7g
Monounsaturated Fat: 16g
Trans Fat: 1g
Cholesterol: 29mg
Sodium: 322mg
Potassium: 534mg
Fiber: 8g
Sugar: 9g
Vitamin A: 589IU
Vitamin C: 33mg
Calcium: 60mg
Iron: 2mg

Easy Salmon Patties Recipe

PREP TIME: 10 mins, COOK TIME: 30 mins, TOTAL TIME: 40 mins,
SERVINGS: 4

INGREDIENTS

- 1 lb Alaska salmon
- 4 tablespoon olive oil partitioned
- 1 shallot finely cleaved
- ½ yellow onion finely cleaved
- 2 cloves garlic minced
- ½ red ringer pepper diced
- ½ cup olives slashed
- 3 eggs
- 1 cup of bread scraps
- 1 teaspoon sumac
- ½ teaspoon cumin
- ½ teaspoon pink salt
- 1 teaspoon dried dill
- 1 teaspoon Dijon mustard
- Tzatziki sauce to serve

PREPARATION

•Preheat the stove to 400F. Cover a baking sheet with a nonstick splash.
•Put salmon pieces on the baking sheet and brush with olive oil and sprinkle some salt and pepper on the salmon.
•Prepare the salmon on the stove for 20 minutes.
•In the meantime, heat two tablespoons of olive oil in a dish and saute shallot, onion, garlic, and chime pepper until vegetables are delicate and onions are clear.
•When the salmon is cooked, piece it involving a fork and spot it in an enormous bowl.
•Add cooked shallots, onions, garlic, and ringer pepper to the chipped salmon and blend well.
•Add olives, eggs, and bread pieces to the blend and blend well, so every one of the fixings is all-around integrated.
•Include sumac, cumin, salt, dried dill, and Dijon mustard, and mix well.
•Heat the excess olive oil in a dish over medium intensity.
•Scoop out the salmon patties and shape them with your hand.
•Sear the patties in the dish for four minutes on each side until they are firm and brilliant outwardly.
•Present with additional olive, rice, or a side serving of mixed greens.

NUTRITION
Calories: 482kcal
Carbohydrates: 24g
Protein: 31g
Fat: 29g
Saturated Fat: 5g
Cholesterol: 185mg
Sodium: 865mg

Potassium: 726mg
Fiber: 3g
Sugar: 4g
Vitamin A: 770IU
Vitamin C: 21mg
Calcium: 101mg
Iron: 3mg

Best Salmon Marinade Mediterranean Style

PREP TIME: 10 mins, COOK TIME: 20 mins, SERVINGS: 4

INGREDIENTS

- •2 lb salmon
- •2 lemon juice of
- •4 tablespoon olive oil
- •2 tbsp honey
- •6 cloves of garlic cut
- •½ teaspoon salt
- •1 teaspoon dried oregano
- •¼ tsp dull pepper
- •1 teaspoon dried dill
- •½ teaspoon red pepper pieces

PREPARATION

- •Clear off the salmon and put it on a baking sheet or a compartment.
- •In a bowl, mix lemon juice, olive oil, honey, cut garlic, salt, oregano, pepper, dill, and red pepper drops. Pour the marinade over the salmon.

•Cover and refrigerate to marinade for 30 minutes to 4 hours.
•Exactly when ready to warm, preheat the oven to 400°F and line a baking sheet with aluminum foil or coat it with a nonstick cooking sprinkle.
•Eliminate the salmon from the refrigerator and move it to the baking sheet.
•Set up the salmon in the oven for 20 minutes. The salmon is arranged when it chips really and is dark.
•Present with a side plate of leafy greens.

NUTRITION
Calories: 503kcal
Carbohydrates: 16g
Protein: 46g
Fat: 29g
Saturated Fat: 4g
Cholesterol: 125mg
Sodium: 398mg
Potassium: 1204mg
Fiber: 2g
Sugar: 10g
Vitamin A: 179IU
Vitamin C: 30mg
Calcium: 62mg
Iron: 3mg

POULTRY RECIPES

CREAMY LEMON CHICKEN PICCATA

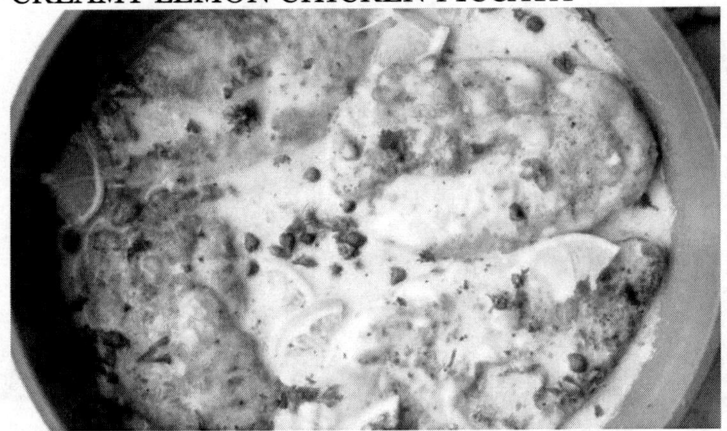

Prep Time: 10 minutes, **Cook Time**: 15 minutes, **Total Time:** 25 minutes,
Servings: 4,

INGREDIENTS
For the chicken:
•2 chicken bosoms (1 lb. complete) boneless and skinless
•1 teaspoon salt
•1 teaspoon ground dark pepper
•1 teaspoon Italian flavoring
•¼ cup regular flour
•2 tablespoons vegetable oil
•For the sauce:
•2 tablespoons spread
•2 teaspoons garlic, minced
•1 cup chicken stock (or 1 tablespoon chicken bouillon powder + 1 cup water)
•½ tablespoon of regular flour
•⅓ cup weighty cream
•2 tablespoons tricks

•1 tablespoon lemon juice
•1 tablespoon new parsley, finely hacked (for decorate)
•1 tablespoon lemon wedges, daintily cut (for decorate)
•For serving (discretionary):
•6 to 8 oz. dry pasta
•pureed potatoes

PREPARATION

•Cut every chicken bosom cautiously in half the long way (on a level plane) and spot each in turn, between 2 sheets of plastic grip wrap or in a Ziploc cooler sack. Cautiously level the chicken bosoms with a moving pin until they are roughly ¼-inch thick. Try not to pound the bosoms excessively hard, as it could destroy them. In a perfect world, you need straightened chicken bosoms with uniform thickness.

•Season the two sides of every chicken bosom with salt, pepper, and Italian flavoring. Then, dunk the chicken in a shallow bowl of flour and uniformly coat the two sides. Put away on a plate.

•Heat oil in a huge skillet over medium-high for 2 minutes until the oil is sizzling and shining.

•Sear the chicken for around 5 minutes for every side until brilliant brown and completely cooked through. The inside temperature for the chicken ought to reach 165F. Contingent upon the size of your skillet, you might need to do this in two groups. Lay the chicken on a plate.

•In a similar skillet, liquefy spread and sauté the garlic until fragrant, around 1 moment. Mix in chicken stock and flour and blend well until the sauce is smooth and uniform.

•Include weighty cream, escapades, and lemon juice. Turn the intensity down to medium-low and carry the sauce to a stew until thickened to an ideal consistency, around 2-3 minutes. Mix persistently, assuming the cream coagulates on account of lemon juice, until smooth.

•Return the chicken to the skillet and throw well to cover. Let the chicken cook with the sauce for one more moment, and trim with lemon wedges and parsley.

•Serve quickly with a side of pasta.

NUTRITION FACTS
Total Fat 16.9g 13%
Cholesterol 38.1mg 40%
Sodium 924.5mg 3%
Total Carbohydrate 9.2g
Sugars 0.8g 10%
Protein 5.2g 12%
Vitamin A 110.3μg 6%
Vitamin C 5mg

ONE PAN OF GARLIC ROASTED CHICKEN AND BABY POTATOES

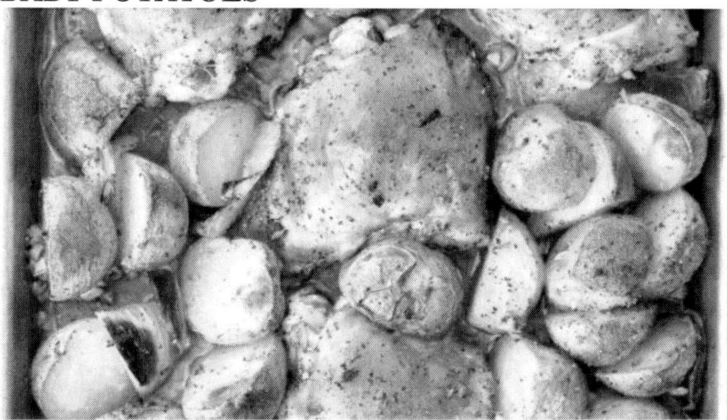

Prep Time: 10 minutes, **Cook Time:** 1 hour 25 minutes, **Total Time:** 1 hour 35 minutes

Servings: 6

INGREDIENTS

•5 to 6 chicken thighs, bone-in, and skin on (2 lbs. absolute)

•15-20 child potatoes, divided

•2 medium carrots, cut into 1-inch pieces (discretionary)

•½ onion, quartered

•4 cloves garlic, minced

•2 to 3 tablespoons olive oil

•2 teaspoons salt (or to taste)

•½ teaspoon ground dark pepper (or to taste)

•1 tablespoon dried rosemary

PREPARATION

•Preheat the broiler to 350 degrees F.

•In an enormous simmering skillet or goulash dish, add chicken, potatoes, carrots (if utilized), onion, garlic, and olive oil. Season with salt and pepper and throw to cover.

•Organize in the middle of between the potatoes. Then, at that point, sprinkle dried rosemary on top of the chicken and vegetables.
•Place the skillet in the broiler and cook for 1 hour and 25 minutes until the skin is fresh and brilliant brown and the potatoes are delicate when punctured with a fork.
•For crispier and more cooked skin, turn the grill on high and sear for 3-4 minutes until fresh. Make certain to watch out for the oven as things can consume rapidly.
•Eliminate from broiler and serve.

NUTRITION FACTS
Total Fat 12.2g 47%
Cholesterol 140.1mg 69%
Sodium 1582.5mg 17%
Total Carbohydrate 46.4g
Sugars 3.9g 69%
Protein 34.3g 1%
Vitamin A 11.7µg 31%
Vitamin C 27.5mg

BAKED CHICKEN BREAST WITH GREEK SOUVLAKI MARINADE

Prep Time: 10 minutes, **Cook Time:** 25 minutes, **Total Time:** 1 hour 35 minutes,
Serving: 4

INGREDIENTS

•2 tablespoons olive oil
•lemon juice from a piece of a lemon
•2 cloves garlic, squeezed or minced
•2 tablespoons new parsley, hacked
•1 tablespoon dried oregano
•1 teaspoon dried mint (or dill)
•1 teaspoon paprika (discretionary)
•½ teaspoon salt
•½ teaspoon ground faint pepper
•2 chicken chests, boneless and skinless

PREPARATION

•In a medium bowl, go along with one olive oil, lemon juice, garlic, parsley, oregano, dill, paprika, salt, and pepper.

•Place chicken chests in a huge shallow bowl and pour the marinade up and over. Throw the chicken in the marinade to guarantee that they are covered.
•Cover the bowl with plastic hold wrap and spot in the cooler for 1 hour to permit the chicken to marinate.
•Preheat the broiler to 450 F. Put chicken on a quarter sheet baking skillet and power for 20-25 minutes, until chicken is long, not pink inside, and inside temperature appears at 165 F in the thickest piece of the chicken chest (as analyzed on a meat thermometer).
•Clear out the chicken off of the stove and grant it to sit for 5 minutes. Serve warm with a side of a Greek plate of salad greens, pita bread, rice pilaf, and Greek lemon singed potatoes. Also, review the tzatziki sauce.

NUTRITION FACTS
Total Fat 10.7g 33%
Cholesterol 99.3mg 15%
Sodium 353.6mg 1%
Total Carbohydrate 2.1g
Sugars 0.4g 62%
Protein 30.9g 2%
Vitamin A 20.9µg 8%
Vitamin C 7.6mg

ROASTED SPATCHCOCK CHICKEN (BUTTERFLIED CHICKEN)

Prep Time: 15 minutes, **Cook Time:** 40 minutes, **Total Time:** 55 minutes,
Serving: 6

INGREDIENTS

- •1 whole chicken (3 to 4 lbs.)
- •2 tablespoons olive oil, detached
- •1 tablespoon salt
- •½ tablespoon ground dull pepper
- •3 cloves garlic, stripped (+ 1 tablespoon minced)
- •1 twig rosemary
- •2-3 parts of thyme (+1 tablespoon cut)

PREPARATION

Spatchcock the Chicken:

•Clear off the whole chicken and dry with a paper towel before adding preparation. This makes extra new skin while cooking.

•Put chicken chest side down on an ideal and dry slicing board (wearing nonessential gloves helps with basically dealing with).

•Cut along the spine in the middle with kitchen scissors and dispose of the spine, which is around 1-inch wide.
•Make a somewhat cut with a sharp edge along the white tendon that interfaces the breastbone and kills the breastbone by getting it out through the cut.
•Turn the chicken over with the chest side up and even out it out. Overlay the wings under the chicken chests.
•Clear off the spatchcock chicken again to take out any excess liquid.
Season the Spatchcock Chicken:
•In a little bowl, blend one tablespoon of olive oil, salt, and pepper, until joined.
•Generously smeared the enhancing mix over the whole chicken all around and permitted it to lay on a perfect plate for something like 15 minutes. Guarantee the enhancement covers the entire chicken, including inside the pit.
Cook the Chicken:
•Preheat the oven to 450F.
•Heat a cast-iron skillet on the stove for 5 minutes over medium-extreme focus (or preheat the iron skillet on the grill for 5 minutes). At the point when the skillet is sizzling hot, burn the chicken by putting chicken chest side down in the hot skillet for 3-5 minutes, until the skin gets fairly firm.
•Move the skillet to the oven and set up the chicken for 30 minutes until the skin on the chest becomes brown. You can add a grill-safe burden over the chicken, for instance, a Dutch oven cover, to progress caramelizing.
•Kill the skillet from the grill and turn the chicken over with the chest side up. Crease whole garlic cloves and twigs of rosemary and thyme under the chicken to add flavor.
•Join the overabundance of oil, hacked thyme, and minced garlic in a little bowl and brush the enhancing mix over the chicken chests.

•Move the skillet back into the oven and continue to prepare the chicken for 10 extra minutes until the inside temperature comes to 165F.
•Dispose of the chicken from the oven and put it on a gigantic plate. Let the chicken rest for 15 minutes. Then, at that point, cut and serve.

NUTRITION FACTS
Total Fat 11g 14% 52%
Cholesterol 154.7mg 57%
Sodium 1305.2mg 0%
Total Carbohydrate 1.1g
Sugars 0g 80%
Protein 40g 2%
Vitamin A 16.8µg 1%
Vitamin C 1.1mg

CHICKEN MARSALA

Prep Time: 10 minutes, **Cook Time:** 20 minutes,
Total Time: 30 minutes,
Servings: 4

INGREDIENTS
For the Chicken:
•2 chicken chests, boneless and skinless (around 1 lb.)
•½ teaspoon salt
•½ teaspoon ground dim pepper
•¼ cup standard baking flour
•2 tablespoons olive oil
•For the Creamy Mushroom Sauce:
•2 tablespoons margarine, unsalted
•2 cups gritty shaded mushrooms, pitifully cut
•1 teaspoon ordinary flour
•½ teaspoon Italian seasoning
•1 tablespoon garlic, minced
•½ cup dry marsala wine
•1 cup chicken stock
•⅓ cup profound cream

•1 tablespoon new parsley, finely severed (for embellishing)

PREPARATION

•Slice each chicken chest warily down the middle longwise (uniformly) and place one by one between 2 sheets of grasp wrap or in a Ziploc cooler sack. Carefully level the chicken chests with a moving pin until they are generally ¼ inch thick. Do whatever it takes not to pound the chests exorbitantly hard as it could annihilate the chest. Ideally, you want evened-out chicken chests to a uniform thickness.

•Season the different sides of every chicken chest with salt and pepper. Set up a shallow plate with flour and dive the chicken into the flour, consistently covering the different sides. Set aside.

•Heat oil in a huge skillet over medium-high for 2 minutes until the hot oil sizzles. Consume the chicken for about 5 minutes for each side until splendid brown and cooked through. The inside temperature for the chicken should reach 165F. Move the chicken to a plate.

•In a comparable skillet, melt spread and sauté mushrooms until splendid brown on the different sides, close to 5 minutes. Add to some degree more olive oil, if vital.

•Blend in flour, Italian enhancing, and garlic and sauté until fragrant, around 1 second.

•Pour in Marsala wine, chicken stock, and cream and whisk well until the sauce is smooth and uniform. Reduce force to medium and convey the sauce to a stew until thickened to an optimal consistency, around 4-5 minutes.

•Return the chicken to the skillet and toss well to cover, allowing the chicken to cook and ingest the sauce for 1-2 minutes.

•Improve with parsley and serve rapidly with pasta, rice, or over pureed potatoes.

NUTRITION FACTS
Total Fat 19.6g 37%
Cholesterol 110.5mg 101%
Sodium 2323.5mg 4%
Total Carbohydrate 10g
Sugars 1.4g 57%
Protein 28.4g 12%
Vitamin A 107.4µg 1%
Vitamin C 0.8mg

GENERAL TSO'S CHICKEN

Prep Time: 10 minutes, **Cook Time:** 20 minutes, **Total Time:** 30 minutes,
Servings: 3
INGREDIENTS
Chicken:
•1 lb. chicken thighs or bosoms, boneless and skinless, cut into 1-inch shapes
•½ tablespoon salt
•1 teaspoon ground dark pepper
•1 tablespoon olive oil
•½ cup regular baking flour (or cornstarch)
•cooking oil shower
•1 teaspoon sesame seeds (for decorating)
•Sauce:
•2 tablespoons soy sauce
•2 tablespoons dark vinegar
•1 tablespoon Chinese Shaoxing cooking wine (or mirin)
•1 tablespoon granulated sugar
•½ cup chicken stock
•2-3 dried red bean stew peppers, cut into 1-inch pieces
•1 teaspoon garlic, minced
•1 teaspoon ginger, newly ground

•1 green onion, cut into 1-inch pieces
•1 teaspoon sesame oil
•2 teaspoons cornstarch (or regular flour)
PREPARATION
•Preheat stove to 400F.
•Wipe off the chicken totally with a paper towel and cut it into 1-inch 3D squares. Place into a medium blending bowl and season it with salt, pepper, and oil. Throw well to consolidate and set to the side for no less than 5 minutes.
•In a huge Ziploc pack, add flour and cubed chicken. Seal the sack and shake well to equitably cover.
•Put covered chicken on a huge half-sheet baking skillet fixed with material paper. Softly shower the chicken with cooking splash oil to assist with making a fresh covering outwardly.
•Prepare for 20 minutes until brilliant brown. Put away on a plate in the wake of baking.
•In another medium blending bowl, whisk together all the sauce fixings until sugar and cornstarch are completely consolidated.
•In a shallow pot or wok, heat the sauce over medium intensity for 3-4 minutes. Continue to mix until thickened to the ideal consistency. Add the prepared chicken and throw well to cover.
•Decorate with sesame seeds on top and serve quickly with a bowl of steamed rice or boiled rice.
NUTRITION FACTS
Total Fat 14g 16%
Cholesterol 47.5mg 72%
Sodium 1655.6mg 10%
Total Carbohydrate 28.3g
Sugars 5.2g 28%
Protein 14g 4%
Vitamin A 33.9µg 2%
Vitamin C 1.5mg

BAKED QUESO CHICKEN

Prep Time: 5 minutes, **Cook Time:** 30 minutes, **Total Time:** 35 minutes,
Servings: 6

INGREDIENTS

•4 chicken bosoms (around 2 lb. all out), skinless and boneless

•2 tablespoons olive oil, isolated

•1 teaspoon ground cumin

•1 teaspoon bean stew powder

•1 teaspoon paprika

•½ teaspoon garlic powder

•½ teaspoon dried oregano or Italian flavoring

•½ teaspoon salt (or to taste)

•¼ teaspoon ground dark pepper

•1 medium onion, finely slashed

•1 medium tomato, diced

•jalapeño, diced (discretionary)

•2 cups queso sauce, natively constructed or locally acquired

•1 tablespoon new cilantro (for decorating)

PREPARATION

•Preheat broiler to 400 F. Organize broiler rack on the first rate.

•In an enormous Ziploc sack, join chicken bosoms with 1 tablespoon olive oil and all preparations, including cumin, stew powder, paprika, garlic powder, oregano, salt, and pepper. Press air out of the pack and seal firmly. Press the flavoring around the chicken to cover. Allow it to marinate for something like 15 minutes, up to expedite in the cooler.

•At the point when prepared to cook, heat the excess 1 tablespoon oil in an enormous cast-iron skillet for 2 minutes over medium-high intensity until the hot oil sizzles. Burn the chicken bosoms until well caramelized on the two sides, around 4-5 minutes on each side. Once finished, move onto a plate.

•In a similar skillet, add onion, tomato, and jalapeño and sauté until delicate, around 2-3 minutes.

•Return the chicken to the skillet and top with sautéed onion and tomato. Spread queso sauce uniformly over every chicken bosom. (If you don't have a solid metal skillet, utilize a 9x13-inch dish container).

•Prepare on the top rack of the broiler for 20-25 minutes until completely cooked through and the queso becomes brilliant brown. The interior temperature for the chicken ought to arrive at 165F as perused on a meat thermometer.

•Embellish with new cilantro and present with cilantro lime rice, dried-up bread, or over pasta whenever wanted.

NUTRITION FACTS

Total Fat 21.7g 57%

Cholesterol 172.4mg 37%

Sodium 850.4mg 2%

Total Carbohydrate 4.4g

Sugars 1g 99%
Protein 49.3g 15%
Vitamin A 132µg 2%
Vitamin C 2.2mg

OVEN-BAKED CHICKEN BREAST

Prep Time: 15 minutes, **Cook Time:** 25 minutes, **Total Time:** 40 minutes,
Servings: 4

INGREDIENTS

•4 boneless and skinless chicken bosoms (around 2 pounds all out)

•1 tablespoon olive oil

•½ teaspoon garlic powder

•½ teaspoon paprika

•½ teaspoon Italian flavoring

•½ teaspoon salt

•½ teaspoon ground dark pepper

PREPARATION

•Preheat the broiler to 450F.

•In an enormous blending bowl or Ziploc sack, join chicken bosoms with oil, garlic powder, paprika, Italian flavoring, salt, and pepper. Rub well to cover equitably and put away until the stove is prepared.

•Place the chicken bosoms in a meal dish or enormous half-sheet baking skillet. Prepare for 20 minutes until

completely cooked through. The interior temperature for the chicken ought to arrive at 165F as perused on a meat thermometer.
•Freely cover with aluminum foil and let the chicken rest at room temperature for 5 minutes.
•Sprinkle with lemon juice whenever wanted. Cut and serve warm.

NUTRITION FACTS
Total Fat 9.5g 55%
Cholesterol 165.5mg 17%
Sodium 393.3mg 0%
Total Carbohydrate 0.8g
Sugars 0g 102%
Protein 51.2g 4%
Vitamin A 35.1µg 0%
Vitamin C 0.1mg

APPLE CIDER CHICKEN WITH BUTTERNUT SQUASH

Prep Time: 15 minutes, **Cook Time:** 25 minutes, **Total Time:** 40 minutes,
Servings: 6

INGREDIENTS
- •5 chicken bosoms, boneless, skin-on
- •2 tablespoons olive oil, isolated
- •2 tablespoons paprika
- •1 tablespoon salt
- •½ tablespoon ground dark pepper
- •1 cup apple juice (NOT apple juice vinegar)
- •2 tablespoons margarine, mellowed
- •1 tablespoon mustard
- •1 tablespoon earthy-colored sugar
- •1 tablespoon soy sauce
- •2 cups butternut squash, diced into ¼-inch blocks (new or defrosted from frozen)
- •1 apple, cut
- •1 tablespoon new thyme, slashed

PREPARATION

•Preheat the broiler to 420F.
•Prep the chicken. Wipe off every chicken bosom with a paper towel before adding preparation. This makes extra fresh skin while singing and simmering.
•Season, the chicken. Join olive oil, paprika, salt, and pepper in a little bowl and blend well in with a spoon to consolidate. Liberally smear the flavoring combination over the chicken bosoms and let it lay on a spotless plate for something like 15 minutes.
•Burn the chicken. Heat a broiler-safe or cast-iron skillet in the oven for 5 minutes over medium-high intensity. When the skillet is sizzling hot, singe the chicken bosoms by putting them skin side down until the skin becomes brown, around 4-5 minutes. Move the chicken bosoms on a plate to rest.
•Get ready for apple juice sauce. On a similar skillet, turn down the intensity to medium and add apple juice, spread, mustard, earthy-colored sugar, and soy sauce. Mix to consolidate. Carry the sauce blend to a stew and mix until it frames a smooth surface. Eliminate the intensity and move the chicken bosoms back to the skillet with the skin side up.
•Plan butternut squash. In an enormous blending bowl, add butternut squash, cut apples, thyme, and the remaining tablespoon of olive oil. Throw to join. On the off chance that you are utilizing frozen butternut squash, try to thaw it out first and wipe it off to eliminate the overabundance of water. Move the butternut squash and apple blend to the skillet and spread it around the chicken.
•Prepare. Move the whole skillet onto the preheated stove and heat for 20 minutes until the skin is firm and brilliant brown and the inner temperature for the chicken arrives at 165F on a meat thermometer.

•Serve. Serve the chicken and butternut squash on a plate and sprinkle some apple juice sauce from the skillet on top.

NUTRITION FACTS
Total Fat 15.1g 59%
Cholesterol 176.5mg 60%
Sodium 1369.2mg 6%
Total Carbohydrate 16.6g
Sugars 10.3g 108%
Protein 53.8g 40%
Vitamin A 359.6µg 12%
Vitamin C 11.2mg

DUTCH OVEN WHOLE ROAST CHICKEN

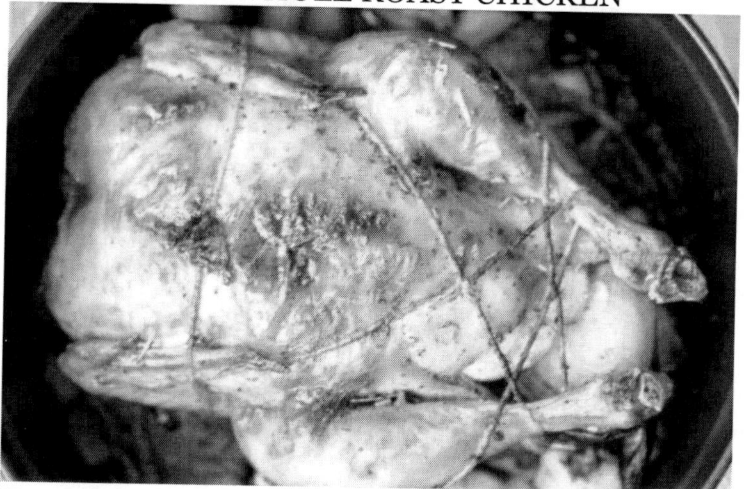

Prep Time: 15 minutes, **Cook Time:** 1 hour, **Total Time:** 1 hour 15 minutes,
Serving: 6

INGREDIENTS

•1 entire chicken (3 lbs.)
•2 tablespoons olive oil
•½ tablespoon Italian flavoring
•1 tablespoon salt
•½ tablespoon ground dark pepper
•1 apple, cut
•1 huge yellow onion, cut
•1 head of garlic, cut down the middle
•juice from ½ lemon
•2 tablespoons dissolved spread, partitioned
•2 carrots, hacked into 2-inch long pieces
•1 medium potato, stripped and cut into 1-inch 3D squares
•1 teaspoon parsley, finely hacked

PREPARATION

•Preheat the stove to 400 F. Deliver the chicken once again from the refrigerator and permit it to come to room temperature (around 30 minutes); this will guarantee, in any event, cooking. Wipe off the entire chicken totally with a paper towel before adding preparation. This makes an extra fresh skin while simmering.
•In a little bowl, add olive oil, Italian flavoring, salt, and pepper, and blend well in with a spoon to join. Liberally smear the flavoring combination over the entire chicken all around. Utilizing dispensable gloves to make it more straightforward. Ensure the flavoring covers all around the entire chicken, including within the pit of the chicken.
•Stuff the pit of the chicken with around 50% of the apples, a big part of the onion, and a big part of the garlic.
•Support the chicken by tying the chicken cozily with kitchen string, so the wings and legs remain nearby the body. This helps cook the entire chicken equally.
•In a huge blending bowl, consolidate lemon juice, 1 tablespoon liquefied spread, and remaining vegetables (carrots, apples, onions, garlic, and potatoes). Throw to consolidate.
•Spread the vegetables uniformly inside the Dutch stove and put the entire chicken on top. Ensure the bosoms of the chicken face up. Brush the chicken equitably with the leftover tablespoon of liquefied spread. Cover the top and dish the chicken for 30 minutes.
•Eliminate the cover and keep on cooking until the interior temperature arrives at 165F, around 20-25 minutes more. You can take a look at the inward temperature by staying a meat thermometer into the thickest piece of the bosom.

•To make chicken skins extra firm and carmelized, turn on the cook set to HI and let it sear in the broiler for extra 5 minutes. Brush extra softened margarine over the skin.
•Eliminate the Dutch stove from the broiler and allow it to sit at room temperature for something like 10 minutes before serving because the chicken is as yet cooking bit by bit because of the remaining intensity.
•Present with the vegetables, a sprinkle of parsley, and a shower of additional juices from the skillet on top.

NUTRITION FACTS
Total Fat 15.2g 55%
Cholesterol 164.8mg 59%
Sodium 1346.1mg 9%
Total Carbohydrate 25.8g
Sugars 7.4g 86%
Protein 42.8g 47%
Vitamin A 421.3μg 27%
Vitamin C 24.5mg

EASY CHICKEN PARMESAN

Prep Time: 15 minutes, **Cook Time:** 35 minutes,
Total Time: 50 minutes,
Servings: 5

INGREDIENTS
For the chicken:
•2-3 chicken bosoms, cut in half longwise
•2 teaspoons salt, separated
•2 cups Panko breadcrumbs
•½ cup Parmesan cheddar, ground
•1 tablespoon garlic powder
•2 eggs, beaten
•⅓ cup vegetable oil (for sautéing)
•For the sauce:
•1 cup onion, finely slashed
•2 tablespoons garlic, minced
•2 cups pureed tomatoes
•2 tablespoons tomato glue
•1 teaspoon Italian flavoring
•¼ cup new parsley, hacked
•½ teaspoon salt

•For the fixing:
•5 cups of mozzarella cheddar
•1/4 cup Parmesan cheddar, ground
•1 tablespoon new parsley, finely hacked
PREPARATION
Set up the Chicken:
•Preheat stove to 425 F.
•Cut every chicken bosom cautiously in half longwise. Place each split chicken bosom between 2 sheets of cling wrap or in a cooler sack. Cautiously straighten the chicken bosoms with a moving pin to accomplish uniform thickness, about 1/2-inch thick. Try not to pound the bosoms excessively hard. It could destroy them.
•Wipe off each bosom totally with a paper towel and season with 1 teaspoon salt. Put away for no less than 10 minutes.
•On a shallow plate, whisk together Panko breadcrumbs, Parmesan cheddar, garlic powder, and the leftover 1 teaspoon salt. Put away. Add beaten eggs to another shallow plate.
•Plunge the two sides of each divided chicken bosom into the eggs to equally cover them, and afterward, dunk it into the breadcrumb blend. The breadcrumbs will adhere to the egg wash.
•Heat oil in a nonstick cast-iron skillet over medium-high intensity for 2 minutes until the hot oil is sizzling and sparkling. Sear the chicken bosoms for around 4-5 minutes on each side until brilliant and firm. Put away on a plate. The chicken ought to be completely cooked, and the inner temperature ought to arrive at over 155 F.
Set up the Sauce:
•Eliminate everything except 2 tablespoons of the hot oil in the skillet. Add onions and sauté for 2 minutes

until delicate and delicate. Add garlic and sauté for an additional 2 minutes until fragrant.
•Add pureed tomatoes, tomato glue, Italian flavoring, parsley, and salt. Mix well to join and carry the sauce to a stew. Go to low intensity and let it stew for 5 minutes. Eliminate from intensity and move sauce into a bowl.
Collect and Bake:
•In a similar skillet, or one more solid metal skillet or baking dish, equitably spread ½ cup of the sauce on the base. Place the chicken bosoms separated equitably separated over the sauce.
•Cover each bosom with ¼ cup sauce, and top each bosom with a cut of mozzarella cheddar and 1 tablespoon Parmesan cheddar. Sprinkle finely hacked parsley on top.
•Prepare on the preheated stove at 425F for 15-20 minutes until the cheddar melts and becomes brilliant brown.
•Present with spaghetti and trimming with more parsley on top.

NUTRITION FACTS
Total Fat 26g 62%
Cholesterol 186.3mg 85%
Sodium 1955.4mg 16%
Total Carbohydrate 44.8g
Sugars 9g 106%
Protein 52.9g 17%
Vitamin A 154µg 19%
Vitamin C 16.9mg

AIR FRYER CHICKEN BREAST

Prep Time: 5 minutes, **Cook Time:** 25 minutes, **Total Time:** 30 minutes,
Serving: 3

INGREDIENTS

•3 chicken chests, skinless and boneless (around 1.5 pounds)

•½ tablespoon vegetable oil

•½ teaspoon salt

•¼ teaspoon ground dull pepper

•½ teaspoon Italian seasoning

•½ teaspoon paprika

•½ teaspoon garlic powder

PREPARATION

•Use a paper towel to wipe the chicken chests off. Generously smear oil consistently generally around the chicken. Center on all the seasoning, including salt, pepper, Italian enhancing, paprika, and garlic powder, and coat the chicken consistently. You can, in like manner, unite the chicken by setting it up in a gigantic Ziploc pack and shake well to cover. Set aside for somewhere near 15 minutes to marinate, or refrigerate until further notice.

•Place the marinated chicken chests in a single layer in the air fryer bushel.
•Air fry at 375 F for 22-25 minutes until cooked through, and the internal temperature for the chicken ranges 165F. You can investigate the inside temperature by remaining a meat thermometer into the thickest piece of the chest.
•Give rest for 5-10 minutes to get to the air fryer before serving.

NUTRITION FACTS
Total Fat 9.5g 66%
Cholesterol 198.6mg 22%
Sodium 510.7mg 0%
Total Carbohydrate 0.9g
Sugars 0.1g 123%
Protein 61.4g 5%
Vitamin A 44µg 0%
Vitamin C 0.1mg

CREAMY TUSCAN CHICKEN

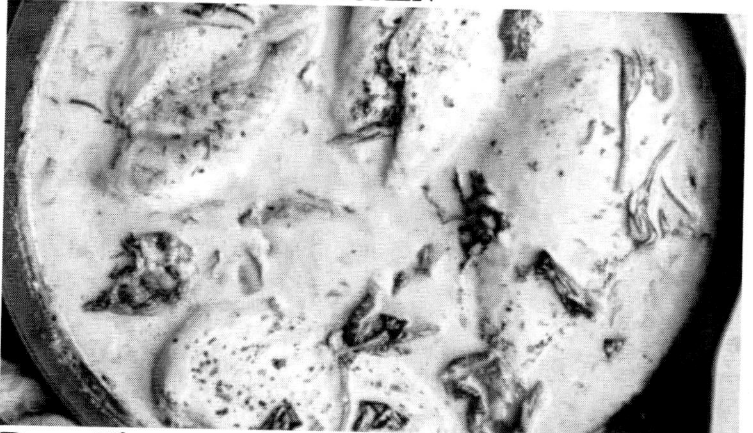

Prep Time: 5 minutes, **Cook Time:** 25 minutes, **Total Time:** 30 minutes,
Servings: 6

INGREDIENTS
For the chicken:

•4 boneless and skinless chicken chests (around 2 pounds)
•½ teaspoon salt
•¼ teaspoon ground dim pepper
•½ teaspoon Italian enhancing
•2 tablespoons vegetable oil
•For the sauce:
•2 tablespoons spread
•2 tablespoons garlic, finely minced
•1 cup of significant cream
•½ cup chicken stock
•1 tablespoon tomato stick
•¼ cup Parmesan cheddar, recently ground
•3 cups youngster spinach
•½ cup sun-dried tomatoes
•¼ teaspoon salt (or to taste)

PREPARATION

•Use a paper towel to wipe the chicken chests off. Season with salt, pepper, and Italian enhancement.

•In an immense skillet, heat oil over medium-focused energy until the hot oil sizzles, around 1-2 minutes. Add chicken and consume until splendid brown, 6-8 minutes for each side. Set aside on a plate.

•In a comparative skillet, add spread and garlic and sauté until fragrant, around 1 second. Add significant cream, chicken stock, tomato paste, and Parmesan cheddar. Mix well until smooth and convey the sauce to a stew over medium power, around 3-4 minutes.

•Blend in spinach and sun-dried tomatoes and cook until the spinach has wilted, around 1 second.

•Return the chicken to the skillet and spoon some sauce over to cover. Give the chicken stew admittance to the sauce until the sauce has thickened to an optimal consistency, around 3-4 minutes. Season with salt to taste.

•Serve quickly with pasta, rice, or potatoes.

NUTRITION FACTS

Total Fat 20.9g 27%

Cholesterol 145.9mg 49%

Sodium 517mg 22%

Total Carbohydrate 5.4g 2%

Sugars 2.8g

Protein 37.4g 75%

Vitamin A 215.2µg 24%

Vitamin C 7.6mg 8%

ONE POT OF SPANISH CHICKEN AND RICE

Prep Time: 15 minutes, **Cook Time:** 30 minutes, **Total Time:** 45 minutes,
Servings: 6

INGREDIENTS
•1 tablespoon olive oil
•5 boneless, skinless chicken thighs (or 1 lb.), cut into 1–2-inch pieces
•½ teaspoon salt
•½ teaspoon ground dark pepper
•½ medium onion, diced
•1 red chime pepper, diced
•2 cloves garlic, minced or squeezed
•1 cup long grain white rice, washed
•½ tablespoon paprika
•1 + ½ cups chicken stock
•1 cup pureed tomatoes (canned or natively constructed)
•spot of saffron
•salt and pepper to taste

•½ cup little stuffed green olives with pimento
•½ cup new hacked cilantro
•lemon wedges to serve
PREPARATION
•Heat oil over medium intensity in a huge non-stick skillet or pot. Add chicken and season with salt and pepper. Cook for around 5-6 minutes until the chicken starts to brown somewhat.
•Add onion, red pepper, and garlic and cook for a couple of moments until they somewhat relax.
•Add the rice and mix to join. Cook for 1-2 minutes.
•Blend in the paprika and keep on cooking for one more moment.
•Add chicken stock and pureed tomatoes and heat to the point of boiling. Turn down the intensity to low and add the saffron. Cover the skillet and cook for 25 minutes until the rice is completely cooked.
•Add salt and pepper to taste, olives, and cilantro. Throw and present with a lemon wedge.

NUTRITON FACTS
8% Total Fat 6.5g
6% Cholesterol 19mg
30% Sodium 686.6mg
12% Total Carbohydrate 32.2g
Sugars 4g
20% Protein 10.1g
8% Vitamin A 69.4µg
40% Vitamin C 36.1mg

BAKED CAPRESE CHICKEN

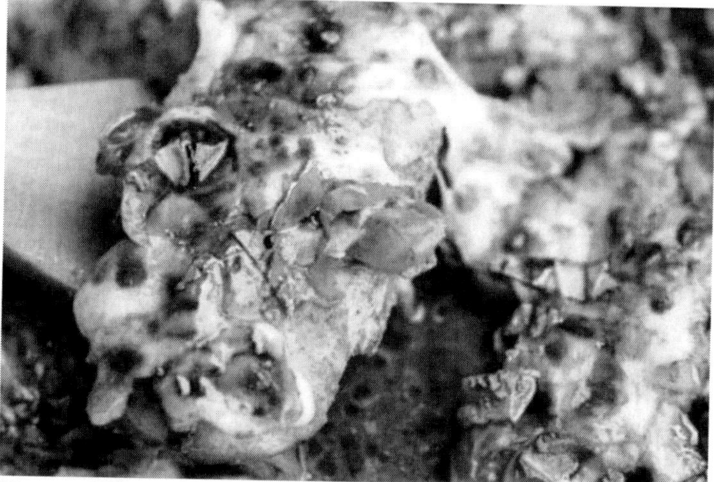

Prep Time: 10 minutes, **Cook Time:** 35 minutes, **Total Time:** 45 minutes,
Servings: 5

INGREDIENTS

- •5 chicken bosoms (around 2.5 lbs.), skinless and boneless
- •2 tablespoons olive oil, partitioned
- •½ tablespoon Italian flavoring
- •1 teaspoon salt
- •½ teaspoon ground dark pepper
- •½ cup balsamic vinegar, partitioned
- •2 cups cherry tomatoes, divided
- •2 cups bocconcini (mozzarella balls), divided
- •1 tablespoon new basil, cleaved

PREPARATION

•In an enormous Ziploc sack, join chicken bosoms with olive oil, Italian flavoring, salt, pepper, and 2 tablespoons of balsamic vinegar. Press air out of the pack and seal firmly. Press the flavoring around the chicken to cover. Allow it to marinate for somewhere around 15 minutes, up to expedite in the refrigerator. You can likewise marinate in a huge. Blending bowl and covering it with plastic grip wrap.

•Preheat the broiler to 400 F.

•Organize marinated chicken in an 8-inch square baking dish. Add tomatoes and disseminate them equally in the skillet. Heat for 20 minutes until the tomatoes are delicate.

•Eliminate the skillet from the stove and add mozzarella balls equitably over the chicken. Return the skillet to the stove and keep baking for another 10-15 minutes until the softened cheddar becomes brilliant brown. The interior temperature for the chicken ought to likewise arrive at 165F as perused on a meat thermometer.

•In the interim, make the balsamic coating by adding the excess balsamic vinegar to a little pot. Allow it to stew for over low intensity until thickened and diminished considerably (around 5-7 minutes), blending periodically.

•Permit the heated chicken to rest for 10 minutes. Then, at that point, shower the balsamic decrease on top. Embellish with basil and serve warm.

NUTRITION FACTS
15% Total Fat 11.7g
58% Cholesterol 173.6mg
40% Sodium 912.1mg
3% Total Carbohydrate 8.7g
Sugars 6.1g
132% Protein 66.1g
14% Vitamin A 122.3µg
9% Vitamin C 8.5mg

CREAMY CHICKEN ROULADE WITH SPINACH AND MUSHROOMS

Prep Time: 15 minutes, **Cook Time:** 25 minutes, **Total Time:** 40 minutes,
Servings: 3

INGREDIENTS
Chicken Roulade:
•1 cup + 1 tablespoon vegetable oil, isolated
•1 cup onions, finely slashed
•1 cup earthy-colored mushrooms, finely slashed
•3 chicken bosoms, boneless and skinless
•3 teaspoons dark pepper, isolated
•3 teaspoons salt, isolated
•3 teaspoons Italiano preparing, isolated
•1 cup child spinach, slashed and isolated
•2 eggs, beaten
•1-2 cups panko breadcrumbs
•Velvety Alfredo Sauce:
•3 tablespoons margarine
•⅓ cup parsley, finely slashed
•3 tablespoons cream cheddar

•2 teaspoons garlic powder
•½ cup milk
•½ cup Parmesan cheddar, ground
•½ teaspoon ground dark pepper

PREPARATION

Set up the Chicken Roulade:

•Heat 1 tablespoon of oil in a skillet over medium-high intensity. Add onions and mushrooms. Mix well and cook for 2-3 minutes. Move the combination into a bowl and let it cool at room temperature for no less than 20 minutes.

•Season the two sides of every chicken bosom with 1 teaspoon of dark pepper, salt, and Italiano preparation.

•Place every chicken bosom, each in turn, between 2 sheets of cling wrap or in a Ziploc cooler pack. Cautiously level the chicken bosoms with a moving pin until they are roughly ¼-inch thick and 6-inches wide. Try not to pound the bosoms excessively hard. It could destroy the bosom. In a perfect world, you need to be leveled chicken bosoms with uniform thickness.

•Put one chicken bosom on another sheet of cling wrap. Add ⅓ cup child spinach on top of the chicken bosom.

•Save 1-2 tablespoons of the mushroom and onion blend, and afterward, add 33% of the mushroom and onion combination on top. Make a point to spread the filling equally, leaving a ½-inch line around the edges.

•Firmly fold the chicken into a log, and wrap the moved chicken firmly in saran wrap. Once wrapped, get the two finishes of the cling wrap and roll to contort them and make it extra close. Utilize plastic clasps to get the two finishes. Rehash these means with the leftover two chicken bosoms.

•Move the chicken rolls to the fridge and let them set for 30-an hours.

Make the Creamy Alfredo Sauce:

•Dissolve margarine in a non-stick pot over medium intensity. Add hacked parsley and the held onion and mushroom blend. Cook for 2 minutes until it sizzles and becomes fragrant.
•Add cream cheddar and garlic powder. Mix well and cook for one more moment. Add milk and keep mixing, so the sauce shapes a uniform surface. Include Parmesan cheddar and dark pepper. Mix well to join and cook briefly. You will see the combination begin to thicken a little.
•Eliminate from intensity, and move the sauce to a perfect bowl.
Make the Chicken Roulade:
•Remove the chicken rolls from the refrigerator and eliminate the cling wrap. Take two shallow plates and add eggs to one and panko breadcrumbs to the next. Dunk every chicken roll into the beaten eggs (beaten eggs behave like paste to cover the chicken rolls with bread pieces). Then, roll in the panko and completely coat. If you like a thicker breaded covering, you can go for seconds in beaten eggs and afterward breadcrumbs once more.
Cook the breaded chicken rolls in one of 3 ways:
•Broil: Heat 1 cup of oil in a pot over medium intensity for 3-4 minutes until it comes to 325°F (170°C). Sear the breaded chicken rolls in the hot oil for around 5 minutes on each side, or until the outside is an even brilliant brown and the inward temperature comes to 166°F (74°C).
•Air Fry: Spray some oil over the chicken rolls to guarantee that they get that brilliant earthy-colored covering. Cook in the air fryer at 350 F for 25 minutes. Turn the chicken turns over part of the way through baking.
•Prepare: Spray some oil over the chicken rolls to guarantee that they get that brilliant earthy-colored

covering. Cook in a preheated 375 F broiler for 25 minutes. Turn the chicken turns over partially through baking.
•Cool the chicken rolls on a wire cooling rack for 5 minutes. Cut and pour the rich Alfredo sauce on top.

NUTRITION FACTS
36% Total Fat 27.9g
81% Cholesterol 241.6mg
231 %Sodium 5315.2mg
15% Total Carbohydrate 40.5g
Sugars 8.1g
77% Protein 38.4g
41% Vitamin A 365.9µg
37% Vitamin C 33.4mg

SKILLET CHICKEN THIGHS AND POTATOES

Prep Time: 10 minutes, **Cook Time:** 35 minutes, **Total Time:** 45 minutes,
Servings: 4

INGREDIENTS

•2 lbs. chicken thighs, bone-in, skin on (around 4 colossal thighs)

•2 teaspoons Italian enhancing

•½ teaspoon paprika

•½ tablespoon salt

•1 teaspoon ground dim pepper

•1 + ½ tablespoons margarine (or olive oil)

•½ medium onion cut

•4 cloves garlic, minced

•2 cups youngster potatoes, separated (around 20 kid potatoes)

•2 medium carrots, cut

PREPARATION

•Preheat oven to 400 F. Clears off each chicken thigh with a paper towel before adding preparation. This makes additional firm skins while singing.

•In a medium bowl, add Italian enhancing, paprika, salt, and pepper mix well to join. Generously rub ¾ of the enhancing mix by and large around the chicken thighs, on the different sides.
•Incorporate onions, garlic, potatoes, and carrots in the bowl with the overabundance seasoning mix. Toss to join.
•Mellow the spread in a cast-iron skillet over medium-extreme focus for 1-2 minutes until hot. Place the chicken thighs with the skin side down on the skillet, and sear for 2-3 minutes until the skin becomes brown and firm. Flip the chicken over and cook on the contrary side for 2 extra minutes. Dispense with the chicken thighs from the skillet and put them on a plate.
•On a comparative skillet, add the vegetables and blend well to join. Cook for 3-4 minutes until onions are sensitive and start to brown to some degree. Dispense with the power and put chicken thighs on top, skin side up.
•Move the skillet into the preheated oven and intensity for 30-40 minutes until the internal temperature for the chicken thighs comes to 165F. Kill the skillet from the oven and let it rest for 10 minutes before serving.

NUTRITION FACTS
18% Total Fat 14g
75% Cholesterol 224.5mg
49% Sodium 1123.3mg
7% Total Carbohydrate 18.1g
14% Sugars 3g
93% Protein 46.7g
39% Vitamin A 348.1μg

CHICKEN MADEIRA

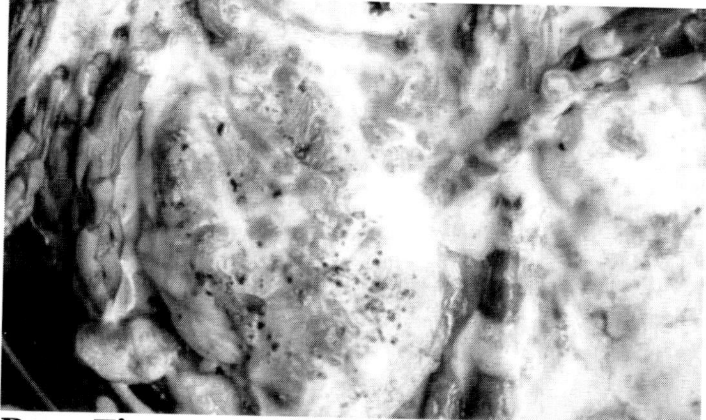

Prep Time: 10 minutes, **Cook Time:** 30 minutes, **Total Time:** 40 minutes,
Servings: 4

INGREDIENTS

•1-pound medium asparagus, closes managed
•¼ cup spread, separated
•1-pound white mushrooms, cut
•¼ teaspoon salt
•¼ teaspoon ground dark pepper
•1 medium yellow onion, diced
•1 tablespoon garlic, minced
•2 tablespoons new parsley, finely cleaved
•2 huge chicken bosoms, boneless and skinless
•½ cup Madeira wine
•1 cup chicken stock
•½ cup weighty cream
•1 cup mozzarella cheddar, destroyed

PREPARATION

Cook the asparagus:

•In a huge pot of bubbling water, add asparagus and whiten until somewhat yet radiant green, around 2-3 minutes. Wash the asparagus under cool running water to stop the cooking system and channel in a colander. Put away.

Set up the mushrooms:

•Liquefy 2 tablespoons spread in a huge skillet over medium-high intensity until it begins to rise, around 1 moment. Add mushrooms and sauté until the dampness dissipates from them, around 5 minutes. Season with salt and pepper and keep cooking for another 2-3 minutes until the mushrooms become brilliant brown. (Salt will additionally remove additional water from the mushrooms, giving them a pleasant earthy colored tone).

•Mix in onion, garlic, and parsley and cook until delicate, around 2 minutes. Move the mushroom blend to a plate and put it away.

Set up the chicken:

•Cut every chicken bosom in half longwise (on a level plane) and season with salt and pepper to taste (about ¼ teaspoon of each).

•Utilize a paper towel to clean a similar skillet off. Dissolve the excess spread over medium intensity until it begins to rise, around 1 moment.

•Sing the chicken until brilliant brown and completely cooked through, around 5 minutes for every side. The inner temperature for the chicken ought to arrive at 165F on a meat thermometer. Eliminate the chicken from the intensity and move to a similar plate with mushrooms.

Gather the chicken, Madeira:

•In a similar skillet, add wine and mix well to deglaze the lower part of the dish. Mix in chicken stock and weighty cream. Blend well and carry the sauce to a stew. Keep on stewing until thickened to an ideal consistency, around 2-3 minutes. Switch off the intensity.

•Return the chicken to the skillet and throw it to cover in the sauce. Orchestrate the mushrooms and asparagus around the chicken. Top with destroyed mozzarella cheddar.

•Move the dish to the stove and sear on HI for 3-4 minutes (or prepare in a preheated 450F broiler for 5-7 minutes) until the liquefied cheddar becomes brilliant brown.

•Serve warm with pasta or rice whenever wanted.

NUTRUTION FACTS
27% Total Fat 21.2g
51% Cholesterol 153.1mg
29% Sodium 665.9mg
5% Total Carbohydrate 13.3g
Sugars 6.7g
94% Protein 47g
29% Vitamin A 257.8µg
16% Vitamin C 14.2mg

INSTANT POT WHOLE CHICKEN

Prep Time: 10 minutes, **Cook Time:** 40 minutes, **Total Time**: 50 minutes,
Servings: 6

INGREDIENTS

- •1 medium entire chicken (3 pounds)
- •½ tablespoon vegetable oil
- •½ teaspoon salt
- •¼ teaspoon ground dark pepper
- •½ teaspoon paprika
- •½ teaspoon Italian flavoring
- •½ teaspoon garlic powder
- •½ lemon
- •3-4 branches of thyme or rosemary
- •½ cup chicken stock
- •For the sauce:
- •2 tablespoons regular flour
- •½ cup chicken stock
- •2 tablespoons spread
- •½ teaspoon salt (or to taste)

•¼ teaspoon ground dark pepper (or to taste)
PREPARATION

•Pat the entire chicken dry utilizing a paper towel. Rub on oil, salt, pepper, paprika, Italian flavoring, and garlic powder equally to prepare. Put away on a plate for no less than 30 minutes or refrigerate for the time being. At the point when prepared to cook, it's ideal to carry the marinated chicken to room temperature to accomplish, in any event, cooking more delicate and juicier meat.

•Stuff the lemon half and new thyme into the cavity of the chicken.

•Bracket the chicken by tying the chicken cozily with cooking twine, so the wings and legs remain nearby the body. This helps cook the entire chicken uniformly.

•Place a rack that can be fitted into the moment pot into pot and add the stock. The stock will be utilized to make sauce later; it additionally prevents the chicken drippings from consuming.

•Place the chicken (bosom side up) on the rack and seal the cover (the steam discharge handle should be gone to the fixed position). Set the chicken on pressure, cooking for 25 minutes. For every additional pound of chicken, cook 6 additional minutes.

•When the time is up, let the moment pot gradually discharge the strain, around 15 minutes. The inner temperature of the thickest piece of the bosom ought to arrive at 165F as perused on a meat thermometer.

•To make chicken skin extra firm and cooked, turn on the stove oven and set it to high. Sear the chicken on a baking sheet for 5-7 minutes. Watch out for the oven since things can warm up and consume rapidly. Eliminate the container from the stove and let the chicken sit at room temperature for something like 15 minutes.

Set up the sauce:

•On the Instant Pot, switch the Sauté capability on high. Add flour, chicken stock, and margarine to the chicken drippings in the pot. Whisk well until smooth and cook until thickened to an ideal consistency, around 2-3 minutes. Season with salt and pepper to taste.
•Cut the chicken and present with sauce on top.

NUTRITION FACTS
16% Total Fat 12.8g
67% Cholesterol 200.3mg
30% Sodium 701.4mg
2% Total Carbohydrate 4.1g
Sugars 0.7g
97% Protein 48.5g
7% Vitamin A 60.9µg
9% Vitamin C 8.4mg

PARMESAN CRUSTED CHICKEN

Prep Time: 10 minutes, **Cook Time:** 30 minutes, **Total Time:** 40 minutes,
Servings: 4
INGREDIENTS
•4 chicken bosoms, boneless and skinless
•1 teaspoon salt
•1 teaspoon ground dark pepper
•1 teaspoon Italian flavoring
•2 tablespoons regular baking flour
•1 cup breadcrumbs
•¼ cup Parmesan, ground
•1 teaspoon garlic powder
•¼ cup new parsley, finely cleaved
•1 tablespoon olive oil
•1 egg, beaten
PREPARATION
•Preheat the broiler to 400 F.
•Utilizing a paper towel, wipe off every chicken bosom totally and place, each in turn, between 2 sheets of grip wrap or in a Ziploc cooler pack. Cautiously level the chicken bosoms with a moving pin until they are roughly ½-inch thick. Try not to pound the bosoms excessively hard as it could destroy the bosom. In a

perfect world, you need straightened chicken bosoms with uniform thickness.

•Season the two sides of every chicken bosom with salt, pepper, and Italian flavoring. Put away on a plate.

•In a blending bowl, whisk together breadcrumbs, Parmesan, garlic powder, parsley, and olive oil until smooth. You can likewise join these fixings into a food processor and heartbeat blend until recently consolidated. Move the breadcrumb blend into a shallow plate.

•Set up one more shallow plate with flour and a shallow plate with the beaten egg.

•Dunk each piece of chicken into the flour to cover on all sides uniformly. Then, at that point, dunk into the egg to cover and afterward coat it in the breadcrumb blend equitably. The flour will adhere to the chicken, the egg adheres to the flour, and the breadcrumbs adhere to the egg. Shake off any abundance of breadcrumbs.

•Move the breaded chicken on a huge half-sheet baking dish fixed with material paper. Prepare for 30 minutes until the covering is brilliant brown and the inward temperature for the chicken arrives at 165F as perused on a meat thermometer. You can likewise flip the chicken once part of the way through baking, assuming that you believe that the two sides should be fresh.

•Cut into strips and serve promptly over salad or pasta.

NUTRITION FACTS

Total Fat 14.7g 19%

Cholesterol 248.7mg 83%

Sodium 1006.9mg 44%

Total Carbohydrate 24.1g 9%

Sugars 1.8g 138%

Protein 69g

Vitamin A 86.9µg 10%

Vitamin C 5.2mg 6%

VEGETABLE

Roasted Vegetables

Prep Time: 15 minutes, **Cook Time:** 30 minutes, **Total Time:** 45 minutes

INGREDIENTS

•1 medium head cauliflower (2 pounds)

•1 crown broccoli (1/2 pound)

•1 medium red onion

•2 medium yams (1 1/2 pounds)

•1 red pepper

•1 yellow pepper

•4 tablespoons olive oil

•2 teaspoons garlic powder

•2 teaspoons Old Bay flavoring

•1 teaspoon legitimate salt

PREPARATION

•Change the stove racks for simmering 2 plates. Preheat the stove to 450 degrees Fahrenheit.

•Hack the vegetables: Chop the cauliflower and broccoli into florets. Hack the onion into 1/2-inch cuts. Slice the yam down the middle longwise, in half again the long way, and afterward cut each quarter into flimsy pie-formed cuts (see the photograph). Slash the peppers into 1/2-inch strips, then cut the strips down the middle.
•Line two baking sheets with material paper (we favor this over silicone baking mats since it brings about crispier veggies). Spread the vegetables equitably onto each sheet. Sprinkle around 50% of the olive oil onto every plate, then, at that point, with a portion of the flavors onto every plate. Blend in with your hands until equally covered.
•Place into the stove and prepare for 20 minutes (don't mix!). Eliminate the dish from the stove, pivot them, and meal an additional 10 minutes (for 30 minutes all out) until delicate and gently caramelized on one side. Move to a serving bowl or dish and serve right away.

NUTRITION FACTS
Total Fat 7.5g 10%
Saturated Fat 1.2g
Total Carbohydrate 26.8g 10%
Dietary Fiber 6g 22%
Sugars 7.1g
Protein 4.6g 9%
Vitamin A 616.5pg 69%
Vitamin C 83.6mg 93%
Calcium 70mg 5%
Iron I.3mg 7%
Vitamin D Ogg 0%
Magnesium 47.Img 11%
Potassium 752.8mg 16%
Vitamin B6 0.5mg 27%
Vitamin B12 Ogg 0%

Ultimate Sauteed Vegetables

Prep Time: 7 minutes, **Cook Time:** 13 minutes, **Total Time:** 20 minutes

INGREDIENTS

•2 multi-hued chime peppers (we utilized red and yellow)

•1 medium red onion

•1 enormous carrot

•1 head broccoli (8 ounces, stem on)

•2 tablespoons olive oil, partitioned

•1 teaspoon dried oregano

•½ teaspoon genuine salt

•Fresh ground black pepper

PREPARATION

•Meagerly cut the peppers. Cut the onion. Cut the carrot into slight rounds, on the predisposition. Cut the broccoli into little florets.

•Throw the vegetables in a bowl with 1 tablespoon olive oil and the oregano, genuine salt, and a lot of new ground dark pepper.

•In an enormous skillet, heat the leftover 1 tablespoon olive oil over medium-high intensity. Cook for 10 to 12 minutes until delicate and gently scorched, mixing sporadically. Taste and add a couple of portions of extra salt to taste. Serve right away.

NUTRITION FACTS
Total Fat 7.4g 9%
Saturated Fat Ig
Total Carbohydrate I0.3g 4%
Dietary Fiber 3.Ig 11%
Sugars 5.5g
Protein I.8g 4%
Vitamin A 274.3,ug 30%
Vitamin C 118.5mg 132%
Calcium 28.2mg 2%
Iron 0.6mg 3%
Vitamin D Ogg 0%
Magnesium 18.6mg 4%
Potassium 326.8mg 7%
Vitamin B6 0.3mg 18%
Vitamin B12 0,ug 0%

Perfect Roasted Cauliflower

Prep Time: 10 minutes **Cook Time:** 30 minutes, **Total Time:** 40 minutes

INGREDIENTS

•1 medium head cauliflower (2 pounds or around 6 to 7 storing cups florets)

•2 tablespoons olive oil

•¾ teaspoon fit salt, in addition to more to taste

•1 medium garlic clove

•1 teaspoon lemon zing, discretionary (and additionally destroyed Parmesan cheddar)

PREPARATION

•Preheat the broiler to 450 degrees Fahrenheit.

•Clean and slash the cauliflower into medium florets. In a bowl, join the cauliflower with olive oil and legitimate salt.

•Line a baking sheet with material paper. Spread the cauliflower on a baking sheet and heat for 30 to 35 minutes or until sautéed and firm at the edges, blending once.

•At the point when the cauliflower is finished, eliminate the skillet from the broiler. Grind the garlic and lemon zing onto the dish and utilize a spoon to delicately throw it all together (isolating any ground garlic that clusters together). Taste, and if the flavor doesn't pop, a couple of additional squeezes fit salt. Serve right away.

NUTRITION FACTS
Total Fat 7.4g 10%
Saturated Fat I.2g
Total Carbohydrate 7.3g 3%
Dietary Fiber 2.9g 11%
Sugars 2.SE
Protein 2.Sg 6%
Vitamin A 0,ug 0%
Vitamin C 70.9mg 79%
Calcium 32.3mg 2%
Iron 0.6mg 3%
Vitamin D Ogg 0%
Magnesium 22.1mg 5%
Potassium 439.5mg 9%
Vitamin B6 0.37,2g 16%
Vitamin B12 0,ug 0%

Bulanglang

Prep Time: 5 minutes, **Cook Time:** 15 minutes, **Total Time:** 20 minutes

INGREDIENTS

•1 piece of minimal Green Papaya cut

•2 cups calabaza squash cut

•Loofah Patola, cut

•Lemongrass Optional

•3 medium tomatoes cut

•10 to 15 little Okra

•1 cup malunggay moringa leaves

•4 cloves of garlic gently crushed

•1 thumb ginger severed

•1 to 2 teaspoons of salt

•4 to 6 cups rice Washing

PREPARATION

•Heat a cooking pot and pour-in rice washing. Let bubble.

•Add garlic, ginger, and lemongrass. Bubble for 5 to 7 minutes.

•Dispense with lemongrass. Add papaya and calabaza squash. Bubble for 6 minutes.

•Add tomatoes, okra, and loofah. Cook for 3 to 4 minutes.
•Put in the malunggay and salt. Blend. Switch the force off.
•Move to a serving bowl and serve. Share and appreciate!

NUTRITION FACTS
Serving Size: 241 g
Calories: 97
CalSugar: 9.5 g
Sodium: 784 msg
Fat: .7g
Saturated Fat: .2g
Carbohydrates: 14.9g
Fiber: 4.8g
Protein: 6.6g
Cholesterol: 14 mg

Ginataang Hipon Sitaw at Kalabasa

Prep Time: 10 minutes, **Cook Time:** 40 minutes, **Total Time:** 50 minutes

INGREDIENTS

•1 lb shrimp cleaned

•10 strings beans stew, cut into 2 1/2-inch length

•2 cups kalabasa squash, cubed

•2 cups coconut milk

•1 medium yellow onion cut

•2 tablespoons bagoong alamang shrimp stick

•1 cup malunggay leaves

•3 cloves of garlic crushed

•Salt and pepper to taste

•3 tablespoons cooking oil

•Salt and pepper to taste

PREPARATION

•Heat oil in a cooking pot.

•Sauté the garlic and onion until the onion ends up being sensitive.
•Put in the shrimp. Cook for 1 to 2 minutes. Dispose of from the pot and set aside.
•Meanwhile, put in the bagoong alamang and pour in the coconut milk. Blend and let bubble.
•Add the kalabasa. Cook for 8 to 12 minutes or until fragile.
•Put the shrimp in a difficult spot in the pot. Blend and cook momentarily.
•Add the string beans (sitaw) and malunggay leaves. Cook for 2 to 3 minutes.
•Add salt and pepper to taste.
•Move to a serving plate. Serve.
•Share and appreciate!

NUTRITION FACTS
Serving: 4g | Calories: 429kcal | Carbohydrates: 19g | Protein: 13g | Fat: 36g | Saturated Fat: 22g | Polyunsaturated Fat: 3g | Monounsaturated Fat: 8g | Trans Fat: 1g | Cholesterol: 86mg | Sodium: 283mg | Potassium: 660mg | Fiber: 1g | Sugar: 2g | Vitamin A: 815IU | Vitamin C: 142mg | Calcium: 338mg | Iron: 5mg

Utan Nga Langka

Prep Time: 10 minutes, **Cook Time:** 35 minutes, **Total Time:** 45 minutes

INGREDIENTS

- •2 lbs. unripe jackfruit cut
- •1 Knorr Shrimp 3D shape
- •3 cups coconut milk
- •2 cups bago leaves cut
- •1 cup dried fish Dulong
- •2 onions cleaved
- •5 cloves of garlic cleaved
- •3 Thai stew pepper
- •2 tablespoons vinegar
- •Fish sauce to taste
- •3 tablespoons cooking oil

PREPARATION

•Heat oil in a huge wok.
•Sauté onion and garlic.
•Add the dried fish once the onions are mellow. Cook for 1 moment.
•Add unripe jackfruit. Cook while blending for 2 to 3 minutes.
•Add bean stew peppers and bago leaves. Mix.
•Season with 1 tablespoon fish sauce, and afterward, pour in the coconut milk. Let bubble.
•Add vinegar. Cook for 5 to 8 minutes.
•Add Knorr Shrimp Cube. Keep cooking until the fluid vanishes totally.
•Season with ground dark pepper and fish sauce, depending on the situation.
•Move to a serving plate. Present with warm rice.
•Share and appreciate!

NUTRITION FACTS
Calories: 522kcal | Carbohydrates: 48g | Protein: 14g | Fat: 34g | Saturated Fat: 23g | Polyunsaturated Fat: 3g | Monounsaturated Fat: 6g | Trans Fat: 0.03g | Cholesterol: 23mg | Sodium: 196mg | Potassium: 1138mg | Fiber: 3g | Sugar: 31g | Vitamin A: 205IU | Vitamin C: 33mg | Calcium: 258mg | Iron: 13mg

Chopsuey with Chicken and Broccoli

Prep Time: 5 minutes, **Cook Time:** 25 minutes, **Total Time:** 35 minutes

INGREDIENTS

•4 ounces chicken bosom cut
•1 piece Knorr Chicken Cube
•1 1/2 cups broccoli florets
•1 ½ cups cauliflower florets
•2 pieces of carrot cut across
•12 pieces of snow peas
•2 cups cabbage cleaved
•1 piece red chime pepper cut
•1 piece green chime pepper cut
•12 pieces of quail eggs bubbled
•14 ounces of youthful corn
•1 cup water
•5 cloves of garlic cleaved
•1 piece onion cut

•2 tablespoons soy sauce
•2 tablespoons shellfish sauce
•1 tablespoon cornstarch weakened in ¾ cup of water
•3 tablespoons cooking oil
•Salt and ground dark pepper to taste
PREPARATION
•Heat oil on a skillet. Saute onion until layers are independent.
•Add garlic. Continue sautéing until the onion begins to mellow.
•Add chicken, and pan sear until the external part becomes light brown.
•Pour soy sauce, clam sauce, and water. Mix. Cover the skillet and let the fluid bubble.
•Add Knorr Chicken Cube. Mix. Cover and cook utilizing medium intensity until the sauce decreases to half.
•Add the carrot. Cook for 3 minutes.
•Pour the cornstarch and water blend. Mix.
•Add your corn, cauliflower, chime pepper, broccoli, snow peas, and cabbage. Throw. Cover and cook for 1 ½ minute.
•Throw and season with ground dark pepper and salt.
•Add bubbled quail eggs.
•Move to a serving plate. Serve. Share and appreciate!

NUTRITION FACTS
Calories: 308kcal | Carbohydrates: 38g | Protein: 14g | Fat: 14g | Saturated Fat: 1g | Polyunsaturated Fat: 4g | Monounsaturated Fat: 7g | Trans Fat: 1g | Cholesterol: 44mg | Sodium: 1062mg | Potassium: 809mg | Fiber: 7g | Sugar: 11g | Vitamin A: 1691IU | Vitamin C: 134mg | Calcium: 73mg | Iron: 2mg

Bok Choy in Garlic Sauce

Prep Time: 5 minutes, **Cook Time:** 12 minutes, **Total Time:** 17 minutes

INGREDIENTS

•1 pound Bok Choy
•1 tablespoon vegetable oil
•1 tablespoon sesame oil
•1/4 cup water
•1 teaspoon ground new ginger root
•2 cloves garlic minced
•1 tablespoon shellfish sauce
•1 tablespoon soy sauce
•1 tablespoon earthy-colored sugar

PREPARATION

•Consolidate soy sauce, water, garlic, ginger, shellfish sauce, and sugar, and blend well. Put away.
•Heat a wok or skillet, then, at that point, put in the cooking oil.
•While the cooking oil is sufficiently hot, pour in the sesame oil.

•Pan sear the Bok Choy. Put the stalks first and pan-fried food for around 2 minutes, then add the leaves and pan-fried food for 2 to 4 minutes.
•Switch off the intensity and move the cooked Bok Choy to a serving plate.
•Heat a similar wok or griddle, then pour in the sauce blend. Cook for around 2 minutes or until the sauce thickens.
•Switch off the heat, then, at that point, top the sauce over the Bok Choy.
•Serve. Share and appreciate!

NUTRITION FACTS
Total Fat 3.6g 5%
Saturated Fat 0.3g 1%
Polyunsaturated Fat 1g
Cholesterol 0mg
Sodium 220mg 10%
Total Carbs 2g 1%
Dietary Fiber 0g 1%
Total Sugars 0g
Protein 0g 1%
Vitamin A 1,503mcg 167%
Vitamin C 1mg 1%
Vitamin D 0mcg (0iu)
Vitamin B-12 0mcg
Calcium 0mg
Magnesium 4mg 1%

Laing with Shrimp" Natong"

Prep Time: 10 minutes, **Cook Time:** 45 minutes, **Total Time:** 55 minutes

INGREDIENTS

•1 pack of dried taro leaves
•1/2 lb. pork cut into shaky strips
•1/2 lb. shrimp with head (optional)
•1/2 cup shrimp stick
•1 medium onion cut
•6 PCs Thai bean stew
•1/4 cup ginger cut into strips
•1 tbsp garlic minced
•3 cups Coconut milk
•2 tbsp fish sauce
•Salt and pepper to taste

PREPARATION

•In a tremendous skillet, pour in the Coconut milk and intensity with the result of bubbling
•Add the garlic, onion, and ginger. Stew for 10 minutes

•Add the pork meat and shrimp paste and blend incessantly
•Put in the Thai bean endlessly stew for 10 extra minutes
•Add the fish sauce and dried Taro leaves and stew for 15 to 20 minutes
•Put the shrimps in and stew for 5 minutes
•Serve hot. Appreciate

NUTRITION FACTS
Calories 380
Calories from Fat 329 %
Total Fat 37g 57%
Saturated Fat 27g 135%
Trans Fat 0.1g
Cholesterol 25mg 8%
Sodium 425mg 18%
Potassium 547mg 16%
Total Carbohydrates 7.4g 2%
Dietary Fiber 1g 4%
Sugars 1.4g
Protein 10g
Vitamin A 19%
Vitamin C 25%
Calcium 6%
Iron 29%

Pinakbet Ilocano

Prep Time: 10 minutes, **Cook Time:** 40 minutes, **Total Time:** 50 minutes

INGREDIENTS

•4 pieces of round eggplant are cut down the middle
•2 pieces of little severe melon ampalaya, quartered
•½ pack of string beans cut into 2-inch length
•1 piece yam kamote, quartered
•8 pieces okra
•1 piece tomato cubed
•1 piece onion cubed
•1½ cup water
•1 lb magnet
•1/4 cup Anchovy sauce bagoong is

PREPARATION

•In a huge dish, place water and let bubble
•Yet again, put in the anchovy sauce and trust that the blend will bubble

•Include the vegetables beginning with the yam, then, at that point, put in the okra, unpleasant melon, eggplant, string beans, tomato, and onion, and stew for 15 minutes
•Add the Bagnet or Lechon kawali (cooking system accessible in the recipe area) and stew for 5 minutes
•Serve hot. Share and Enjoy!

NUTRITION FACTS
Calories: 58kcal | Carbohydrates: 12g | Protein: 2g | Sodium: 1166mg | Potassium: 401mg | Fiber: 3g | Sugar: 3g | Vitamin A: 5100IU | Vitamin C: 46.5mg | Calcium: 37mg | Iron: 0.6mg

Vegetable Biryani

Prep Time: 20 mins, **Cook Time:** 1 hrs, 15 mins, **Total Time:** 1hrs, 35 mins

INGREDIENTS

•1/4 cup (60ml) entire milk

•20 strands of saffron

•2 cups (400g) basmati rice

•2 huge yellow or white onions, divided and cut meagerly

•1/4 cup in addition to 2 teaspoons (70ml) ghee or oil, for example, grapeseed

•2 1/2 teaspoons (8g) Diamond Crystal legitimate salt, separated, in addition to more to taste; if involving table salt, utilize half as much by volume.

•12 dried apricots (125g), cleaved

•1/2 cup (70g) entire cashews

•1/4 cup (35g) brilliant raisins

•10 garlic cloves, ground

•3-to 4-inch piece of new ginger stripped and ground (around 4 tablespoons; 50g)

•1 green chile, like jalapeno or serrano, minced
•1 1/2 teaspoons garam masala
•1 entire star anise unit
•1 teaspoon ground caraway
•1/2 teaspoon ground turmeric
•1/2 cup (120g) plain unsweetened yogurt
•1 little cauliflower, isolated into 1/2-inch florets
•1 Yukon gold potato, stripped and diced into 1/2-inch (2.5 cm) 3D squares
•1 medium carrot, managed, stripped, and diced
•1 cup (240ml) water
•1/2 cup (60g) green peas, new or frozen
•1 cup new cilantro, delicate stems, and leaves
•1 cup new mint, delicate stems, and leaves
•1/4 cup (60ml) lemon or lime juice
•3 green cardamom units gently broke
•A 2-inch (5cm) stick of cinnamon
•4 cloves
•2 huge narrow leaves
•2 teaspoons (10ml) rosewater
•2 teaspoons (10ml) pandan (kewra/screwpine) water

PREPARATION

•Warm the milk up in a little pot set over medium intensity until steaming hot, or around 110°F (43°C) as enrolled on a moment-read thermometer, around 1-2 minutes. (On the other hand, place milk in a microwave-safe bowl and intensity on high until steaming hot, around 30 seconds to 1 moment). Grind half of the saffron strands to a fine powder utilizing a mortar and pestle. Add the ground saffron and remaining saffron strands to the hot milk, cover, and let steep until prepared to utilize.

•Clean the rice of any garbage. Place rice in a fine-network sifter and wash it under cool running faucet water until the water runs clear. Move rice to a medium blending bowl, cover with new virus water, and let it drench for no less than 30 minutes and as long as 60 minutes. Channel rice completely.

•While the rice drenches, add 1/4 cup (60ml) ghee to a 5-quart Dutch stove and intensity over medium intensity until shining. Add onions, season with a spot of salt, and cook until the onions caramelize and turn a dim shade of brilliant brown, around 15 to 20 minutes, blending with a huge wooden spoon or spatula sporadically. (The sautéing time might fluctuate impressively.) Reduce intensity to medium-low. Move half of the onions to a little bowl. Add apricots, cashews, and raisins to the onion staying in the dish and cook until the organic product becomes stout, and the nuts become light brilliant brown, around 2 minutes. Eliminate the intensity and move to a different little bowl; this will be utilized for the embellishment.

•Return the onions from the little primary bowl to the Dutch stove; assuming that the blend looks dry, amount to 1 tablespoon (15ml) oil. Add the garlic, ginger, chile, garam masala, star anise, caraway, and turmeric and sauté until fragrant, around 30 to 45 seconds. Mix in the yogurt, cauliflower, potato, carrot, and water, alongside 1 teaspoon of salt. Increment intensity to medium-high and heat the items in the pot to the point of boiling, then decrease intensity to medium-low, cover with a top, and cook, frequently mixing to keep the sauce from singing, until the vegetables are sufficiently delicate to be penetrated with a blade, around 20 minutes. When the vegetables are delicate, mix in the peas and cook until warmed through and delicate, around 5 minutes.

•Switch off heat, taste for preparation, and season with salt, if necessary. Crease in cilantro and mint, then move items in the pot to a medium blending bowl. Flush and wipe the Dutch broiler clean.

•In the meantime, set up the rice. Join flushed rice with 4 cups (960 ml) water, lemon juice, 1 1/2 teaspoons salt, green cardamom cases, cinnamon, cloves, sound leaf, and 1 teaspoon of ghee or oil in a huge pot and heat to the point of boiling over medium-high intensity. Cook for 2 minutes, then, at that point, strain rice and flavors through a fine-network sifter; dispose of the cooking water. The rice will be, to some extent, cooked — a rice grain broken in half will uncover a clear external ring and a small, inward misty ring.

•Brush the base and the sides of the Dutch stove with the leftover 1 teaspoon of ghee. Utilizing a perfect, enormous wooden spoon or spatula, spread out a portion of the rice in an even layer in the lower part of the Dutch stove. Add the cooked vegetables with any fluids from the bowl over the rice and spread them cautiously in a solitary layer. Top the vegetables with the excess rice. Sprinkle the saffron-injected milk over the rice, trailed by the rosewater and the pandan water. Decorate the highest point of the rice with the held caramelized onions, dried natural product, and cashew blend. Cover the Dutch broiler with two sheets of aluminum foil, pleat the shade to frame a tight seal, and put the top on top. Place Dutch stove over medium-low intensity and cook until the rice is completely cooked, around 15 minutes.

•Switch off the intensity and let the Dutch broiler sit for 5 minutes. Cautiously strip off the aluminum seal. There ought to be next to zero fluid left at the lower part of the pot; to check, make a profound well in the rice the entire way to the foundation of the pot utilizing a chopstick or the handle of a wooden spoon. Assuming there is any fluid left at the base, reseal the pot, return it to the oven, and cook it over medium-low intensity for an extra 5-10 minutes until the fluid has been consumed.

•Utilizing a fork, relax the rice a bit and serve out of the Dutch stove, or move to a platter and serve.

NUTRITION FACTS
Total Fat 8g 10%
Saturated Fat 6g 30%
Trans Fat 0g
Polyunsaturated Fat 0g
Monounsaturated Fat 0g
Cholesterol 0mg
Sodium 100mg 4%
Total Carbs 34g 12%
Dietary Fiber 7g 25%
Total Sugars 15g
Sugar Alcohols 0g
Protein 4g 8%
Alcohol 0g
Caffeine 0mg

Easy Utan Bisaya

Prep Time: 5 minutes, **Cook Time:** 20 minutes, **Total Time:** 25 minutes

INGREDIENTS

- 3/4 lb squash
- 2 pieces taro
- 1 piece Knorr Shrimp Cube
- 4 thumbs ginger
- 2 stalks lemongrass
- 1 piece Chinese eggplant cut
- 10 pieces of string beans cut into 2-inch pieces
- 12 pieces okra
- 2 cups spinach
- 3 1/2 cups of water
- Salt and ground dark pepper to taste

PREPARATION

- Bubble water in a cooking pot. Add lemongrass and ginger. Cook for 5 minutes.
- Add taro and squash. Cover and keep bubbling for 5 to 7 minutes.
- Eliminate lemongrass from the pot. Add okra, string beans, and eggplant. Mix. Cover and keep cooking for 7 minutes.

•Add Knorr Shrimp Cube. Mix and cook for 3 minutes.
•Add spinach. Cook for 2 minutes.
•Season with salt and ground dark pepper.
•Move to a serving bowl. Serve.
•Share and appreciate!

NUTRITION FACTS
Calories: 160kcal | Carbohydrates: 37g | Protein: 7g | Fat: 1g | Saturated Fat: 1g | Polyunsaturated Fat: 1g | Monounsaturated Fat: 1g | Cholesterol: 1mg | Sodium: 282mg | Potassium: 1246mg | Fiber: 12g | Sugar: 14g | Vitamin A: 12221IU | Vitamin C: 56mg | Calcium: 174mg | Iron: 4mg

Sautéed vegetables

Prep Time: 10 mins, Cook Time: 15 mins, Total Time: 25 mins

INGREDIENTS

- •2 Tbsp olive oil
- •3 garlic cloves, minced
- •1 cup carrots, cut
- •1 lb asparagus, close managed and cut into 1-inch pieces
- •1 zucchini, cut
- •1 red ringer pepper, cut
- •8 oz mushrooms, cut
- •1 tsp genuine salt
- •1/2 tsp Italian flavoring
- •1/2 tsp onion powder
- •1/4 tsp paprika
- •1/4 tsp dark pepper
- •Spot of red pepper pieces

PREPARATION

•In an enormous skillet over medium-high intensity, sprinkle olive oil and sauté garlic for about a moment, mixing continually with the goal that it doesn't consume.

•Next, add the carrots and asparagus and sauté for around 6 minutes, mixing periodically. Then include zucchini, ringer pepper, mushrooms, and flavors. Cook an extra 8 to 10 minutes, mixing periodically so every one of the vegetables will equitably cook.

•Taste veggies, adjust seasonings as needed, and serve immediately. Enjoy!

NUTRITION FACTS
CALORIES: 124
SUGAR: 7.2 G
SODIUM: 415 MG
FAT: 7.2 G
SATURATED FAT: 1.1 G
CARBOHYDRATES: 12.5 G
FIBER: 4.9 G
PROTEIN: 4.6 G

SAUTEED SWISS CHARD

Prep Time: 20 minutes, **Cook Time:** 15 minutes, **Total Time:** 35 minutes

INGREDIENTS

•1 bundle Swiss chard new or rainbow chard

•2 tablespoons olive oil

•2-3 cloves of garlic coarsely slashed

•squeeze squashed red pepper or more-as indicated by taste

•1-2 tablespoons water discretionary

•salt and pepper to taste

•olive oil for showering

•Parmesan cheddar shavings discretionary

PREPARATION

•Set a huge pot of salted water to bubble.

•In the meantime, appropriately flush the chard to eliminate soil and sand.

•Trim off the finishes. Remove the ribs from the verdant part.

•When the water has begun bubbling, toss in the ribs. Bubble for 3-5 minutes or until starting to mellow.

•Add the green passes on and keep on bubbling for roughly 1-2 minutes.

•Channel completely in a colander

•Add the olive oil, the slashed garlic, and a spot of red pepper drops (if utilizing) to a huge skillet.

•Turn the intensity on to medium and sauté for 2 to 3 minutes.

•When the garlic starts to turn a light brilliant brown, eliminate the intensity and add the parboiled Swiss chard. Watch for splattering.

•Use utensils to surrender it to appropriately cover it with garlic-imbued oil.

•Put the container back on the intensity, and season with salt and pepper as per taste.

•Cover the skillet and permit it to concoct for 5 minutes or until delicate yet at the same time somewhat fresh if essential, add a couple of tablespoons of water.

•Taste and adapt to flavors.

•Put on the serving dish and shower with olive oil and shavings of Parmesan cheddar.

NUTRITION FACTS

Calories: 78kcal | Carbohydrates: 3g | Protein: 1g | Fat: 7g | Sodium: 160mg | Potassium: 284mg | Fiber: 1g | Vitamin A: 4585IU | Vitamin C: 22.9mg | Calcium: 41mg | Iron: 1.4mg

Crispy Garlic Sautéed Brussels sprouts

Prep Time: 5 minutes, **Cook Time:** 10 minutes, **Total Time:** 15 minutes

INGREDIENTS

•6 cloves garlic, minced

•2 tablespoons vegetable oil

•1 lb. (0.4 kg) Brussels sprouts, base managed and quartered

•1/2 teaspoon chicken bouillon powder, norr Granulated Bouillon Chicken

•1/2 teaspoon salt or to taste

PREPARATION

•Mince the garlic and put it away.

•Heat a skillet (cast-iron liked) with the oil on medium-high intensity. Add the minced garlic and saute until they turn fresh and brown. Because surely you don't consume garlic.

•Channel the garlic and oil IMMEDIATELY through a sifter. Separate the firm garlic and the garlic-mixed oil.

•Add the oil once more into the skillet on high intensity. At the point when the skillet is exceptionally hot, add the Brussels sprouts and immediately sauté. Throw to and fro with a spatula. The external leaves of the Brussels fledglings ought to turn dull and fresh.

•Add the fresh garlic, chicken bouillon powder, and salt. Mix to join well with the Brussels sprouts. Switch off the intensity and serve right away.

NUTRITION FACTS
Calories 116
Total Fat 7g
Saturated Fat 5g
Cholesterol 0mg
Sodium 379mg
Carbohydrates 11g
Fiber 4g
Sugar 2g
Protein 4g

Celery Salad with Apples

Prep Time: 15 minutes, **Cook Time:** 0 minutes
Total Time: 15 minutes

INGREDIENTS

•8 celery ribs in addition to ½ cup celery leaves
•1 red apple
•1 tablespoon white wine vinegar
•½ tablespoon Dijon mustard
•1 teaspoon maple syrup or sugar
•½ teaspoon fit salt
•3 tablespoons olive oil
•¼ cup shaved Parmesan cheddar

PREPARATION

•Meagerly cut the celery ribs. Measure out the celery leaves. Meagerly cut the red apple.
•In a medium bowl, whisk together the white wine vinegar, Dijon mustard, maple syrup or sugar, and fit

salt. Bit by bit, race in the olive oil, each tablespoon in turn.
•In another bowl, throw together the celery and celery leaves with the apple, dressing, and Parmesan cheddar shavings. Serve right away or refrigerate until serving. These preferences are best on the day of making; however, you can refrigerate extras for a couple of days (revive them with just the right amount of vinegar or salt if necessary).

NUTRITION FACTS
Total Fat 8.2g 11%
Saturated Fat 1.6g
Total Carbohydrate 9.1g 3%
Dietary Fiber 2.9g 10%
Sugars 5.7g
Protein 2.3g 5%
Vitamin A 38.2pg 4%
Vitamin C 5.6mg 6%
Calcium 98.7mg 8%
Iron 0.3mg 2%
Vitamin D Ogg 0%
Magnesium 18.4mg 4%
Potassium 389.1mg 8%
Vitamin B6 0.1mg 7%
Vitamin B12 Ogg 2%

Caprese Salad

Prep Time: 10 minutes, **Cook Time:** 0 minutes **Total Time:** 10 minutes

INGREDIENTS

•6 to 8 prepared treasure tomatoes of different assortments and sizes

•4 ounces new mozzarella cheddar or burrata cheddar

•1 little bundle of basil leaves

•Extra-virgin olive oil

•Balsamic lessening (optional)

•Sea salt

•New ground pepper

PREPARATION

•Cut the tomatoes and put them on a plate.

•Top with torn mozzarella cheddar and basil leaves. Sprinkle with extra-virgin olive oil. At whatever point is needed, sprinkle with balsamic decline. Top with sea salt and new ground pepper. Serve immediately.

(Doesn't save well; tomatoes should not be taken care of refrigerated.)

NUTRITION FACTS
Total Fat 17g 26%
Saturated Fat 7.9g 40%
Trans Fat 0g
Cholesterol 44mg 15%
Sodium 439mg 18%
Potassium 254mg 7%
Total Carbohydrates 4.7g 2%
Dietary Fiber 1.1g 4%
Sugars 2.8g
Protein 13g
Vitamin A 24% Vitamin C 20% Calcium 30% Iron 3%

Edamame

Prep Time: 10 minutes, **Cook Time:** 5 minutes, **Total Time:** 15 minutes

INGREDIENTS

- •1 pound frozen edamame in units (in the shell)
- •1/2 tablespoon toasted sesame oil
- •1 little garlic clove
- •3/4 teaspoon genuine or fine ocean salt, as well as something else for the water
- •Enthusiastic variety: add around 1 tablespoon of stew garlic sauce to taste
- •Optional fixing: Toasted sesame seeds

PREPARATION

•Heat an enormous pot of water with the inevitable consequence of foaming. Add the edamame and 1 teaspoon of genuine salt. Heat the edamame until splendid green and delicate, around 4 to 5 minutes, then, at that point, channel.
•Place the edamame in a bowl. Add the toasted sesame oil and salt, then pulverize the garlic clove into the bowl (utilizing a Microplane). Throw cautiously until everything is fairly covered, detaching any bunches of the garlic that stay together. Move to a serving bowl and serve warm, with an honest bowl for the disposed of cases.

NUTRITION FACTS
Total Fat 7.1g 9%
Saturated Fat 0.2g
Total Carbohydrate 8.6g 3%
Dietary Fiber 5.4g 19%
Sugars 2.8g
Protein 12.7g 25%
Vitamin A 0,ug 0%
Vitamin C Deng 12%
Calcium 68mg 5%
Iron 2.4mg 13%
Vitamin D 0,ug 0%
Magnesium 69.2mg 16%
Potassium 546.6mg 12%
Vitamin B6 0.2n2g 9%
Vitamin B12 0,ug 0%

Roasted Asparagus with Lemon

Prep Time: 10 minutes, **Cook Time:** 10 minutes, **Total Time:** 20 minutes

INGREDIENTS

•1 pound asparagus

•1 tablespoon olive oil

•½ teaspoon fit salt

•1 little garlic clove

•1 lemon (Zest and 1 teaspoon juice from half, notwithstanding cuts from the other half)

PREPARATION

•Preheat the grill to 425 degrees Fahrenheit.

•Clear out the serious base terminations of the asparagus. Add the asparagus stalks to a foil-lined baking sheet. Give them olive oil, and add the certified salt and a couple of drudgeries of dull pepper. Add the punch of ½ lemon and mix in with your hands. Softly cut 4 lemon wheels from the lemon, then, at that point, add them right to the plate.

•Plan for 10 to 15 minutes until fragile when invaded by a fork at the thickest part. The timing will depend on the thickness of the asparagus spears. Toss with the 1 teaspoon lemon juice, then serve.

NUTRITION FACTS
Total Fat 3.6g 5%
Saturated Fat 0.5g
Total Carbohydrate 4.4 2%
Dietary Fiber 2.4g 9%
Sugars 2.Ig
Protein 2.5g 5%
Vitamin A 43.1pg 5%
Vitamin C 6.4mg 7%
Calcium 27.4mg 2%
Iron 2.4mg 13%
Vitamin D Opg 0%
Magnesium 15.9nig 4%
Potassium 229.1mg 5%
Vitamin B6 0.1mg 6%
Vitamin B12 Opg 0%

Baked Vegetables

Prep Time: 10 mins, Cook Time: 30 mins, Total Time: 40 mins

INGREDIENTS

- Stove Temp: 325F-160C
- 2 tbsp Butter
- 1 cup Onions, finely cleaved
- 250-gram Mixed vegetables (cooked till chomp like), hacked
- 2 tsp Salt
- 1 tsp Black pepper, powdered
- 3 cups Cheese, ground
- For embellishing Tomato cuts
- For the white sauce:
- 2 cups Milk
- 2 tbsp Maida
- 2 tbsp Butter

PREPARATION

- Combine every one of the fixings as one and continue to mix to keep away from bumps.
- Liquefy the spread add onions, and sautéed food till they look polished.

•Add the blended vegetables and keep on mixing fry over high intensity till vegetables seem as though they are covered with the spread.
•Take it off the intensity and blend in the salt, pepper, and white sauce.
•Move blend into a piece of stove evidence serving dish.
•Sprinkle the cheddar to cover the blend, embellish with the tomato cuts and prepare on a pre-warmed stove for 30 minutes, or till the cheddar is somewhat brown.

NUTRITION FACTS
Calories 113
Total Fat9.26g 12%
Saturated Fat1.293g 6%
Trans Fat-
Polyunsaturated Fat1.046g
Monounsaturated Fat6.578g
Cholesterol0mg 0%
Sodium779mg3 4%
Total Carbohydrate7.47g 3%
Dietary Fiber1.8g 6%
Sugars2.41g
Protein1.48g
Vitamin D0mcg 1%
Calcium17mg 1%
Iron0.64mg 4%
Potassium249mg 5%
Vitamin A46mcg 5%
Vitamin C108mg 120%

SIDES RECIPES

ZESTY CHARGRILLED BROCCOLINI

Prep time: 10 minutes, servings 4

INGREDIENTS

•Avocado oil, depending on the situation for cooking

•10½ ounces (300g) of broccoli

•1 lemon

•Legitimate salt and newly ground dark pepper

•Sunflower and pumpkin seeds to serve

PREPARATION

•Set a frying pan or barbecue skillet over high intensity and add a sprinkle of avocado oil. Place the broccoli in the dish with the goal that the barbecue imprints will run flat. Cook for 5 minutes, flipping part of the way through, then grind the zing from the lemon on top and season with salt and pepper.

•To serve, add a crush of lemon juice and the sunflower and pumpkin seeds.

NUTRITION

53 calories

3g fat

7g carbs

3g protein

2g sugars

QUICK GUACAMOLE QUINOA SALAD

Prep time: 30 minutes, Servings: 4

INGREDIENTS

- •1 cup quinoa, flushed
- •2 avocados, divided and pitted
- •½ little white or red onion, finely diced
- •½ cup inexactly pressed slashed new cilantro
- •2 tablespoons newly crushed lime juice
- •½ teaspoon legitimate salt
- •One 15-ounce can of dark beans, depleted and flushed
- •1 cup cherry tomatoes, quartered
- •Extra-virgin olive oil for showering
- •Romaine lettuce, minced garlic, hot sauce, red-pepper drops, and lime wedges for serving

PREPARATION

- •Cook the quinoa as indicated by bundle guidelines. Permit it to cool to room temperature.
- •Score the avocado tissue (still in the skin) with a paring blade, then, at that point, scoop the tissue into a huge bowl. Coarsely squash about a portion of the avocado with a fork, leaving a lot of pieces flawless. Blend in the onion, cilantro, lime squeeze, and salt.

•Delicately crease in the dark beans, tomatoes, and quinoa. Taste and change the flavors whenever wanted and sprinkle with olive oil.
•Serve on a bed of romaine lettuce finished off with garlic, hot sauce, and red-pepper chips close by lime wedges.

NUTRITION
431 calories
18g fat
57g carbs
15g protein
3g sugars

STUFFED EGGPLANT

Prep time: 1hour 20 minutes,

INGREDIENTS

•2 medium eggplants, split

•3 tablespoons olive oil, disengaged

•1 red onion, diced

•2 garlic cloves, minced

•1 16 ounces cremini mushrooms, quartered

•2 cups torn kale

•2 cups cooked quinoa

•1 tablespoon hacked new thyme

•Punch and crush 1 lemon (despite extra lemon wedges for serving)

•Salt and, as of late, ground dull pepper

•½ cup plain Greek yogurt

•3 tablespoons hacked new parsley for decorating

PREPARATION

•Preheat the broiler to 400°F. Line a baking sheet with material paper.

•Utilizing a spoon, scoop out 33% of the tissue inside the eggplants (you can save it for different purposes or dispose of it). Rub every eggplant half with 1½ teaspoons olive oil and move to the planned baking sheet.

•Add the additional 1 tablespoon olive oil to a giant skillet and power over medium power. Add the onion and sauté until delicate, 3 to 4 minutes. Add the garlic and cook until fragrant, brief more.
•Add the mushrooms and cook until they are delicate, 4 to 5 minutes. Mix in the kale and quinoa, and cook until the kale is shriveled subtly for 2 to 3 minutes. Season the blend in with thyme, and lemon punch, and pulverize, salt, and pepper.
•Spoon the filling into the set-up eggplants and dish until the eggplants are delicate yet not self-destructing, 17 to 20 minutes. Let cool for 5 minutes.
•Serve the eggplant right away, wrapped up with parsley and joined by the yogurt and extra lemon wedges.

NUTRITION
339 calories
15g fat
46g carbs
12g protein

Minty-Fresh Zucchini Salad with Marinated Feta

Prep time: 15 minutes, Serving 4

INGREDIENTS

•1/4 pound block of feta cheddar, cut into squares

•Adequate bundle of new mint leaves, in addition to additional torn leaves for decorating

•Newly ground dark pepper, to taste

•2 or 3 (1-inch) strips orange strips, in addition to ground zing for decorating

•Squashed red-pepper drops, to taste (optional)

•Extra-virgin olive oil, depending on the situation

•2 medium zucchinis, cut into 1 1/2-by-1/2-inch cudgel (around 5 1/2 cups)

•1 teaspoon flaky salt (like Maldon)

•1/2 cup shelled salted broiled pistachios

•1/4 cup dried currants

PREPARATION

•MARINATE THE FETA: At least 1 day and as long as about fourteen days before serving, place the feta in a 16-ounce container. Add a liberal measure of new mint leaves, pressing them in as firmly as you can without separating the cheddar. Add dark pepper, the orange strip, and a squeeze or two of red-pepper pieces if utilizing. Fill the container with enough extra-virgin olive oil to simply cover the contents; it is lowered to ensure the cheddar. Close the container and turn it more than a couple of times. Assuming that you intend to utilize the cheddar the following day, you can keep the container out at room temperature. In any case, place it in the fridge.

•MAKE THE SALAD: Place the zucchini in a huge serving bowl and season it with the salt; prepare to cover. Add the pistachios and the currants and throw to consolidate.

•Eliminate the cheddar from the marinade, allowing any overabundance of olive oil to deplete once again into the container; disintegrate it into the plate of mixed greens, and throw to join. The cheddar will begin to cover the zucchini as you blend everything.

•Shower 1 tablespoon of the marinating oil over the serving of mixed greens and throw to cover. Embellish the serving of mixed greens with torn new mint leaves, extra dark pepper, and some ground orange zing.

NUTRITION
228 calories
16g fat
16g carbs
9g protein
11g sugars

Keto Instant Pot Greek Cauliflower Rice

Prep time: 10 minutes, Serving 8

INGREDIENTS

•1 little head cauliflower, oversaw and cut into quarters
•2 tablespoons olive oil, isolated
•½ cup diced red onion
•1 tablespoon minced garlic
•1 cup split grape tomatoes
•½ cup cut English cucumber
•½ cup split kalamata olives
•½ cup deteriorated feta cheddar
•¼ cup cut new parsley
•Ground punch and squeeze 1 lemon
•¼ teaspoon fine sea salt
•¼ teaspoon dim pepper
•¼ cup cut walnuts, toasted at whatever point needed

PREPARATION

•Void 1 cup of water into the Instant Pot. Put the cauliflower on a trivet with handles and lower the trivet into the pot. Secure the top on the pot and close the strain release valve. Set the pot to High Pressure for 0 minutes (see note). Around the completion of the cooking time, quick conveyance of the strain. Move the

cauliflower to a huge bowl and set it aside. Discard the liquid from the pot and wipe dry.
•Select Sauté on the Instant Pot. Right when the pot is hot, add 1 tablespoon of olive oil. Add the onion and garlic to the hot oil and cook until sensitive, something like 4 minutes. Select Cancel. Return the cauliflower to the pot and use a potato masher or wooden spoon to break the knots into close-to-nothing, rice-size pieces.
•Move the cauliflower to a serving bowl. Add the tomatoes, cucumber, olives, feta, parsley, lemon punch, and lemon press, and toss softly to merge. Season with salt and pepper. Not well before serving, cross over the walnuts and sprinkle with the abundance 1 tablespoon of olive oil.

NUTRITION
09 calories
9g fat
6g carbs
3g protein
2g sugars

Citrus, Fennel, and Avocado Salad

Prep time: 35 minutes, Serving 4 to 6

INGREDIENTS

•3 tablespoons extra-virgin olive oil

•Juice of 1 lemon

•1 tablespoon divided new mint

•2 tablespoons divided new parsley

•1 teaspoon certified salt

•½ teaspoon ground dim pepper

•6 cups arugula

•2 oranges, stripped and divided

•2 blood oranges, stripped and divided

•1 ruby-red grapefruit, stripped and divided

•1 bulb fennel, quartered and pitifully cut (fronds held, optional)

•2 avocados, isolated, pitted, and pitifully cut

PREPARATION

•In a little bowl, whisk the olive oil with lemon juice, mint, parsley, salt, and pepper to join.

•In a tremendous bowl, toss the arugula with the dressing. Segment the arugula similarly among plates.

•Top each serving of leafy greens with ¼ cup of every kind of citrus and about ¼ cup of fennel. Finish 4 or 5 avocado cuts. Serve immediately.

NUTRITION
369 calories
25g fat
38g carbs
5g protein
20g sugars

Greek Wedge Salad

Prep time: 15 minutes, Serving 4

INGREDIENTS

DRESSING

- •½ cup extra-virgin olive oil
- •1 tablespoon Dijon mustard
- •1 garlic clove, minced
- •1 teaspoon dried oregano
- •1 teaspoon salt
- •¾ teaspoon, as of late, ground dull pepper
- •⅓ cup red wine vinegar

SALAD

- •1 headpiece of ice lettuce — washed, cored, and quartered
- •1 16 ounces cherry tomatoes, quartered
- •½ cucumber, delicately cut
- •½ red onion, delicately cut
- •½ cup separated feta cheddar
- •1 cup kalamata olives
- •4 peperoncino peppers

PREPARATION

•MAKE THE DRESSING: In a medium bowl, whisk the olive oil with the mustard, garlic, oregano, salt, and

pepper. Unendingly rush in the red wine vinegar and blend well to consolidate.
•MAKE THE SALAD: Place a fourth of a chunk of ice lettuce on each plate and consequently sprinkle with an even extent of the tomatoes, cucumber, and red onion. Give each wedge salad dressing to taste.
•Embellish with 2 tablespoons feta, ¼ cup olives, and pepperoncino pepper. Serve right away.

NUTRITION
Dressing
248 calories
27g fat
1g carbs
0g protein
0g sugars
Salad
153 calories
8g fat
18g carbs
6g protein
10g sugars

Grilled Peach and Halloumi Salad with Lemon-Pesto Dressing

Prep time: 30 minutes, Serving 4

INGREDIENTS

•1½ cup basil leaves, finely hacked

•1 garlic clove, minced

•3 tablespoons lemon juice

•1 tablespoon rice vinegar

•⅓ cup + 4 tablespoons extra-virgin olive oil

•Genuine salt and recently ground dim pepper

•6 ounces of green beans

•3 peaches, hollowed and split

•6 ounces halloumi, cut

•4 cups mixed greens

•½ cup pine nuts, toasted

PREPARATION

•In a little bowl, whisk together the basil, garlic, lemon press, and rice vinegar. Little by little, race in ⅓ cup olive oil. Season with salt and pepper to taste.

•Heat a medium pot of salted water with the result of bubbling over focused energy. Add the green beans and brighten for 1 to 2 minutes. Move to a bowl of ice water to cool.

•Preheat a grill or grill dish over focused energy. Brush the extra olive oil consistently over the peaches and halloumi. Working in bundles, grill the peaches and halloumi until by and large around seared, about 3 minutes for each side.
•Organize the mixed greens on an enormous platter. Top with the green beans, peaches, and halloumi. Sprinkle with the dressing and trim with the pine nuts.

NUTRITION
696 calories
66g fat
21g carbs
11g protein
14g sugars

Rainbow Vegetable Skewers

Prep time: 23 minutes, Serving 6

INGREDIENTS

LEMON-PARSLEY DRESSING

•⅓ cup recently squeezed lemon juice

•Punch of 1 lemon

•1 tablespoon Dijon mustard

•½ cup extra-virgin olive oil

•¼ cup divided new parsley

•¾ teaspoon garlic powder

•1 press of cayenne pepper

•Salt and recently ground dull pepper

•Sticks

•3 red onions, cut into gigantic pieces

•2 summer squash, cut

•4 orange toll peppers, cut into squares

•2 pints of cherry tomatoes

•2 zucchini, cut

•1 eggplant, cut into gigantic strong shapes

•Salt and recently ground dull pepper

•2 tablespoons separated new parsley

PREPARATION

•MAKE THE LEMON-PARSLEY DRESSING: In a medium bowl, whisk the lemon juice with the lemon punch and Dijon mustard to combine. One small step at a time adds the olive oil, whisking perfect for joining. Add the parsley, garlic powder, and cayenne; season with salt and pepper.

•MAKE THE SKEWERS: Arrange the red onions immovably onto two sticks. Reiterate with various veggies.

•Brush the sticks with the dressing on the different sides and season with salt and pepper. Working in gatherings, cook on a preheated grill or grill dish until very much scorched, 3 to 5 minutes for each side.

•Adorn with parsley. Serve quickly with extra dressing as an idea in retrospect.

NUTRITION
Lemon-Parsley Dressing
170 calories
18g fat
3g carbs
0g protein
1g sugars
Skewers
119 calories
1g fat
26g carbs
5g protein
15g sugars

Yellow Tomato Gazpacho

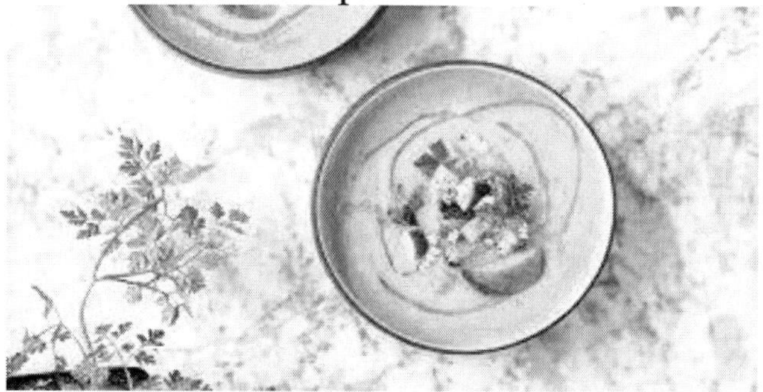

Prep time: 45 minutes, Serving 4 to 6

INGREDIENTS

CROUTONS

•1 tablespoon extra-virgin olive oil

•3 or 4 thick cuts of white or sourdough bread, cut into little solid shapes

•Ocean salt and newly ground dark pepper

GAZPACHO

•4 enormous, firm, ready orange or yellow tomatoes, coarsely slashed

•6 basil leaves, in addition to a modest bunch of little basil, lemon basil, or opal basil leaves, for embellishing

•1 or 2 garlic cloves, coarsely slashed

•Ocean salt

•1 seedless cucumber, stripped and finely slashed

•1 pound (455g) firm, ready legacy tomatoes, finely slashed

•1 little purple onion or shallot, finely cleaved (optional)

•1 red or yellow ringer pepper, cultivated and finely slashed

•2 firm, ready peaches, stripped and finely slashed

•Extra-virgin olive oil, for sprinkling

•Newly ground dark pepper

•Chervil (optional) for embellishing

PREPARATION

•MAKE THE CROUTONS: Heat the olive oil in a little skillet over medium intensity. Throw the bread blocks in the oil, turning with utensils or an intensity-resistant spatula to toast on all sides, around 4 minutes. Season with salt and pepper. Move to a plate to cool. (You can make these as long as a day ahead of time; simply make certain to cool totally and store them in an impenetrable compartment.)

•MAKE THE GAZPACHO: Combine the tomatoes, basil, and garlic in an enormous bowl; season with salt. Cover and refrigerate for 30 minutes. Cool the singular serving bowls.

•Eliminate the basil from the chilled tomato combination and dispose of it. Move the combination to a blender or utilize a submersion blender to process until foamy and smooth, 2 to 3 minutes.

•Spoon the soup into the chilled bowls and hill a touch of the cucumber, treasure tomatoes, onion (if utilizing), chime pepper, and peaches in the middle. Top with little basil leaves, chervil (if utilized), and the bread garnishes. Shower with olive oil and season with salt and pepper. Serve cold or at room temperature.

NUTRITION

Croutons

326 calories

5g fat

58g carbs

12g protein

5g sugars

Gazpacho

142 calories

6g fat

21g carbs

4g protein

11g sugars

Black Fig and Tomato Salad

Prep time: 10 minutes, Serving 4

INGREDIENTS

•8 new and arranged dull figs

•4 medium-sized arranged tomatoes

•Ocean salt and newly ground pepper

•1 tablespoon of extraordinary red wine or champagne vinegar

•2 tablespoons olive oil

•12 basil leaves

PREPARATION

•With clean hands, tear the figs into fifths. Cut the tomatoes into quarters a similar size as the fig parts.

•Place tomato wedges in a medium bowl and season well with salt and pepper. Shower with vinegar and olive oil and throw.

•Add the figs and basil to the tomatoes and throw again tenderly. Gather the part of salad greens on a serving dish or individual plates.

NUTRITION

159 calories

7g fat

25g carbs

2g protein

20g sugars

Pearl Couscous with Chickpeas, Eggplant, and Peaches

Prep time: 35 minutes, Serving 6

INGREDIENTS

•1 pound (about 3 medium peaches), destroyed and cut into ½-inch wedges.
•1 negligible red onion, cut into ½-inch wedges.
•One pound of eggplant, cut into 1-inch shapes.
•One 15½-ounce compartment of chickpeas was rinsed, depleted, and cleared.
•4 pieces of new thyme
•8 tablespoons additional virgin olive oil
•1 teaspoon smoked paprika
•¼ teaspoon cayenne pepper
•2 teaspoons fine salt
•1½ teaspoons newly ground black pepper
•3 cups vegetable broth
•2½ cups pearl couscous
•½ cup leafless kalamata olives, chopped
•½ cup chopped new parsley
•½ cup minced fresh mint
•1 teaspoon lemon punch
•2 tablespoons new lemon juice
•2 tablespoons tahini

PREPARATION

•Preheat grill to 425°F. In a large bowl, combine peaches, onion, eggplant, chickpeas, thyme sprigs, 5 tablespoons olive oil, paprika, cayenne, 1 teaspoon salt, and 1 teaspoon black pepper. Divide the combination between two rimmed baking sheets and spread in a single layer. Heat until vegetables are weak, 18 to 20 minutes. Remove the thyme sprigs.
•Meanwhile, in a huge saucepan, heat the broth until frothy, add the couscous, cover, and lower the heat to keep it stewed. Cook until the liquid is retained and the couscous is still fairly firm 8 to 10 minutes.
•In a goliath serving bowl, consolidate the couscous, cooked vegetables, peaches, olives, parsley, mint, lemon punch, lemon juice, tahini, remaining 3 tablespoons oil, remaining teaspoon salt, and remaining ½ teaspoon pepper. Serve hot, cold, or at room temperature.

NUTRITION
633 calories
25g fat
88g carbs
17 protein
12g sugars

Citrus, Shrimp, and Quinoa Salad with Feta

Prep time: 20 minutes, Serving 4

INGREDIENTS

•1 cup uncooked quinoa
•16 medium shrimp, stripped and deveined
•2 tablespoons additional virgin olive oil
•½ teaspoon authentic salt
•⅛ teaspoon chipotle stew powder or smoked paprika
•2 cold grapefruits, stripped and cut into changed or isolated pieces.
•4 cold clementines, stripped and partitioned
•4 ounces feta cheddar, crumbled
•12 dried Moroccan or kalamata olives, cored and cut
•1 lime, slashed

PREPARATION

•Preheat the oven to 425°F. In a medium pan, add 2 cups of water and quinoa and heat until bubbling. Lessen to a stew, cover, and cook until quinoa is delicate, 12 to 15 minutes. Eliminate from the intensity and let stand, covered, for 5 minutes. When conscious, circulate air through with a fork and move it to a huge bowl.

•In the meantime, on a baking sheet, throw shrimp with oil, salt, and chipotle powder or smoked paprika.

Cook until shrimp are dazzling pink, 7 to 10 minutes. Add shrimp to the bowl with quinoa, alongside grapefruit, clementine, feta, and olives. Delicately throw to join.

•Split the blended greens between plates or bowls and top with lime pieces. Leafy greens can be put away in the fridge for as long as two days.

NUTRITION
398 calories
17g fat
50g carbs
15g protein
17g sugars

15-Minute Gazpacho with Cucumber, Red Pepper, and Basil

Prep time: 15 minutes, Serving 4

INGREDIENTS

•2¼ pounds tomatoes, diced

•1 red ringer pepper, diced

•1 European cucumber, stripped and diced

•1 clove garlic

•1 red onion, minced and partitioned

•4 tablespoons cleaved basil, isolated

•Genuine salt and newly ground dark pepper

•2 cups cherry tomatoes, cleaved

•2 tablespoons additional virgin olive oil

PREPARATION

•In a blender or food processor, join tomatoes, red ringer pepper, cucumber, garlic, a big part of the red onion, and a big part of the basil. Puree the blend until smooth.

•Season gazpacho with salt and pepper to taste and mix to consolidate.

•Empty gazpacho into serving bowls and top with outstanding onion and basil, cherry tomatoes, and a little sprinkle of olive oil. Serve right away.

NUTRITION

159 calories

8g fat

22g carbs

4g protein

13g sugars

Broccoli Rabe and Burrata with Lemon

Prep time: 10 minutes, serving: 4

INGREDIENTS

•1 bundle broccoli rabe, stem closes cut off

•1 to 2 tablespoons extra-virgin olive oil, in addition to a little oil for showering

•2 cloves garlic, minced

•¼ teaspoon red pepper drops

•4 ounces new burrata or mozzarella cheddar

•½ tablespoon new lemon juice

•2 tablespoons squashed and toasted pistachios

•Flaky ocean salt, to serve

PREPARATION

•Heat an enormous pot of salted water to the point of boiling. Bubble broccoli rabe for 3 minutes, then channel.

•In an enormous, profound skillet over medium intensity, heat 1 to 2 tablespoons of olive oil to cover the lower part of the container. Mix in the garlic and cook for 30 seconds; then, at that point, mix in the red pepper chips.

•Add broccoli and sauté, shaking the container and mixing delicately to guarantee in any event, cooking until delicate (particularly the stems), 3 to 5 minutes.

•Eliminate broccoli from the skillet and channel abundance fluid. Orchestrate broccoli on a plate or platter. Tear burrata and partition pieces over broccoli. Sprinkle with lemon juice, pistachios, and salt. Sprinkle with olive oil whenever wanted, and serve.

NUTRITION
198 calories
15g fat
6g carbs
1g sugars
11g protein

Zucchini & Tomato Ragù

Prep time: 20 minutes, Serving 6

INGREDIENTS

•6 tablespoons additional virgin olive oil

•1 onion, peeled and coarsely chopped

•2 cloves garlic, peeled and lightly crushed

•1 medium zucchini, chopped

•1 medium summer squash, chopped

•Real salt and freshly ground black pepper

•7 ounces of delicious ready-to-use tomatoes, chopped

•4 ounces mozzarella cheddar cheese, coarsely torn

•¼ cup parsley leaves, coarsely chopped

•¼ cup basil leaves, torn

PREPARATION

•Heat oil in a huge non-stick skillet over medium heat. Add onion and garlic and cook, frequently stirring, until onion is clear, 8 to 10 minutes.

•Add zucchini and summer squash; season with salt and pepper. Cook, frequently stirring, until zucchini and summer squash are shiny, about 2 minutes.

•Stir in tomatoes and cook until tomatoes begin to soften and zucchini and summer squash are still somewhat firm about 2 minutes. Serve with mozzarella, parsley, and basil.

NUTRITION

204 calories
18g fat
7g carbs
6g protein
4g sugars

Sweet Corn, Tomato, and Zucchini Grain Salad with Peach-Dijon Vinaigrette

Prep time: 15 minutes, Serving 4

INGREDIENTS

•2 tablespoons additional virgin olive oil
•1½ tablespoons peach jam
•1 tablespoon whole grain Dijon mustard
•Salt and freshly ground black pepper
•1 cup cooked wheat pieces
•5 large hard-boiled eggs, peeled and cracked
•2 large tomatoes, chopped
•Raw almonds from an ear of sweet corn
•¼ young zucchini, cut into quarters and pieces
•¼ small red onion, chopped
•¼ cup disintegrated feta cheddar cheese
•Sliced new basil for embellishment
•Fresh dill, thinly sliced, for garnish
•Borage flowers, for garnish (optional)
•Nasturtium flowers, for garnish (optional)

PREPARATION

•In a small bowl, whisk together olive oil, peach jam, and Dijon mustard until emulsified; season with salt and pepper.

•Place wheat pieces on a platter and top with eggs, tomatoes, corn, zucchini, red onion, feta, basil, and dill.

Pour dressing over salad and arrange borage and nasturtium flowers on top (if using).

NUTRITION
260 calories
15g fat
20g carbs
12g protein
7g sugars

Whole Roasted Radishes

Prep time: 35 minutes, Serving 4

INGREDIENTS

•2 bunches of radishes, ends, and tops were cut off

•3 tablespoons of olive oil

•1 tablespoon lemon juice

•1½ teaspoons real salt

•1 teaspoon freshly ground pepper

PREPARATION

•Preheat the grill to 400°F.

•In a colossal bowl, toss the radishes with olive oil and lemon juice. Season with salt and pepper and mix.

•Bake until radishes are tender and hot around the edges, 25 to 30 minutes. Serve hot.

NUTRITION

101 calories

10g fat

3g carbs

0g protein

1g sugars

Whole Roasted Carrots

Prep time: 1hour 15minutes, Serving 4

INGREDIENTS

•2 lots of carrots, stripped and stemmed
•1 red onion, stripped and cut into 8 wedges
•3 tablespoons olive oil
•2 tablespoons red wine vinegar
•1 tablespoon ground cumin
•1 teaspoon legitimate salt
•1 teaspoon newly ground dark pepper
•3 tablespoons hacked new mint
•Zing of one lemon

PREPARATION

•Preheat the stove to 400°F. In a medium baking dish, consolidate carrots and onions.
•In a little bowl, consolidate olive oil with red wine vinegar, cumin, salt, and pepper. Pour combination over carrots and onions; throw delicately to cover.
•Broil until carrots and onions are delicate and cooking at the edges, 30 to 35 minutes. Decorate with mint and lemon zing. Serve hot.

NUTRITION

177 calories
11g fat
20g carbs
2g protein
9g sugars

Cauliflower with Roasted Tomatoes, Parsley and Bread Crumbs

Prep time: 55 minutes, Serving 4

INGREDIENTS

GARLIC BREAD CRUMBS

•¼ cup impartial oil, for example, canola or safflower oil.

•4 cloves garlic, minced

•½ teaspoon salt

•1 cup bread pieces or panko

CAULIFLOWER

•1 head cauliflower, cored and cut into florets.

•3 tablespoons additional virgin olive oil, partitioned

•Legitimate salt and newly ground dark pepper

•2 quarts cherry tomatoes or 10 plum tomatoes, cut down the middle or quarters if huge.

•½ pack parsley, coarsely cleaved

•½ cup pitted olives, coarsely slashed (optional)

•½ cup garlic breadcrumbs

PREPARATION

•MAKE THE GARLIC BREAD CRUMBS: In an enormous skillet, heat the oil until extremely hot, then, at that point, add the garlic and salt.

•Eliminate from heat, so the garlic doesn't consume, and let represent 10 minutes (or cook garlic on low intensity for 5 minutes, observing cautiously to abstain from consuming).

•Add the bread morsels and blend them in. Return the skillet to the intensity and toast the sleek breadcrumbs until brilliant and fragrant, around 3 minutes.

•Eliminate the intensity and let it cool. Put away in an impenetrable compartment.

•MAKE THE CAULIFLOWER: Preheat the broiler to 425°F. Throw cauliflower with 1½ tablespoons olive oil and sprinkle with salt and pepper. Organize on a foil-lined baking sheet; don't swarm cauliflower.

•Broil until cauliflower is brilliant brown, fresh outwardly, and delicate when punctured with a blade, around 25 minutes.

•Leave the cherry tomatoes crudely or throw them with the excess 1½ tablespoons olive oil and a spot of salt; then, at that point, cook in the broiler, blending consistently, until the fluid is decreased and sweet, 15 to 25 minutes.

•Throw cauliflower with tomatoes, parsley, and olives, if utilized. Top with garlic breadcrumbs and serve.

NUTRITION
246 calories
12g fat
31g carbs
8g protein
13g sugars

BEANS RECIPES

White bean salad

Prep Time: 15 minutes, **Cook Time:** 0 minutes **Total Time:** 15 minutes

INGREDIENTS

- •2 jars of white beans (cannellini), drained and rinsed well
- •1 English cucumber, diced
- •10 oz grape or cherry tomatoes, divided
- •4 green onions, sliced
- •1 cup new parsley, cut into strips
- •15-20 mint leaves, slivered
- •1 lemon, zest, and juice
- •salt and pepper
- •Flavorings (1 teaspoon of Za'atar and ½ teaspoon of Sumac and Aleppo).
- •Additional virgin olive oil

•Cheddar feta cheese, optional

PREPARATION

•Add white beans, cucumbers, tomatoes, green onions, parsley, and mint to a huge mixing bowl.

•Add lemon zest. Season with salt and pepper, then add the za'atar, sumac, and Aleppo pepper.

•Wrap the whole with lemon juice and a generous drizzle of extra virgin olive oil (2 to 3 tablespoons). Stir the plate of mixed greens to combine. Taste and adjust the mixture. Add feta cheddar cheese, if desired. (For best flavor, let the salad sit in the dressing for about 30 minutes before serving.

NUTRITION FACTS

Calories 205
Total Fat 6g 8%
Sodium 679mg 30%
Total Carbohydrate 31.4g 11%
Sugars 5.8g
Protein 9.7g 19%
Vitamin A 14%
Vitamin C 62%
Calcium 9%
Iron 21%
Vitamin D 0%
Magnesium 24%
Potassium 8%
Zinc 22%
Phosphorus 14%
Thiamin (B1) 76%
Riboflavin (B2) 19%
Niacin (B3) 5%
Vitamin B6 8%
Folic Acid (B9) 21%
Vitamin B12 2%
Vitamin E 4%
Vitamin K 345%

Bean Soup with Tomato Pesto

Prep Time: 10 mins, Cook Time: 27 mins, Total Time: 37 mins

INGREDIENTS

•Extra virgin olive oil

•1 huge earthy potato, trimmed and cut into minimal 3D shapes

•1 medium yellow onion, chopped

•1 15 oz can of diced tomatoes

•1 tablespoon white vinegar

•1 tablespoon ground cilantro

•1 teaspoon Spanish paprika

•salt and pepper

•5 cups of low sodium vegetable broth, or your choice of broth

•80 g frozen spinach; try not to thaw
•15 oz canned kidney beans, drained and rinsed
•15 oz canned cannellini beans, drained and emptied
•15 oz canned chickpeas, drained
•Basil leaves for garnish, optional
•⅓ cup toasted pine nuts for garnish (optional)
•For the tomato pesto sauce
•2-3 colossal cloves of garlic; you can start with less garlic assuming you are not sure.
•1 ½ cups new tomatoes, diced
•15-20 huge basil leaves
•½ cup Private Reserve Greek extra virgin olive oil
•Salt and pepper
•⅓ cup ground Parmesan cheese
PREPARATION
•In a huge Dutch oven or significant pot, heat two tablespoons of olive oil over medium heat until it fizzes but does not smoke. Add the diced potatoes and onions. Cook for 4 to 5 minutes, stirring well.
•Add canned diced tomatoes, vinegar, flavorings, salt, and pepper. Stir to combine. Cover and cook for an additional 4 minutes.
•Uncover, and add vegetable broth and frozen spinach. Increase power to medium-high to bubble for about 4 minutes. Add kidney beans, cannellini beans, and chickpeas. Increase power again until the mixture is bubbling, then reduce power to medium-low. Cover and cook for an additional 15 to 20 minutes (potatoes should be crumbly at this point).
•While the soup is cooking, prepare the tomato pesto. In the bowl of a food processor fitted with a rim, place the garlic and new tomatoes. Pulse several times to solidify. Add the basil and puree. While the food processor is running, add the olive oil a little at a time.

Transfer the thick tomato pesto to a bowl, and stir in the ground parmesan.
•When the soup is ready, remove it from the processor. Stir in the tomato pesto.
•Spoon into serving bowls. Garnish each bowl with two or three basil leaves and toasted pine nuts. Make the most of your #1 evaporated bread!

NUTRITION FACTS
Calories: 366.1kcal
Carbohydrates: 37.3g
Protein: 14g
Fat: 20.2g
Saturated Fat: 3.1g
Cholesterol: 3.7mg
Sodium: 568.1mg
Potassium: 672.3mg
Fiber: 11.2g
Vitamin A: 3792.7IU
Vitamin C: 14.1mg
Calcium: 183.2mg
Iron: 4.5mg

Kidney bean curry

Prep time: 5 mins, Cook time: 30 mins, Total time: 35 mins

INGREDIENTS

•1 tablespoon vegetable oil

•1 onion, finely hacked

•2 cloves garlic, finely hacked

•1 piece ginger, stripped and finely hacked

•1 little bundle coriander, stems finely cleaved, leaves coarsely destroyed

•1 teaspoon ground cumin

•1 teaspoon ground paprika

•2 teaspoons garam masala

•400 g canned hacked tomatoes

•400 g canned red beans in water

•cooked basmati rice to serve

PREPARATION

•Heat oil in a huge skillet over low-medium intensity. Add the onion and a spot of salt and cook gradually, sometimes mixing, until relaxed and starting to take on the variety. Add the garlic, ginger, and coriander stems and cook for an additional 2 minutes, until fragrant.

•Add the flavors to the skillet and cook for 1 more moment until fragrant. Add the cleaved tomatoes and kidney beans to their water and heat to the point of boiling.

•Bring down the intensity and stew for 15 minutes until the curry is thick. Season to taste and present with basmati rice and coriander leaves.

NUTRITION FACTS
Kcal 282
Low in
Fat 8g
Saturates 1g
Carbs 33g
Sugars 13g
Fiber 14g
Protein 13g
Salt 0.1g

Mixed bean chili

PREP TIME: 10 mins, COOK TIME: 50 mins, TOTAL TIME: 1 hrs.

INGREDIENTS

- olive oil
- 1 red onion, diced
- 1 ringer toll pepper, diced
- 3 cloves garlic, crushed
- 3 containers of 400 g mixed beans, drained
- 400 g tomatoes, separated
- 500 mL vegetable stock

Flavors

- 1 teaspoon sweet or smoked chipotle stick
- 1 tablespoon ground cumin
- 1 ½ tablespoons paprika
- 1 tablespoon dried oregano
- 1 tablespoon gritty shaded sugar or honey
- Sea salt and pepper to taste
- Outmaneuvering
- 1 lime, cut into wedges
- 1 unassuming pack of cilantro

PREPARATION

•In a medium dish over medium-low power, sauté onion and ringer pepper for 5 minutes until loose.

•Add garlic and sauté for an additional 2 minutes. Add cumin and paprika, and when you can start to smell the flavors, blend in a chipotle stick, add tomatoes, stock, oregano, sugar, salt, and pepper.

•The intensity with the end result of bubbling, add the beans, cut down the power, and stew for 40-45 minutes. You could need to add a little water as you go on the off chance that the stew ends up being unnecessarily thick.

•At the point when the beans are sensitive, truly check out the seasoning and present with manages.

NUTRITION FACTS
Calories: 259kcal
Carbohydrates: 39g
Protein: 14g
Fat: 4g
Saturated Fat: 1g
Sodium: 738mg
Potassium: 308mg
Fiber: 15g
Sugar: 9g
Vitamin A: 602IU
Vitamin C: 557mg
Calcium: 129mg
Iron: 4mg

Classic Bean Soup

Prep Time: 10 mins, Cook Time: 23 mins, Total Time: 33 mins

INGREDIENTS

- •1 medium yellow onion, diced
- •2 enormous carrots, diced
- •2 celery ribs, diced
- •4 enormous garlic cloves, minced
- •3 tablespoons olive oil
- •28 oz can fire-simmered tomatoes, squashed
- •2 - 15 oz jars white beans*, depleted (or substitute cannellini or pinto beans)
- •1 - 15 oz can kidney beans, depleted
- •1-liter vegetable stock
- •2 tablespoons smoked paprika
- •½ teaspoon cumin
- •1 teaspoon fennel seeds

•2 teaspoons fit salt

PREPARATION

•Dice the onion, carrots, and celery. Slash the garlic.

•In an enormous pot or Dutch stove over medium intensity, sauté onion, carrots, and celery for 5-7 minutes, until onion is clear. Add garlic and cook for 1 moment.

•Add tomatoes, depleted beans, vegetable stock, smoked paprika, cumin, fennel seeds (squash fennel seeds with fingers as you add them), and legitimate salt. Stew for 15 minutes. Taste and change flavors if important. Serve warm: extras save well in the fridge for as long as 3 days or in the cooler for as long as 90 days.

NUTRITION FACTS

Total Fat 9.3g 12%
Saturated Fat I.2g %
Total Carbohydrate 45g 16%
Dietary Fiber 7.3g 26%
Sugars 5.4g
Protein 16.Ig 32%
Vitamin A 218.2pg 24%
Vitamin C 33.9mg 38%
Calcium 93mg 7%
Iron 4.9mg 27%
Vitamin D Ogg 0%
Magnesium 219. ? Mg 52%
Potassium 685.1mg 15%
Vitamin B6 0.4mg 22%
Vitamin B12 Opg 0%

Cuban Black Beans

Prep Time: 10 minutes, **Cook Time:** 25 minutes, **Total Time:** 35 minutes

INGREDIENTS

•1 ½ cups minced sweet yellow onion (around 1 huge onion)

•1/2 green chime pepper

•6 garlic cloves

•1/4 jalapeño pepper

•2 tablespoons salted spread (substitute extra olive oil for veggie lover)

•1 tablespoon olive oil

•2 15-ounce jars of dark beans (or 3 cups cooked or Instant Pot dark beans)

•1 teaspoon cumin

•2 teaspoons oregano

•1 ¼ teaspoon legitimate salt

•New cilantro, for an embellishment

•1 cup dry white or brown long grain rice, to serve

PREPARATION

•Begin the rice as per the bundle directions, or utilize our Instant Pot Rice technique or How to Cook Rice on the Stove.

•Mince the onion and mince the pepper (hack them into little dice). Mince the garlic.
•Eliminate the ribs and seeds from the jalapeño pepper and mince them.
•Utilize a sifter to deplete the dark beans over a glass estimating cup, saving the can fluid. (Don't bother flushing.)
•In an enormous skillet, heat the margarine and olive oil over medium-high intensity. Once softened, add the onion, ringer pepper, jalapeño pepper, and garlic. Cook for 10 minutes, until it is clear and softly sautéed to mix periodically until the onions are. Add the beans, cumin, oregano, and genuine salt and mix to consolidate. Add ½ cup of the fluid from the dark beans. Stew for 15 minutes until beans are delicate.
•Cleave the cilantro for the trimming. Serve the dark beans warm with rice and topping with hacked cilantro.
NUTRITION FACTS
Total Fat 10.7g 14%
Saturated Fat 4.5g %
Total Carbohydrate 77.8g 28%
Dietary Fiber 15.7g 56%
Sugars 5.2g
Protein 15.8g 32%
Vitamin A 80.5pg 9%
Vitamin C 58.3mg 65%
Calcium 143mg 11%
Iron 4.9mg 27%
Vitamin D Ogg 0%
Magnesium 92.9mg 22%
Potassium 841.5mg 18%
Vitamin B6 0.5mg 30%
Vitamin B12 Ogg 1%

3-Bean Healthy Chili

Prep Time: 5 minutes, **Cook Time:** 35 minutes, **Total Time:** 40 minutes

INGREDIENTS

- ¾ cup Simply Nature Organic Quinoa
- 2 little or 1 medium yellow onion
- 3 cloves garlic
- 2 tablespoons olive oil
- ½ cup Simply Nature Organic Ketchup
- ¼ cup bean stew powder
- 2 tablespoons dried oregano
- 1 tablespoon garlic powder
- 1 teaspoon cumin
- 1 cup water
- 3 15-ounce jars of Simply Nature Organic Beans (we did 1 can each dark, pinto, and kidney), depleted
- 2 28-ounce jars of Simply Nature Organic Diced Tomatoes

•1 cup frozen corn
•1 tablespoon yellow mustard
•1 tablespoon Worcestershire sauce, vegetarian whenever wanted
•2 tablespoons ground Simply Nature Flax Seed (optional)
•1 ½ teaspoon legitimate salt
•Optional: 1 tablespoon adobo sauce (from a container of chipotle stews)
•To embellish: Sour cream or Greek yogurt (or Vegan Sour Cream or Cashew Cream for veggie lovers), Mexican mix destroyed cheddar, and Southern Grove Pepitas

PREPARATION

•Cook the quinoa: Place the quinoa in a pot with 1 ½ cups water. Heat to the point of boiling, then diminish the intensity to exceptionally low. Cover the pot and stew where the water is only rising for around 15 to 20 minutes until the water has been assimilated. (Check by pulling back the quinoa with a fork to check whether water remains.) Turn off the intensity and let sit covered to steam for 5 minutes.
•Dice the onions. Mince the garlic.
•In a huge pot or Dutch stove, heat the olive oil over medium intensity. Add the onions and saute for 5 to 7 minutes, until delicate. Add the garlic and cook for 2 minutes until delicately seared. Add the ketchup and flavors and cook for 1 moment until fragrant.
•Add any remaining fixings, and toss in the quinoa at whatever point it is cooked. Stew for 25 minutes. Serve promptly with fixings. Store extras refrigerated for as long as 3 days or frozen for quite some time.

NUTRITION FACTS
Total Fat 6.7g 9%
Saturated Fat ig %

Carbohydrate 53.7g 20%
Dietary Fiber 15.8g 56%
Sugars 7Ig
Protein 14.3g 29%
Vitamin A 109.2pg 12%
Vitamin C 13.6ntg 15%
Calcium 107.7mg 8%
Iron 5.4mg 30%
Vitamin D Opg 0%
Magnesium 117.3mg 28%
Potassium 878.9mg 19%
Vitamin B6 0.4mg 23%
Vitamin 612 Ogg 0%

Black Bean Burger

Prep Time: 10 minutes, **Cook Time:** 50 minutes, **Total Time:** 1 hrs

INGREDIENTS

For the black bean burger

•1 little yam (½ pound)

•¾ cup Bob's Red Mill without gluten dated moved oats

•2 green onions

•15-ounce can of dark beans

•½ cup sunflower seeds (shelled)

•½ teaspoon fit salt

•½ teaspoon garlic powder

•2 teaspoons smoked paprika

•1 ½ tablespoons soy sauce

•1 ½ tablespoons mirin

•For the shiitake mushrooms or substitute Shiitake Bacon

•4 shiitake mushrooms

•1 sprinkle every olive oil, mirin, and soy sauce.

PREPARATION

•Preheat broiler to 375°F.

•Wash the yam and prick it with a fork. Microwave until cooked through, around 8 minutes, turning partially through. Cut open and permit to cool until the steam disperses and it is cool to the touch.
•Put oats on the cutting board and generally slash with a blade to get a blended surface. Daintily cut green onions. Channel and wash the beans.
•In a bowl, consolidate onions, oats, beans, sunflower seeds, fit salt, garlic powder, smoked paprika, soy sauce, and mirin. Blend in with your hands and daintily pound the beans with your fingers. Add ½ cup yam and blend to consolidate.
•Line a baking sheet with material paper. Structure into 4 patties and put on the baking sheet. Prepare 20 minutes on one side, then, at that point, flip and heat for 20 minutes on the opposite side. Cool somewhat before serving.
•Eliminate the stems and cut the shiitake mushroom covers. In a little skillet, add a sprinkle of olive oil, mirin, and soy sauce, then, at that point, saute the mushrooms until delicate, around 1 moment.
•Make the Spicy Mayo.
•To serve, put the burgers on toasted English biscuits and top with mushrooms, hot mayo, and hay sprouts.

NUTRITION FACTS
Total Fat 10.4g 13%
Saturated Fat 1.3g %
Total Carbohydrate 41.1g 15%
Dietary Fiber 11.4g 41%
Sugars 5.9g
Protein 13.4g 27%
Vitamin A 241.7gg 27%
Vitamin C 5.3mg 6%
Calcium 62.8mg 5%
Iron 4mg 22%

Vitamin D 0.3pg 1%
Magnesium 85.1mg 20%
Potassium 1070mg 23%
Vitamin B6 0.3mg 19%
Vitamin B12 Ogg 1%

Enchiladas

Prep Time: 15 minutes, **Cook Time:** 15 minutes, **Total Time:** 30 minutes

INGREDIENTS

•3 cups Homemade Red Enchilada Sauce or bought sauce

•2 tablespoons olive oil

•2 huge portobello mushroom covers

•1/2 medium red onion

•1 orange chime pepper

•15-ounce can of dark beans, depleted and washed

•1 teaspoon garlic powder

•2 teaspoons cumin

•1 teaspoon onion powder

•1 teaspoon paprika

•1 teaspoon legitimate salt

•2 tablespoons lime juice

•½ cup vegetable stock (extra from the enchilada sauce recipe) or water

•1 ½ cups guacamole

•12 8-inch flour or corn tortillas

•For the trimming: 1 cup meagerly cut romaine lettuce, 1 to 2 radishes cut into matchsticks, 2 tablespoons minced red onion, and torn cilantro.

PREPARATION

•Preheat the broiler to 400 degrees Fahrenheit.

•Begin the Enchilada Sauce (or for speedier prep, make it the prior night).

•Eliminate the stems from the mushroom covers and meagerly cut them. Meagerly cut the red onion. Meagerly cut the chime pepper.

•In an enormous skillet, heat the olive oil over medium-high intensity. Saute the veggies for 6 to 7 minutes until delicate. Add the dark beans (depleted and flushed), garlic powder, cumin, onion powder, paprika, legitimate salt, lime juice, and vegetable stock or water. Cook for 2 minutes until the fluid is thickened into a sauce.

•Spread 1 cup of the enchilada sauce in the lower part of an enormous baking dish.

•On the off chance that utilizing corn tortillas ONLY: Brush the two sides of every tortilla daintily with olive oil. Heat a huge frying pan to medium-high intensity. Cook the tortillas in groups for 15 seconds for each side until gently seared.

•Fill every tortilla with ¼ cup of vegetable filling and around 2 tablespoons of guacamole, running in a line down the middle (see the photograph). Roll it up and put it in the baking dish crease side down. When the 12 tortillas are all in the dish, pour over the leftover 2 cups of enchilada sauce.

•Prepare for 5 minutes until warmed through. Top with enhancements and serve. (Extras kept very much refrigerated.)

NUTRITION FACTS
Total Fat 10.8g 14%
Saturated Fat I.5g %
Total Carbohydrate 41.2g 15%
Dietary Fiber 6.3g 23%
Sugars 5.4g
Protein 8.8g 18%
Vitamin A 21.9pg 2%
Vitamin C 22.3mg 25%
Calcium 117.4mg 9%
Iron 2.4mg 13%
Vitamin D 0.1,ug 0%
Magnesium 24.6mg 6%
Potassium 372.5mg 8%
Vitamin B6 0.2mg 11%
Vitamin 1312 Dug 0%

Black Bean Tacos

Prep Time: 10 minutes, **Cook Time:** 5 minutes, **Total Time:** 15 minutes

INGREDIENTS

For the black beans

•2 15-ounce cans of dark beans

•2 garlic cloves

•1 tablespoon olive oil

•1 tablespoon margarine (or substitute more olive oil for veggie lovers)

•½ teaspoon cumin

•1 sparse teaspoon of legitimate salt

•For the tacos

•Taco sauce (bought or natively constructed) or salsa

•1 can corn

•Romaine lettuce slashed

•Feta cheddar disintegrates or destroys cheddar

•Cilantro leaves, torn

•Cut red onions or Pickled Red Onions

•Avocado slashed

•Cut jalapeno peppers or salted jalapenos (optional)
•Harsh cream, 5 Minute Cilantro Lime Sauce or Cilantro Sauce (veggie lover), optional**
•8 little tortillas, flour, or corn.
PREPARATION
•Make the dark beans: Drain the beans; however, don't wash them. Mince the garlic. In a medium pan, heat the olive oil and margarine over medium intensity. Add the garlic and sauté for around 30 seconds until fragrant but not yet cooked. Add the beans (depleted but not washed), cumin, legitimate salt, and a few toils of dark pepper. Cook for 3 to 4 minutes until warmed through and the fluid cooks down and thickens. Taste and add extra salt whenever wanted.
•Gather the garnishes: Review the fixings above and prep them as wanted.
•Warm the tortillas: Warm and burn the tortillas by putting them on an open gas fire-on mode for a couple of moments on each side, flipping with utensils, until they are somewhat darkened and warm.
NUTRITION FACTS
Total Fat 11.5g 15%
Saturated Fat 3.5g
Total Carbohydrate 41.4g 15%
Dietary Fiber 9.6g 34%
Sugars 1.9g
Protein 11.7g 23%
Vitamin A 25 lig 3%
Vitamin C 4.4mg 5%
Calcium 158.8mg 12%
Iron 3.7mg 20%
Vitamin D 0.1pg 0%
Magnesium 53.3mg 13%
Potassium 479mg 10%
Vitamin B6 0.2mg 9%
Vitamin B12 0.2lig 7%

Classic Three Bean Salad

Prep Time: 15 minutes, **Cook Time:** 0 minutes, **Total Time:** 15 minutes

INGREDIENTS

•15-ounce can of kidney beans

•15-ounce can of white beans or pinto beans

•15-ounce can of green beans

•15-ounce can of wax beans (or another 15-ounce can of green beans)

•1/2 medium white onion

•1/4 medium red onion (optional)

•2 tablespoons cleaved wavy parsley (or Italian parsley)

•½ cup white vinegar*

•¼ cup olive oil

•2 tablespoons granulated sugar

•1/4 teaspoon each dried dill and garlic powder
•1 teaspoon genuine salt
•New ground dark pepper
PREPARATION
•Channel and flush the beans.
•Meagerly cut the onions into fragments (go to minute 1:40 of this How to Cut an Onion video to perceive how!). Finely hack the parsley.
•In an enormous bowl, whisk together the white vinegar, olive oil, sugar, dill, garlic, powder, and legitimate salt. Add the beans, onions, and parsley and mix until covered. You can eat right away; however, for best outcomes, refrigerate for 1 hour to permit the plate of mixed greens to marinate. Store extras refrigerated for as long as 5 days.

NUTRITION FACTS
Total Fat 7.9g 10%
Saturated Fat 1g
Total Carbohydrate 25.7g 9%
Dietary Fiber 7.6g 27%
Sugars 4.5g
Protein 7.8g 16%
Vitamin A 0.4 pg 0%
Vitamin C 2.3mg 3%
Calcium 52.3mg 4%
Iron 2.4mg 13%
Vitamin D Oug 0%
Magnesium 65mg 15%
Potassium 181.2mg 4%
Vitamin B6 Omg 3%
Vitamin 1312 0,ug 0%

Black Bean Salsa

Prep Time: 10 minutes, **Cook Time:** 0 minutes, **Total Time:** 10 minutes

INGREDIENTS

•1 pound of ready tomatoes

•½ cup red onion, minced

•¼ cup cilantro, finely cleaved

•1 jalapeño pepper

•15-ounce can of dark beans (or 1 ½ cups cooked or Instant Pot dark beans)

•1 lime (2 tablespoons juice)

•½ teaspoon genuine salt, in addition to more to taste

PREPARATION

•Dice the tomatoes. Mince the red onion. Finely cleave the cilantro. Eliminate the ribs and seeds of the jalapeño pepper and finely cleave them. Channel and wash the dark beans. Juice the lime.

•In a bowl, add tomato, red onion, cilantro, jalapeño, dark beans, lime juice, and genuine salt. Mix to join, and add genuine salt to taste.

NUTRITION FACTS
Calories 215
Calories from Fat 61 %
Total Fat 6.8g 10%
Saturated Fat 19 5%
Trans Fat Og
Cholesterol 0mg 0%
Sodium 737mg 31%
Potassium 682mg 19%
Total Carbohydrates 32g 11%
Dietary Fiber 11g 44%
Sugars 4.8g
Protein 9.6g
Vitamin A 19%
Vitamin C 28%
Calcium 7%
Iron 19%

Refried Beans

Prep Time: 5 minutes, **Cook Time:** 15 minutes, **Total Time:** 20 minutes

INGREDIENTS

•2 garlic cloves

•2 15-ounce jars of pinto beans or 3 cups cooked pinto beans, in addition to ¾ cup can fluid or water

•2 tablespoons olive oil

•1 teaspoon cumin

•½ teaspoon stew powder

•½ teaspoon legitimate salt

PREPARATION

•Mince the garlic. Channel the beans and save the can fluid in a glass estimating cup. (Use water if utilizing cooked beans.)

•In a medium pot, heat the olive oil over medium intensity. Add the garlic and sauté for 1 moment until fragrant yet before its earthy colors.

•Turn the intensity to medium-low and cautiously add the beans (fluid hitting oil can make it spit!), ½ cup of the saved can fluid, cumin, stew powder, and fit salt. Cook for 10 to 15 minutes, mixing at times, adding the excess ¼ cup could fluid when it starts to at point become drier. (How long you cook will rely upon the bean brand or whether you're utilizing beans cooked from dry.) When the fluid gets thick, and the beans become simple to pound, eliminate the intensity. Pound with a potato masher until the ideal surface is reached. If you might want to relax the surface, add more water. Serve right away.

NUTRITION FACTS
Total Fat dg 10%
Saturated Fat 12g
Total Carbohydrate 34.5g 13%
Dietary Fiber 11.7g 42%
Sugars 0.5g
Protein 11.8g 24%
Vitamin A 5.3pg 1%
Vitamin C 1 .5mg 2%
Calcium 67.9mg 5%
Iron 3.1mg 17%
Vitamin D 0µg 0%
Magnesium 66.9mg 16%
Potassium 581.2mg 12%
Vitamin B6 0.3mg 19%
Vitamin B12 0,ug 0%

Dal Makhani

Prep Time: 15 minutes, **Cook Time:** 15 minutes, **Total Time:** 30 minutes

INGREDIENTS

•1 huge yellow onion

•8 garlic cloves

•¼ cup minced ginger

•6 ounces tomato glue

•2 ½ cups milk, partitioned

•3 tablespoons olive oil

•2 teaspoons every cumin seeds, stew powder, and coriander

•1 ½ tablespoons garam masala

•½ teaspoon cayenne pepper

•2 tablespoons spread

•2 15-ounce jars of dark lentils, depleted (or 3 cups of cooked dark lentils)

•15-ounce can of dark beans

•1 ½ teaspoon fit salt

•Naan or basmati rice, for serving

•Acrid cream, to embellish

•New cilantro to embellish

PREPARATION

•Dice the onion. Mince the garlic. Strip and mince the ginger.

•In a little bowl, combine one tomato glue and ½ cup of milk until smooth.

•In a huge skillet, heat the olive oil. Sauté the cumin seeds until they simply begin to brown, around 1 moment. Add the onion, garlic, and ginger, and sauté for 1 to 2 minutes.

•Add the bean stew powder, coriander, garam masala, cayenne pepper, margarine, tomato glue, milk blend, and another ½ cup of milk. Add the beans and lentils and the fit salt.

•Intensity and mix, steadily adding the rest of the milk (1 ½ cups or more) north for a couple of moments until a thick sauce structure.

•Serve warm, with naan for plunging, or present with basmati rice. Top with acrid cream and hacked cilantro.

NUTRITION FACTS

Calories 308Calories from Fat 117

% Daily Value*

Fat 13g20%

Saturated Fat 8g50%

Cholesterol 35mg12%

Sodium 433mg19%

Potassium 353mg10%

Carbohydrates 35g12%

Fiber 12g50%

Sugar 4g4%

Protein 13g26%

Vitamin A 987IU20%

Vitamin B1 (Thiamine) 1mg67%

Vitamin B2 (Riboflavin) 1mg59%

Vitamin B3 (Niacin) 1mg5%
Vitamin B6 1mg50%
Vitamin B12 1μg17%
Vitamin C 17mg21%
Vitamin D 1μg7%
Vitamin E 1mg7%
Vitamin K 7μg7%
Calcium 61mg6%
Vitamin B9 (Folate) 60μg15%
Iron 4mg22%
Magnesium 31mg8%
Phosphorus 77mg8%
Zinc 1mg7%

Creamy White Beans with Kale and Wild Rice

Prep Time: 10 mins, Cook Time: 45 mins, Total Time: 55 mins

INGREDIENTS

- •1 cup (~180g) wild rice (I utilized a bowl of wild rice + earthy colored rice mix)
- •1 1/2 cups (360 mL) vegetable stock or water for Instant Pot strategy (utilize 3 cups (710 mL) vegetable for burner technique)
- •1 yellow onion, diced
- •1/3 cup (80 mL) water
- •6 cloves garlic, minced
- •1 tablespoon new thyme leaves, minced
- •1 (13.5-ounce/400 mL) can "light" or diminished fat coconut milk
- •1 tablespoon white or yellow miso glue
- •1/4 cup (60 mL) pureed tomatoes
- •3 tablespoons tomato glue

•2 (15-ounce/440g) jars of cannellini beans, depleted and washed
•1 teaspoon ground cumin
•1 teaspoon hot or sweet paprika (not smoked)
•1/2 teaspoon red bean stew chips (add more to taste if you need it hot)
•1 teaspoon genuine salt + more to prepare
•Dark pepper to taste
•6-8 cups (400-540g) destroyed Tuscan (lacinato) kale, extreme stems eliminated
PREPARATION
•Make the Wild Rice (Instant Pot technique): Add the wild rice and 1 1/2 cups of vegetable stock to the internal pot of the Instant Pot. Secure the top and select the Pressure Cook/Manual setting for 25 minutes. Permit a characteristic strain delivery and channel off any leftover fluid.
•Make the Wild Rice (Stovetop strategy): Place the wild rice and 3 cups of vegetable stock in a pan over medium-high intensity. Heat to the point of boiling, then, at that point, turn the intensity down and cover. Stew for 40-45 minutes, or until the bits have burst open. Channel off any leftover fluid.
•While the rice is cooking, make the Creamy White Beans and Kale. Heat a profound nonstick container over medium intensity. Add the diced onion and a touch of salt and mix for 1 moment. Then add the water and carry the blend to a stew. Cook for 5 minutes, or until the onion relaxed and the water vanished.
•Add the garlic and thyme passes on to the container. Mix much of the time for 2-3 minutes to keep the garlic from consuming.
•Mix in the coconut milk, miso, pureed tomatoes, tomato glue, cannellini beans, cumin, paprika, pepper drops, salt, and pepper. Mix to consolidate and cover

every one of the beans in the sauce. Then, at that point, add the kale and mix again to integrate.

•Carry the bean blend to a stew. Keep on cooking a stew for 10 minutes until it has thickened and is velvety.

•Serve the beans and kale on top of the cooked wild rice.

NUTRITION FACTS

Calories: 577kcal | Carbohydrates: 100g | Protein: 28g | Fat: 9g | Saturated Fat: 7g | Polyunsaturated Fat: 1g | Monounsaturated Fat: 1g | Sodium: 478mg | Potassium: 1924mg | Fiber: 15g | Sugar: 5g | Vitamin A: 10662IU | Vitamin C: 130mg | Calcium: 355mg | Iron: 10mg

PASTE, GRAIN, RICE RECIPES

One-Pot Tomato Basil Pasta

Prep time: 5 minutes, **Cook time:** 30 minutes, **Total time:** 35 minutes

INGREDIENTS

•8 ounces of entire wheat rotini

•1 cup water

•2 cups low-sodium "no-chicken" stock or chicken stock

•1 (15-ounce) can of no-salt-added diced tomatoes

•2 tablespoons extra-virgin olive oil

•1 ½ teaspoon Italian flavoring

•½ teaspoon onion powder

•½ teaspoon garlic powder

•½ teaspoon salt

•¼ teaspoon squashed red pepper

•6 cups child kale or child spinach

•½ cup fragmented basil

•Ground Parmesan cheddar for embellish
PREPARATION
•Consolidate pasta, water, stock, tomatoes, oil, Italian flavoring, onion powder, garlic powder, salt, and squashed red pepper in a huge pot.
•Cover and heat to the point of boiling over high intensity. Uncover, decrease intensity to medium-high, and cook, blending much of the time, for 10 minutes.
•Mix in kale and cook, frequently blending, until the greater part of the fluid has been consumed, 5 to 7 minutes more. (In the case of utilizing spinach, add it after around 10 minutes, so it cooks in the excess 2 to 3 minutes.) Stir in basil. Decorate with Parmesan whenever wanted.

NUTRITION FACTS
339 calories; protein 11.4g; carbohydrates 55.3g; dietary fiber 7.9g; sugars 5.5g; fat 9.9g; saturated fat 1.4g; vitamin a in 3343.5IU; vitamin c 47.1mg; folate 70.4mcg; calcium 87.3mg; iron 3.8mg; magnesium 100.3mg; potassium 308.2mg; sodium 465.2mg; thiamin 0.3mg.

One-Pan Chicken Parmesan Pasta

Prep Time: 5 minutes, **Cook Time:** 40 minutes, **Total Time:** 45 minutes

INGREDIENTS

- •2 tablespoons extra-virgin olive oil, isolated
- •1/4 cup whole wheat panko breadcrumbs
- •1 tablespoon notwithstanding 1 teaspoon minced garlic, isolated
- •1 pound boneless, skinless chicken chest, cut into 1/2-inch pieces
- •1 teaspoon Italian enhancing
- •1/4 teaspoon salt
- •3 cups low-sodium chicken stock
- •1 1/2 cups crushed tomatoes
- •8 ounces of whole wheat penne
- •1/2 cup obliterated mozzarella cheddar
- •1/4 cup obliterated Parmesan cheddar
- •1/4 cup hacked new basil

PREPARATION

•Heat 1 tablespoon oil in a tremendous ovenproof skillet over medium-extreme focus. Add panko and 1 teaspoon of garlic. Cook, blending until the panko is splendid brown, 1 to 2 minutes. Move to a little bowl and save. Get out the holder.

•Heat the abundance of 1 tablespoon oil in the skillet over medium-focused energy. Add chicken, Italian enhancing, salt, and the extra 1 tablespoon of garlic. Cook, blending as frequently as could be expected, until the chicken is, as of now, not pink obviously, something like 2 minutes. Add stock, tomatoes, and penne. The intensity with the result of bubbling and cooking, revealed, occasionally blending, until the penne is cooked and the sauce has reduced and thickened, 15 to 20 minutes.

•Meanwhile, position an oven rack in the upper third of the grill. Preheat the barbecue to high. Exactly when the pasta is cooked, sprinkle mozzarella over the penne mix. Place the dish under the barbecue; sing until the mozzarella is murmuring and beginning to brown, around 1 second. Top with the panko mix, Parmesan, and basil.

NUTRITION FACTS

538 calories; protein 41g; carbohydrates 55.8g; dietary fiber 7.3g; sugars 6.6g; fat 17.1g; saturated fat 4.8g; cholesterol 77.3mg; vitamin a in 488.5IU; vitamin c 9.8mg; folate 18mcg; calcium 212.7mg; iron 4.6mg; magnesium 49.1mg; potassium 874.8mg; sodium 611.6mg; thiamin 0.1mg.

Bruschetta Chicken Pasta

PREP TIME: 10 minutes, **COOK TIME:** 40minutes, **TOTAL TIME:** 50minutes

INGREDIENTS

•8 ounces entire wheat spaghettini

•3 tablespoons extra-virgin olive oil

•1 pound boneless, skinless chicken bosoms, cut into 1-inch pieces

•1 teaspoon dried Italian flavoring

•2 pints of colorful cherry tomatoes

•3 cloves garlic, finely hacked

•1 teaspoon salt

•¼ teaspoon ground pepper

•¼ cup dry white wine

•1 tablespoon in addition to 1 teaspoon of balsamic coating

•1 ounce Parmesan cheddar, ground on the littlest openings of a box grater (around 1/4 cup)

•¼ cup daintily cut new basil

PREPARATION

•Cook pasta as per bundle bearings, discarding salt. Channel and put away.

•In the meantime, heat oil in a huge high-sided skillet over high intensity. Add chicken and Italian flavoring; cook, infrequently mixing, until just cooked through and sautéed for around 6 minutes. Move the chicken to a plate. (Try not to clean the skillet off.)

•Decrease intensity to medium-low. Add tomatoes, garlic, salt, and pepper; cook, scratching the lower part of the dish to slacken any sautéed bits, until the tomatoes start to explode, 4 to 5 minutes. Add wine; increment intensity to high and cook, frequently mixing, until somewhat diminished, around 3 minutes, pushing on the tomatoes depending on the situation to pound them. Add the pasta and chicken; throw delicately to join. Split the pasta combination between 4 dishes. Shower equally with balsamic coating; sprinkle with Parmesan and basil.

NUTRITION FACTS

499 calories; protein 34.3g; carbohydrates 52.2g; dietary fiber 1.9g; sugars 8g; fat 17.3g; saturated fat 3.6g; cholesterol 68.8mg; vitamin a in 1466.5IU; vitamin c 21.6mg; folate 66.9mcg; calcium 113.9mg; iron 3.4mg; magnesium 116.7mg; potassium 830mg; sodium 791.3mg; thiamin 0.3mg.

One-Pot Spinach, Chicken Sausage & Feta Pasta

Prep Time: 5 minutes, **Cook Time:** 10 minutes, **Total Time:** 15 minutes

INGREDIENTS

•2 tablespoons olive oil

•3 connections cooked chicken wiener (9 ounces), cut into adjusts

•1 cup diced onion (see Tip)

•1 clove of garlic, minced

•1 (8-ounce) can of no-salt-added pureed tomatoes

•4 cups daintily stuffed child spinach (a big part of a 5-ounce box)

•6 cups cooked entire wheat rotini pasta

•¼ cup cleaved pitted Kalamata olives

•½ cup finely disintegrated feta cheddar

•¼ cup hacked new basil (Optional)

PREPARATION

•Heat oil in a huge straight-sided skillet over medium-high intensity. Add hotdog, onion, and garlic; cook, frequently mixing, until the onion is beginning to brown, 4 to 6 minutes. Add pureed tomatoes, spinach, pasta, and olives; cook, frequently blending, until gurgling hot and the spinach is shriveled, 3 to 5 minutes. Add 1 to 2 tablespoons of water, if important, to hold the pasta back from staying. Mix in feta and basil, if utilizing.

NUTRITION FACTS

487 calories; protein 22.8g; carbohydrates 59.3g; dietary fiber 8.1g; sugars 6.7g; fat 19.6g; saturated fat 4.2g; cholesterol 61.7mg; vitamin a in 1290.6IU; vitamin c 10.3mg; folate 72.2mcg; calcium 142.3mg; iron 3.8mg; magnesium 111.5mg; potassium 464.8mg; sodium 623.3mg; thiamin 0.3mg.

Greek Spaghetti (Makaronia me Kima)

Prep Time: 10 min Cook Time: 30 mins, Total Time: 40 mins

INGREDIENTS

- •2 pounds ground sheep
- •1 medium yellow onion, separated
- •3 cloves garlic, crushed
- •1 cup red wine
- •1 28-ounce container of no-salt-added crushed tomatoes
- •1 cup water
- •1 teaspoon salt
- •½ teaspoon ground pepper
- •½ teaspoon ground cinnamon
- •¼ teaspoon ground allspice
- •20 ounces of whole wheat spaghetti
- •1 tablespoon spread

•Ground Greek hard cheddar, as Kefalotyri or Pecorino (optional)

PREPARATION

•Cook sheep in a gigantic pot over medium-focused energy, blending often and saying one last goodbye to a spoon until, as of now, not pink, 7 to 8 minutes. Add onion and cook, blending, until clear, 4 to 5 minutes. Blend in garlic and cook, mixing, until fragile yet not caramelized, 2 to 3 minutes. Pour in the wine and scrape up any singed pieces. Add tomatoes and their juice, water, salt, pepper, cinnamon, and allspice.

•Reduce force to keep a stew and cook, occasionally blending, until the sauce has diminished and thickened, close to an hour. (Add a little water on the off chance that it gives off an impression of being unnecessarily dry.)

•Something like 20 minutes before the sauce is ready, heat a tremendous pot of water with the result of bubbling. Cook spaghetti according to the package heading. Channel well. Move to a tremendous bowl, add margarine and toss until condensed. Move to a serving platter. Spoon the sauce over the spaghetti. Serve polished off with cheddar at whatever point is needed.

NUTRITION FACTS

429 calories; protein 25g; carbohydrates 47.1g; dietary fiber 8.6g; sugars 4.5g; fat 14.1g; saturated fat 5.9g; cholesterol 62.9mg; vitamin a in 692.8IU; vitamin c 5.8mg; folate 21.9mcg; calcium 46.2mg; iron 4.3mg; magnesium 66mg; potassium 551.2mg; sodium 289.6mg; thiamin 0.2mg.

Murgh Koftey Ki Biryani

Prep Time: 15 mins, **Cook Time:** 1 hr 10 mins, **Total Cook Time:** 1 hr 25 mins

INGREDIENTS

•800 gms chicken leg (boneless)
•2 tsp green stew, chopped8 onions, cut
•3 tsp ginger, cut
•4 tbsp coriander, cut
•6 eggs
•1 tsp nutmeg powder
•1 tsp mace powder
•200 gms sheep kidney fat
•to taste salt
•2-liter sheep stock
•8 green cardamom
•6 dim cardamom
•5 sound leaves
•3 cinnamon sticks
•4 mace, sum
•1 tsp cumin seeds
•1 cup hearty shaded onion
•3 tbsp mint, cut

•10 green chillies, julienne
•1 kg yogurt
•1/2 tsp saffron
•2 tsp fennel seeds (saunf)
•400 gms basmati rice, doused
•1 cup ghee
•1 cup cream
•1 1/2 cups milk

PREPARATION

•Take holder. Add chicken leg boneless, cut green bean stew, onion, ginger, coriander, eggs, nutmeg powder, mace powder, and kidney fat, and mix well.

•Right when the chicken is cooked, cool down and mince it. Mix generally around well. Rub fittingly with salt.

•In a skillet, take the sheep stock. Add whole flavors, gritty shaded onion, mint, cut/julienne green chilies, and salt. Stew.

•Make little balls with the chicken mince and brighten them in the stock. Keep aside.

•In the overabundance of stock, add yogurt, a piece of saffron, fennel seeds, and salt.

•Stew it wonderfully and add the soaked basmati rice. Cook for a surprisingly long time.

•Add ghee, cream, milk, mint, gritty shaded onion, and remaining saffron.

•Cook rice in dum and present with brightened chicken mince ball.

Greek Chicken & Feta Pasta

Prep time: 45 mins, Servings: 6

INGREDIENTS

•12 oz pasta

•2 Tbsp olive oil

•12 oz cherry tomatoes, split or quartered

•10 oz cooked chicken bosom, cut into little pieces

•6 new basil leaves, hacked

•½ tsp dried oregano

•3½ oz kalamata olives, cut

•4 oz feta cheddar, disintegrated

•1 Tbsp newly pressed lemon juice

•½ tsp salt

•Pepper

PREPARATION

•In a huge weighty pot with a cover, join pasta, 4 cups water, and olive oil. Heat to the point of boiling over high intensity. Cook pasta, often mixing, until still somewhat firm. The water ought to be almost dissipated; this ought to require around 10 minutes; if water is left in the skillet, channel pasta before adding the excess fixings.

•Add tomatoes, chicken, basil, oregano, olives, and cheddar. Throw together, then, at that point, add lemon squeeze, salt, and pepper.

NUTRITION
Per serving: 440 cal, 17g fat, 50mg chol, 26g prot, 47g carbs, 4g fiber, 740mg sodium

Whole-Grain Spelt Salad with Leeks and Marinated Mushrooms Recipe

Prep time: 20 mins, Total time: 35 mins, Serves: 4 to 6

INGREDIENTS

•1/2 cup in addition to 1 tablespoon extra-virgin olive oil, isolated

•1 pound cremini mushrooms, diced

•1 enormous (12-ounce) leek, diced

•2 medium cloves garlic, meagerly cut

•1 teaspoon picked thyme leaves, minced

•Fit salt and newly ground dark pepper

•1/4 cup in addition to 2 tablespoons juice vinegar, isolated

•6 cups cooked entire grain spelled (from around 24 ounces dry)

•2 little Persian cucumbers, quartered the long way, then cut transversely into 1/4-inch pieces

•1/2 cup minced level leaf parsley

•1/4 cup minced chives

PREPARATION

•In an enormous skillet, heat 3 tablespoons of oil over medium-high intensity until gleaming. Add mushrooms and cook, blending, until delicate and their water has dissipated, around 5 minutes. Add leek, garlic, and thyme, season with salt and pepper, and cook until the spill is delicate, around 4 minutes. Move to an enormous bowl and mix in 1/4 cup juice vinegar. Let stand for 15 minutes.

•In an enormous bowl, mix spelled cucumbers and mushroom-leek blend. Mix in excess 6 tablespoons olive oil, 2 tablespoons juice vinegar, conference, and chives, and season with salt and pepper. Spoon salad into bowls and sprinkle with espelette pepper, if utilizing.

NUTRITION FACTS
241 CALORIES
22g FAT
11g CARBS
3g PROTEIN

Bulgur Salad with Apricots, Radicchio, Herbs, and Walnuts Recipe

Prep time: 20 mins, Total time: 20 mins, Serves: 4

INGREDIENTS

•1 cup bulgur wheat

•1/2 teaspoon salt, in addition to more to taste

•1/2 little head radicchio, cored and meagerly cut (around 1 cup)

•1/2 cup cleaved dried apricots

•1/2 cup cleaved new parsley leaves

•1/2 cup hacked new mint leaves

•3 scallions, white and green parts, finely cut

•1/2 cup hacked pecans, toasted whenever wanted

•1/4 cup newly pressed lemon juice from 2 lemons

•1/4 cup extra-virgin olive oil

•2 1/2 teaspoons agave nectar or honey

•Newly ground dark pepper

PREPARATION

•Heat a pot of water to the point of boiling. Place bulgur in a medium bowl with salt, then pours 1-1/4 cups bubbling water up and over. Cover the bowl firmly with cling wrap and let sit until the water is all retained 25 to 30 minutes

•Join the cooked bulgur with the leftover fixings in general, and throw well. Season to taste with salt and pepper. Serve cold or at room temperature.

NUTRITION FACTS
343 CALORIES
24g FAT
33g CARBS
5g PROTEIN

Toasted Bulgur Salad with Smoked Trout, Radishes, and Green Apple Recipe

Prep time: 45 mins, Total time: 55 mins, Serves: 4

INGREDIENTS

For the Salad:

•3 lemons, cut into suprèmes

•1/2 cup sugar

•1 3/4 cups water, isolated

•1 cup bulgur wheat

•1/2 teaspoon fit salt, in addition to something else for preparing

•8 ounces of smoked trout, skin, and bones eliminated, chipped into 1-inch lumps (around 1 cup)

•4 radishes (around 6 ounces), divided and daintily cut

•1/2 little red onion (around 4 ounces), divided and daintily cut

•1 medium Granny Smith apple (around 8 ounces), split, cored, and daintily cut, cuts cut down the middle across

•1 cup approximately stuffed level leaf parsley leaves, coarsely cleaved

•Newly ground dark pepper

For the Dressing:
•2 tablespoons new squeeze from 1 lemon
•1 tablespoon held lemon drenching syrup
•1/2 teaspoon lemon zing
•1/2 cup in addition to 1 tablespoon extra-virgin olive oil
•Fit salt and newly ground pepper
PREPARATION
•For the Salad: Gently tear every lemon fragment into roughly 1/2-inch pieces and spot them in a heatproof bowl. In a little pot, mix sugar and 1/2 cup of water. Heat to the point of boiling over high intensity, then stew, blending, until the sugar has disintegrated. Pour hot syrup over the lemon pieces and let represent 45 minutes.
•In the meantime, in a medium skillet, toast the bulgur over respectably high intensity, blending as often as possible, until nutty-smelling, around 3 minutes. Move to a medium heatproof bowl. In a little pan, consolidate the excess 1 1/4 cups of water with 1/2 teaspoon salt and heat to the point of boiling. Pour the bubbling water over the bulgur and cover it. Let stand, covered, for 20 minutes, then uncover, cushion with a fork, and let cool to room temperature, around 30 minutes.
•In an enormous bowl, throw trout, radish, onion, apple, and parsley with the cooled bulgur. Channel the lemon sections, saving 1 tablespoon of the lemon splashing syrup for the dressing and the rest for another utilization. Add the depleted lemon parts to the plate of mixed greens and throw tenderly to consolidate.
•For the Dressing: In a medium bowl, whisk the lemon juice with 1 tablespoon of held syrup and lemon zing. In a sluggish sprinkle, pour in the olive oil, whisking continually. Season with salt and pepper.

•Pour the dressing over the serving of mixed greens and throw delicately to consolidate. Season with salt and pepper. Serve immediately or cover and refrigerate for the time being or as long as 2 days. Serve chilled or at room temperature.

Stir-Fried Farro with Garlicky Kale and Poached Egg Recipe

Prep time: 25 mins, Total time: 40 mins, Serves: 4

INGREDIENTS

•1 1/2 cups farro (300g; 10 ounces)

•2 tablespoons extra-virgin olive oil (30ml), in addition to something else for showering

•2 medium shallots (160g; 6 ounces), meagerly cut (around 3/4 cup)

•3 medium cloves garlic, minced

•1 huge pack of lacinato (Tuscan) kale, washed, extreme stems eliminated and disposed of, and generally slashed (around 300g; 10 ounces after de-stemming)

•2 tablespoons red wine vinegar (30ml)

•Legitimate salt and newly ground dark pepper

•4 huge eggs, poached or seared

•Parmigiano-Reggiano cheddar, for shaving (optional)

•Chile sauce, for serving (optional)

PREPARATION

•Heat a huge pot of salted water to the point of boiling and add farro. Lower intensity and stew until farro is delicate yet not soft, around 20 minutes (various brands of farro can have essentially unique cooking times, so begin checking at 20 minutes, and yet be ready to stew longer). Channel and put away.

•Heat the oil in a huge skillet over medium intensity. Add shallots and cook until mellowed, around 4 minutes. Add garlic and cook 30 seconds longer. Add kale and cook, throwing, until shriveled, around 4 minutes. Add farro and vinegar and throw until farro is warmed through. Season with salt and pepper.

•Partition kale and grains into 4 dishes. Top each with an egg, preparing with salt and pepper. Embellish with shaved Parmesan if utilized. Serve, passing stew sauce at the table whenever wanted.

NUTRITION FACTS
424 CALORIES
13g FAT
62g CARBS
19g PROTEIN

Hearty Escarole, Barley, and Parmesan Soup Recipe

Prep time: 20 mins, Total time: 40 mins, Serves: 4 to 6

INGREDIENTS

•1/4 cup extra-virgin olive oil, in addition to something else for serving
•1 medium onion, finely slashed (around 1 cup)
•1 enormous carrot, finely diced (around 1 cup)
•2 medium stems of celery, finely diced (around 1 cup)
•2 tablespoons slashed new rosemary leaves
•3 medium cloves garlic, minced (around 1 tablespoon)
•1 enormous head escarole, hacked into 1-inch pieces
•2 tablespoons tomato glue
•1/2 cup pearled grain
•1 1/2 quarts of low-sodium locally acquired or natively constructed vegetable or chicken stock
•2 cove leaves
•4-inch lump of Parmesan skin
•2 teaspoons soy sauce
•1 teaspoon fish sauce (optional)
•Salt and newly ground dark pepper
•1/4 cup slashed new parsley leaves
•Parmesan cheddar, for serving

PREPARATION

•Heat olive oil in an enormous pot over medium-high intensity until gleaming. Add onions, carrots, and celery. Cook, blending incidentally until mellowed, however not seared, around 4 minutes. Add rosemary and garlic and cook, blending, until fragrant, around 1 moment. Add escarole and cook, blending incidentally, until shriveled, around 5 minutes. Add tomato glue and keep on cooking, blending now and again, until the fluid has dissipated and the combination starts to sizzle, around 5 minutes longer. Add grain and cook, blending, until covered with oil, around 1 moment.

•Mix in stock. Add cove leaves, Parmesan skin, soy sauce, and fish sauce (if utilized), and heat to the point of boiling. Lessen to an exposed stew and cook, mixing periodically, until the grain is mellowed and the soup has consumed flavor from parmesan and sound leaves, around 25 minutes. Season to taste with salt and pepper. Mix in parsley. Serve, showering with olive oil and sprinkling with Parmesan.

NUTRITION FACTS
216 CALORIES
11g FAT
21g CARBS
9g PROTEIN

Beef Barley Soup Recipe

Prep time: 45 mins, Total time: 2 hours, serves: 12

INGREDIENTS

- •2 pounds (1kg) boneless hamburger throw cook, cut into 1 1/2-inch steak, or 3 pounds (1.3kg) bone-in meat short ribs, ribs eliminated and saved (see notes)
- •Fit salt and newly ground dark pepper
- •1 tablespoon (15ml) canola oil
- •3 enormous carrots (10 ounces; 280g), diced
- •1 enormous yellow onion (12 ounces; 340g), diced
- •2 ribs celery (6 ounces; 170g), diced
- •4 medium cloves garlic, generally slashed
- •3 quarts (3L) of natively constructed or locally acquired chicken stock (see notes)
- •Sachet of 2 branches of new thyme, 1 sound leaf, and around 5 entire dark peppercorns
- •1 cup pearled grain (7 ounces; 200g)
- •1/2 teaspoon (3ml) Asian fish sauce (optional)
- •Minced new parsley to decorate

PREPARATION

- •Season hamburger with salt and pepper. In an enormous pot or Dutch stove, heat oil over high intensity until gently smoking. Working in clusters if fundamental, add hamburger and cook, turning every so often, until all around caramelized on all sides, around 5 minutes for each side. Move to an enormous platter.

•Add carrot, onion, celery, and garlic to the pot and cook, mixing and scraping up any caramelized bits from the base, until delicately seared, around 6 minutes. Scratch vegetables into a heatproof bowl and put them away. Add stock to the pot, return to intensity, and scrape up any caramelized bits from the lower part of the pot.

•In the interim, cut meat into lumps and add to the pot, alongside saved bones, if utilized, and a spice sachet. Bring to a stew, then diminish intensity to keep a low stew and cook until hamburger is delicate, 1 to 2 hours; skim any froth that ascents to the top.

•Dispose of bones and spice sachet. Add grain, held vegetables, and fish sauce if utilized, and stew until grain and vegetables are delicate, around 30 minutes. Season with salt and pepper. If soup is excessively dry, top it up with water to accomplish the wanted consistency. Serve, embellishing with parsley.

NUTRITION FACTS
320 CALORIES
16g FAT
19g CARBS
26g PROTEIN

Make-Ahead Quinoa Salad with Cucumber, Tomato, and Herbs Recipe

Prep time: 10 mins, Total time: 30 mins, Serves: 4 to 6

Ingredients

•1 cup quinoa

•1 16 ounces grape tomato split into quarters

•1 colossal cucumber, seeds disposed of, cut into 1/2-inch pieces

•Authentic salt

•2 little shallots, minced

•1/2 cup commonly severed level leaf parsley leaves

•1/4 cup commonly severed new mint leaves

•5 tablespoons extra-virgin olive oil

•2 tablespoons red wine vinegar

•Recently ground dull pepper

PREPARATION

•Solidify quinoa and 2 cups of water in a little pot. The intensity with the eventual result of bubbling, blend, decrease power to low, cover, and cook for 7 minutes. Stop force and let rest until water is polished off, close to 5 minutes longer. Move quinoa to a fine cross-segment sifter and flush under cool water until totally chilled. Let channel for 10 minutes.

•While quinoa cooks, merge tomatoes and cucumbers in a colander set in the sink. Season with salt and toss to cover. Give channel access sink until ready to get together with quinoa.

•In an enormous bowl, toss drained quinoa, exhausted tomatoes and cucumbers, shallots, parsley, mint, olive oil, and red wine vinegar. Season to taste with salt and pepper. Serve immediately, or for best flavor, let rest for the time being in a decent holder in the cooler. Salad can be taken care of in a decent compartment in the refrigerator for up to 5 days

NUTRITION FACTS
172 CALORIES
12g FAT
14g CARBS
3g PROTEIN

Carrot and Rye Berry Salad with Celery, Cilantro, and Marcona Almonds Recipe

Prep time: 15 mins, Total time: 60 mins, Serves: 4

INGREDIENTS

•1 1/2 cups dried rye berries (see note)

•2 sound leaves

•Real salt

•1 pound of little carrots

•1 cup Marcona almonds, by and large hacked

•2 teaspoons whole grain or Dijon mustard

•1 medium garlic clove, minced (around 1 teaspoon)

•2 teaspoons juice from 1 lemon

•2 teaspoons balsamic or sherry vinegar

•3 tablespoons extra-virgin olive oil

•2 stems of celery, stripped, and gently cut on an inclination

•1/2 minimal red onion, gently cut

•1/4 cup cut new cilantro leaves

•Recently ground dim pepper

PREPARATION

•Place rye berries in a medium skillet and cover with water by 2 inches. Add 1 gulf leaf and season strongly with salt. The intensity with the eventual result of bubbling, reduction to a stew, and cooking until rye berries are sensitive, something like 30 minutes. Divert in a fine cross-section sifter and run under cool water until particularly chilled. Discard the limited leaf. Place the sifter over a huge bowl and let channel for something like 15 minutes.

•While rye berries cook, place carrots and remaining river leaf sound leaf in a gigantic pot and cover with cold water by 1 inch. Season seriously with salt. The intensity with the eventual result of bubbling over focused energy, diminishing to a stew, and cooking until fragile, something like 10 minutes. Channel under crisp appearance water and strip to take the skin off under running water. Cut carrots into 1-to-1/2-inch bump on a tendency. Set aside.

•Toast almonds in a medium skillet over medium power, tossing a significant part of the time, until nutty brown and faint in spots, something like 5 minutes. Move to a bowl and set it aside.

•Join mustard, garlic, lemon juice, vinegar, and olive oil in a tremendous bowl and speed to solidify. Add exhausted rye berries, carrots, almonds, celery, onion, and cilantro. Season to taste with salt and pepper. Plan softly with your hands until the plate of leafy greens is shrouded in the dressing. Serve immediately or store in a proper compartment for up to 3 days.

NUTRITION FACTS
467 CALORIES
29g FAT
44g CARBS
14g PROTEIN

Benihana Fried Rice

Prep time: 45minutes, **Cooking time:** 15 minutes, Total **time:** 60 mins **Servings:** 8

INGREDIENTS

•2 cups Botan Calrose rice (or white rice)

•3 cups water

•2 enormous carrots

•1 enormous onion

•1 bundle of green onions

•4 enormous eggs

•2 pounds of protein (chicken bosoms or Jumbo shrimp)

•2 tablespoons safflower oil

•salt and pepper (to taste)

•sesame seeds

•Benihana's garlic margarine:

•1 stick margarine (mellowed)

•2 cloves garlic (minced)

•1 lemon

•2 teaspoons soy sauce

PREPARATION

•Add rice to a pan (or huge pot) with 3 cups of water. Add a spot of salt and mix. Turn the intensity on high.

When you see the rice begin to bubble marginally, give it a decent mix. Cover the pot. Diminish intensity to low and allow it to stew for an additional 20 minutes.
•Eliminate the intensity and allow it to sit (with the cover on) for 20 extra minutes.
•Eliminate the top and cushion the rice with a spoon to isolate the granules however much as could be expected. Then, store it in a shallow holder or a huge baking dish. Refrigerate for the time being, so it gets dried out. Without this step, your broiled rice will be wet and clumpy.
•The subsequent stage is to set up the Benihana garlic spread. Consolidate room temperature spread and two cloves of minced garlic. Sprinkle with a few lemon juices and soy sauce, and blend well.
•Saute the onion and carrots until brilliant brown. As of now or two, add the green onion. Put away.
•Then, heat a few oils and saute your chicken bosom. Take it off the intensity, dice, and spot once again into the skillet as of now or two of cooking; flavor it with some garlic margarine. Blend until the chicken is completely covered. Put away.
•Scramble the eggs and put them away.
•Presently it is the right time to collect the seared rice. Empty safflower oil into a wok or a huge skillet over high intensity. Add the rice and blend it well, so it gets covered with oil. Add the garlic spread. Mix so that the rice gets completely covered in the garlic spread. Include the vegetables, chicken, and egg. Mix well until consolidated.
•Season your seared rice with soy sauce, salt, and pepper (to taste). Top with sesame seeds.
•Appreciate!

MUSHROOM RISOTTO

Prep Time: 10 minutes, **Cook Time:** 20 minutes, **Total Time:** 30 minutes

INGREDIENTS

•2 tablespoons margarine or another vegetarian spread substitute
•1 medium onion, finely diced
•2 cloves garlic, finely minced or squeezed
•1 tablespoon new lemon juice
•1 teaspoon cleaved new thyme (dried thyme likewise works)
•a squeeze or two of salt and pepper
•1/4 cup white wine
•1 cup arborio rice (likewise called risotto rice)
•1 1/2 cups cleaved white mushrooms
•4 cups hot chicken or vegetable stock
•new parsley or thyme and Parmesan cheddar for decorating

PREPARATION

- •Heat an enormous skillet over medium intensity and add the margarine.
- •When the margarine is liquefied, add the onion and garlic and sauté until the onion is delicate and clear.
- •Add the lemon juice, thyme, salt, and pepper.
- •Add the wine and mix as the wine lessens (cook for around 5 minutes until the wine diminishes).
- •Turn the intensity to medium-low and add the rice. Throw the rice in the onion combination until it's covered and move it around the search for gold for 1 moment.
- •Mix in the mushrooms.
- •Add the hot chicken stock (or vegetable stock) around 1/2 cup at once, and hold on until the stock is consumed by the rice until you add another 1/2 cup.
- •Rehash the cycle above until every one of the stock has been added and consumed by the rice and a smooth sauce has been shaped, mixing continually all through.
- •Serve promptly with shaved Parmesan cheddar and newly hacked thyme or parsley.

NUTRITION FACTS

Serving: 1serving | Calories: 275kcal | Carbohydrates: 48g | Protein: 5g | Fat: 6g | Saturated Fat: 4g | Cholesterol: 15mg | Sodium: 994mg | Potassium: 203mg | Fiber: 2g | Sugar: 4g | Vitamin A: 675IU | Vitamin C: 5mg | Calcium: 9mg | Iron: 2mg

Easy coconut milk rice (2-ingredient rice cooker recipe)

Prep time: 3 MINUTES, **Cook time:** 30 MINUTES, **Total time:** 33 MINUTES

INGREDIENTS

- 2 cups jasmine rice (16 ounces absolute)
- 1 (13.66-oz.) container coconut milk
- 2 cups of water
- 1 teaspoon of salt

PREPARATION

- Before opening, fill the container with coconut milk. In the bowl of your rice cooker, add coconut milk, water, rice, and salt.
- Set the rice cooker to the pressure cook setting and start the cycle. If your rice cooker doesn't have this setting, just use the shortest setting anyone can expect.

NUTRITION FACTS
CALORIES: 241 TOTAL FAT: 9.1g SATURATED FAT: 7.5g CHOLESTEROL: 0mg SODIUM: 278.7mg CARBOHYDRATES: 35.3g FIBER: 0.5g SUGAR: 0.6g PROTEIN: 3.8g

Easy Chicken Fried Rice

Prep time: 10 minutes, Cooking time: 15 minutes, Total time: 25 mins, Servings: 8

INGREDIENTS

•2 tbsp margarine

•3 cups cooked white rice (cold)

•1 cup frozen sweet peas

•1/2 cup carrots

•2 eggs (beaten)

•1 little onion, hacked

•2 green onions (hacked)

•1 tsp garlic powder

•2 tbsp soy sauce

•1 pound boneless chicken chest (cooked, hacked into 1/2 inch dice)

•Run of sea salt and dim pepper

PREPARATION

•Disintegrate spread in an enormous nonstick skillet over medium force.

•Add onions, peas, and carrots and cook until sensitive.

•Shove the vegetables aside and pour the beaten eggs on the contrary side. Scramble the eggs until set.

•Join the eggs and vegetables as one.

•Add garlic powder and soy sauce and blend to mix.
•Add the cooked rice and chicken. Mix well.
•You can polish it off with green onions and a smidgen of salt and pepper.
•Appreciate!

Dirty Rice

Prep time: 5 minutes, **COOK TIME:** 25 minutes, **TOTAL TIME:** 30 minutes

INGREDIENTS

•1/2 pound ground pork

•1/2 pound ground hamburger

•1 cup diced yellow onion

•1 cup diced green ringer pepper

•1 cup diced celery

•3 cloves garlic, minced

•2 teaspoons Cajun preparing

•1 1/2 cups long grain white rice

•24 oz chicken stock (or water)

•2 new thyme branches, or 1 tsp dried thyme

•salt, to taste

•green onion, cut, optional topping

PREPARATION

•In an enormous weighty lined pot (like a Dutch stove), over medium-high intensity, cook ground meat until now not pink. Channel oil.

•Include onion, green ringer pepper, and celery. Cook, frequently stirring, until relaxed, around 5 minutes.

•Include garlic and Cajun preparation, and cook for 30 seconds. Add rice, chicken stock, and thyme branches.
•Heat to the point of boiling and afterward lessen the heat. Cover pot with tight fitting top and stew until rice is cooked, around 20 minutes.
•Taste and add salt or extra Cajun preparation to taste. Decorate with green onions whenever wanted. Appreciate!

NUTRITION FACTS
CALORIES: 459 TOTAL FAT: 23g SATURATED FAT: 8g TRANS FAT: 0g UNSATURATED FAT: 11g CHOLESTEROL: 107mg SODIUM: 1511mg CARBOHYDRATES: 29g FIBER: 3g SUGAR: 6g PROTEIN: 34g

SLOW COOKER CHICKEN AND WILD RICE SOUP

Prep time: 15 MINUTES, **Cook time:** 8 HOURS, **Total time:** 8 HOURS 15 MINUTES

INGREDIENTS

•1 1/2 pounds boneless skinless chicken chests
•Season with salt and recently ground slight pepper
•6 cups chicken stock
•1 cup wild rice
•3 garlic cloves, hacked
•1 onion, diced
•3 carrots, stripped and diced
•3 sticks of celery, diced
•1/2 teaspoon dried thyme
•1/2 teaspoon dried rosemary
•2 golf clubs
•1 pound cremini mushrooms, meticulously cut
•1/4 cup unsalted margarine
•1/4 cup standard baking flour
•1 cup of milk
•1 cup half and half
•2 tablespoons divided new parsley

PREPARATION

•Season chicken with salt and pepper to taste. Place chicken in a 6 qt slow cooker.

•Mix in chicken stock, wild rice, garlic, onion, carrot, celery, thyme, rosemary, and a couple of leaves; Season with salt and pepper. Cover and cook on low power for 6-8 hours. Add mushrooms during the latest 30 minutes of cooking.

•Kill the chicken from the drowsy hearth and shred it with two forks.

•Spread thick water in a bowl on medium power. Blend in flour until cooked, something like 1 second. Add milk and cream and cook, mixing consistently, until barely thick, around 4-5 minutes; Season with salt and pepper.

•Join the chicken and milk blend in the languid cooker. Expect that the soup is unnecessarily thick; add more cream, dependent upon the situation, until the ideal consistency is reached.

•Serve immediately, adorning with parsley at whatever point is needed.

Salsa Rice

Prep Time: 5 minutes, **Cook Time:** 15 minutes, **Total Time:** 20 minutes

INGREDIENTS

•2 tablespoons vegetable oil

•1 ½ cups white long-grain rice

•2 teaspoons homemade taco seasoning mix or locally purchased

•2 cups low-sodium chicken or vegetable broth

•1 cup strong salsa, mild or spicy

•Optional Toppings: Corn, beans, shredded cheddar, chopped green onions, olives

PREPARATION

•In a 12-inch skillet, add oil and stir on medium-high. Add the rice and taco preparation and cook until tender and toasted and the flavors are fragrant. Add the broth and salsa and carry the combination to a low bubble.

Reduce the intensity, cover, and cook for 15 minutes or until the stock is gone and the rice is tender.
•Pillow with a fork. Mix in any of the optional add-ins, if you like, and serve.

NUTRITION FACTS
Calories: 234 kcal · Carbohydrates: 40 g · Protein: 5 g · Fat: 5 g · Saturated Fat: 4 g · Sodium: 334 mg · Potassium: 244 mg · Fiber: 1 g · Sugar: 1 g · Vitamin A: 210 IU · Vitamin C: 0.8 mg · Calcium: 29 mg · Iron: 0.7 mg

RICE KRISPIE TREATS

Prep Time: 10 minutes, **Cook Time:** 20 minutes, **Cooling Time:** 30 minutes, **Total Time:** 1 hour

INGREDIENTS

•5 tablespoons salted spread

•1 teaspoon vanilla concentrate

•1/4 teaspoon salt

•6 cups of little marshmallows

•6 cups Rice Krispies grain

PREPARATION

•Oil a 9"x13" baking dish with a cooking splash.

•Dissolve the spread in an enormous sauce pot or Dutch broiler on the burner.

•Mix the vanilla concentrate and salt into the spread.

•Add the little marshmallows to the liquefied margarine combination, mixing until the marshmallows have completely melted.*

•Eliminate the blend from the intensity, and immediately mix in the Rice Krispies oat.
•Spread the Rice Krispies blend into the lubed baking dish and let them cool.
•Cut into serving-size pieces and serve!

NUTRITION FACTS
Calories: 131kcal | Carbohydrates: 24g | Protein: 1g | Saturated Fat: 2g | Cholesterol: 9mg | Sodium: 137mg | Sugar: 11g

Rice Pudding

Prep Time: 5 minutes, **Cook Time:** 25 minutes, **Total Time:** 30 minutes

INGREDIENTS

•⅓ Short grain white rice

•2 ½ cups 2% Milk

•¼ teaspoon Salt

•1 Egg

•¼ cup Brown sugar, stuffed

•½ teaspoon Cinnamon

•⅛ Nutmeg

•1 Vanilla (or almond) remove

•¼-1/3 cup Golden raisins

•Zing of 1 orange

PREPARATION

•Consolidate the milk, rice, and salt in a huge stockpot and heat to the point of boiling over medium intensity;

•Bubble for 20 minutes mixing sporadically to forestall staying and ignite sure the milk doesn't;

•While the rice is cooking, beat an egg with the earthy colored sugar;

•Temper the egg combination with ¼-1/2 rice blend, then add it to the stockpot and mix well to consolidate with the remainder of the rice combination;
•Include the vanilla, cinnamon, nutmeg, orange zing, and raisins and mix to join;
•Let sit to thicken if necessary, then, at that point, serve in a bowl with a cleaning of cinnamon or a cinnamon stick to embellish.

NUTRITION FACTS
Calories: 241Total Fat: 4gSaturated Fat: 2gTrans Fat: 0gUnsaturated Fat: 2gCholesterol: 59mgSodium: 241mgCarbohydrates: 45gFiber: 2gSugar: 35gProtein: 8g

Persian Saffron Rice

Prep Time: 15 mins, **Cook Time:** 1 hr 5 mins, **Total Time:** 1 hr 20 mins

INGREDIENTS

PARBOILED RICE:

•2 cups/360g basmati rice, uncooked

•1 tbsp salt

•3 liters / 3 liters of water

Barberries:

•1/2 cup dried barberries (grade 2)

•2 tbsp/30g unsalted spread

•1 1/2 tsp rosewater (optional)

Saffron rice:

•1 teaspoon saffron threads (grade 3)

•2 tbsp warm water

•1 cup/250g plain yogurt (I use Farmers Union Greek yogurt)

•1/2 cup/125 ml oil, unbiased (or spread!)
•3 egg yolks
•3/4 tsp. salt

PREPARATION

PARBOILED RICE:

Get water to heat a large pot. Add salt and rice. Then bring it back to the air pocket and cook for 5 minutes. Channel and steam dry for 5 minutes.

Barberries:

•In a small compartment, chop margarine on medium power. Add barberries and cook until puffed (see video!), about 1 1/2 minutes.

•Remove from heat (they will shrink quickly), then mix with rosewater (if using).

Saffron rice:

•Preheat the oven to 200°C (standard) or 180°C (convection).

•Gently oil a glass cake pan with oil.

•Grind saffron into powder (optional step). Add water and let flow for 10 minutes.

•Whisk together the yogurt, egg, oil, saffron water, and salt in a large bowl.

•Add rice and mix well.

•Pour about half of the rice into the cake pan on a smooth surface. Garnish with 1/3 of the barberries.

•Cover with rice, smooth the surface and sprinkle another third of the barberries on top. Press down steadily and cover with foil.

•Wait 60-80 minutes until the outer layer is shiny all over.

•Rest for 10 minutes. Kill foil. Place a serving platter on top of the cake pan, then turn it over (it won't stick because of the oil).

•Then sprinkle with the remaining barberries and serve.

NUTRITION FACTS
Calories 360Calories from Fat 162
% Daily Value*
Fat 18g28%
Saturated Fat 3g19%
Cholesterol 75mg25%
Sodium 991mg43%
Potassium 96mg3%
Carbohydrates 42g14%
Sugar 1g1%
Protein 5g10%
Vitamin A 190IU4%
Vitamin C 0.2mg0%
Calcium 55mg6%
Iron 0.5mg3%

SALADS RECIPES

Balela Salad

Prep Time: 15 mins, **Total Time:** 15 minutes
INGREDIENTS

•3 ½ cups cooked chickpeas (or 2 15-ounce jars of chickpeas, depleted and flushed)
•½ green ringer pepper, cored and slashed
•1 jalapeno, finely slashed (optional)
•2 ½ cups grape tomatoes (or cherry tomatoes), cut in equal parts if you like, or leave the entirety
•3-5 green onions, both white and green parts, hacked
•½ cup sun-dried tomatoes (use ones that have been safeguarded in containers with olive oil)
•⅓ cup pitted Kalamata olives
•¼ cup pitted green olives
•½ cup newly slashed parsley leaves
•½ cup newly slashed mint or basil leaves

For Dressing

- ¼ cup Early Harvest Greek additional virgin olive oil
- 2 tbsp white wine vinegar
- 2 tbsp lemon juice
- 1 garlic clove, minced
- Salt and dark pepper, a liberal squeeze as you would prefer
- 1 tsp ground sumac
- ½ tsp Aleppo pepper
- ¼ to ½ teaspoon squashed red pepper.

PREPARATION

- In an enormous bowl, combine as one the serving of mixed greens fixings: chickpeas, vegetables, sun-dried tomatoes, olives, and new spices.
- In a different, more modest bowl or container, combine as one the dressing fixings: additional virgin olive oil, white wine vinegar, lemon juice, minced garlic, salt and pepper, and flavors.
- Shower the dressing over a plate of mixed greens and blend delicate to cover. Leave to the side for 30 minutes before serving, or cover and refrigerate until prepared to serve.
- At the point when prepared to serve, give the serving of mixed greens a speedy blend and taste to change preparing if at all required. Appreciate!

NUTRITION FACTS
Total Fat 7.6g 10%
Sodium 17.6mg 1%
Total Carbohydrate 39.5g 14%
Sugars 8.1g
Protein 12.4g 25%
Vitamin A 5%
Vitamin C2 8%
Calcium 4%
Iron 17%

Vitamin D 0%
Magnesium 13%
Potassium 12%
Zinc1 6%
Phosphorus 13%
Thiamin (B1) 25%
Riboflavin (B2) 11%
Niacin (B3) 8%
Vitamin B6 23%
Folic Acid (B9) 83%
Vitamin E 6%
Vitamin K 21%

Fattoush salad

Prep Time: 20 mins, Total Time: 20 minutes

INGREDIENTS

•2 portions of pita bread

•Additional virgin olive oil

•Fit salt

•2 tsp sumac, isolated, more depending on the situation

•1 heart of Romaine lettuce, slashed

•1 English cucumber, cut down the middle, seeds scratched, then, at that point, cleaved or cut into half moons

•5 Roma tomatoes, slashed

•5 green onions (both white and green parts), slashed

•5 radishes, stems eliminated, meagerly cut

•2 cups slashed new parsley leaves, stems eliminated

•1 cup slashed new mint leaves (discretionary)

Vinaigrette/Dressing

•Juice of 1 lemon or 1 ½ lime

•⅓ cup additional virgin olive oil

•1 to 2 tablespoons pomegranate molasses, discretionary
•Salt and pepper
•1 tsp sumac
•1/4 tsp ground cinnamon
•inadequate 1/4 tsp ground allspice
PREPARATION
•Eat into little scaled-down pieces. Heat 3 tablespoons of olive oil in an enormous skillet until shining, and add the pita bread. Broil momentarily until sautéed, throwing oftentimes. Utilizing a couple of utensils, move the seared pita chips to a plate fixed with a paper towel to deplete. Season with salt, pepper, and sumac.
•In a huge blending bowl, consolidate the cleaved lettuce, cucumber, tomatoes, and green onions with the cut radish and parsley.
•To make the dressing, in a little bowl, whisk together the lemon or lime juice, olive oil, pomegranate molasses (if utilized), salt, pepper, and flavors.
•Pour throw delicately. At last, add the pita chips and more sumac, assuming you like, and throw once again. Move to little serving bowls or plates. Appreciate!

NUTRITION FACTS
Per Serving: 109 calories; protein 2.9g; carbohydrates 13.4g; dietary fiber 2.9g; sugars 2g; fat 5.8g; saturated fat 0.8g; vitamin a iu 2364.8IU; vitamin c 23.5mg; folate 48mcg; calcium 29.6mg; iron 0.8mg; magnesium 20.6mg; potassium 180.6mg; sodium 196.6mg.

Mustard Potato Salad, Mediterranean-Style

PREP TIME: 15 mins, COOK TIME: 6 mins, TOTAL TIME: 21 mins

INGREDIENTS

•1 ½ lb little potatoes like new potatoes, Yukon gold potatoes, or red potatoes

•Water

•teaspoon salt

•¼ cup cleaved red onions

•¼ cup new cleaved parsley

•¼ cup cleaved dill

•2 tablespoon tricks

Dijon Vinaigrette

•⅓ cup additional virgin olive oil

•2 tablespoons white wine vinegar

•2 teaspoon Dijon mustard

•½ teaspoon ground sumac

•½ teaspoon dark pepper

•¼ teaspoon ground coriander

PREPARATION

•Wash and scour the potatoes and dry them well. Cut potatoes are daintily utilizing a mandolin slicer.

•Place potatoes in a pot and add water to cover by 1 inch. Heat to the point of boiling. Add salt. Turn the intensity down and permit the potatoes to stew for around 6 minutes or so until they're delicate (you ought to have the option to jab the potatoes with a fork).
•Add vinaigrette fixings to a little bowl and rush until very much consolidated.
•At the point when the potatoes are prepared, eliminate from intensity and channel well. Place them in a huge blending bowl and quickly dress them in with the Dijon mustard dressing. Delicately throw to cover.
•Add onions, new spices, and escapades. Throw delicately to join.
•Move the potatoes to a serving platter. For best outcomes, permit the potato salad a chance to marinade before serving. You can refrigerate it for 1 hour or so; however, make certain to carry it to room temperature before serving.

NUTRITION FACTS
Calories: 150.9kcal
Carbohydrates: 15.8g
Protein: 2g
Fat: 7.2g
Saturated Fat: 1.1g
Potassium: 386.6mg
Fiber: 2.2g
Sugar: 0.9g
Vitamin A: 271.3IU
Vitamin C: 20.9mg
Calcium: 15.8mg
Iron: 1mg

Blanched Asparagus

PREP TIME: 2 mins, COOK TIME: 4 mins, TOTAL TIME: 6 mins

INGREDIENTS

•1 ½ pound Asparagus, outrageous completions made due (in a perfect world, kid asparagus if open)

•Water

•Punch of 1 lemon

PREPARATION

•In a cooking pot or gigantic pot, bring 8 cups of water, ready with 2 tablespoons of genuine salt, to an air pocket. Have a colossal bowl of ice water arranged near it (this is an ice shower for the brightened asparagus).

•Exactly when water comes to a moving air pocket, add the coordinated asparagus. Bubble until sensitive, 3 to 4 minutes (dependent upon thickness). Wipe out with utensils, or direct in a colander, and immediately move to the bowl of ice water for 1 second to stop the cooking framework. Channel; set aside to chill off a bit (then again, if you like to serve it as a plate of leafy greens, chill in a smidgen).

•Exactly when ready to serve, coordinate the asparagus on a serving platter. Season with salt and pepper. Add a sprinkle of good extra virgin olive oil and lemon punch.

•(Optional) If you like, top your brightened asparagus with this Mediterranean salsa.

NUTRITION FACTS
Calories: 40.2kcal
Carbohydrates: 8.3g
Protein: 3.4g
Fat: 0.3g
Saturated Fat: 0.1g
Sodium: 12.5mg
Potassium: 405mg
Fiber: 3.3g
Vitamin A: 1635.4IU
Vitamin C: 27.9mg
Calcium: 44.9mg
Iron: 3.3mg

Tuna Salad Recipe

PREP TIME: 10 mins, COOK TIME: 10 mins
INGREDIENTS
For the Zesty Dijon Mustard Dressing
•2 ½ teaspoons great quality Dijon mustard
•Zing of 1 lime
•1 ½ lime, juice of
•⅓ cup additional virgin olive oil
•½ teaspoon sumac
•Spot of fit salt and dark pepper
•½ teaspoon squashed red pepper pieces, discretionary
For the Tuna Salad
•3 jars of fish, 5 ounces each (utilization quality fish of your decision)
•2 ½ celery stems, cleaved
•½ English cucumber, cleaved
•4-5 radishes, stems eliminated, cleaved
•3 green onions, both white and green parts, cleaved
•½ medium red onion, finely cleaved

•½ cup pitted Kalamata olives, split
•1 bundle parsley, stems eliminated, slashed (around 1 cup hacked new parsley), 10-15 new mint leaves, stems eliminated, finely cleaved (about ½ cup cleaved new mint)
PREPARATION
•To make the fiery mustard vinaigrette, in a little bowl, whisk together the Dijon mustard, lime zing, and lime juice. Add the olive oil, sumac, salt and pepper, and squashed pepper chips (if utilizing), and whisk again until very much mixed. Put away momentarily.
•To make the fish salad, in a huge plate of mixed greens bowl, join the fish with the cleaved vegetables, Kalamata olives, hacked new parsley, and mint leaves. Blend tenderly with a wooden spoon.
•Pour the dressing over the fish salad. Blend again to ensure the fish salad is uniformly covered with the dressing. Cover and refrigerate for 30 minutes before serving. At the point when prepared to serve, prepare the plate of mixed greens tenderly to invigorate.
NUTRITION FACTS
Calories: 193.7kcal
Carbohydrates: 5.6g
Protein: 12.1g
Fat: 14.7g
Saturated Fat: 1.9g
Polyunsaturated Fat: 1.7g
Monounsaturated Fat: 10.1g
Cholesterol: 20mg
Sodium: 371.8mg
Potassium: 267.7mg
Fiber: 1.9g
Sugar: 1.5g
Vitamin A: 1068.5IU
Vitamin C: 21mg
Calcium: 42.3mg

Mediterranean-Style Grilled Zucchini Salad

PREP TIME: 5 mins, COOK TIME: 10 mins, TOTAL TIME: 15 mins

INGREDIENTS

•4 zucchini squash around 2 lb, cut into adjusts
•Confidential Reserve Greek Extra Virgin Olive Oil
•1 teaspoon natural ground cumin
•Juice of 1 lemon
•1 garlic clove minced
•Salt and pepper
•1 cup pressed cleaved new parsley
•2 teaspoon slashed new tarragon
•Feta or goat cheddar discretionary

PREPARATION

•Place the zucchini into an enormous bowl. Shower around 3 tablespoons of additional virgin olive oil, and sprinkle with cumin. Throw with your spotless hands to join.

•Heat a barbecue or iron until hot, and add zucchini in clumps (don't swarm). Barbecue for 4 minutes or thereabouts, turning over multiple times until zucchini is cooked through and flawlessly roasted.
•Move the barbecued zucchini back to the bowl. Add lemon juice, new garlic, salt, and pepper. Throw to join. Add new spices and throw again delicately.
•Move to a serving platter and top with a sprinkle of feta or goat cheddar, if you like. Serve at room temperature.
•For ideas, see the "what to present with this zucchini salad" segment in the post above.

NUTRITION FACTS
Total Fat 0g
Sodium 350mg 15%
Potassium 160mg 4%
Carbohydrates 4g
Net carbs 3.5g
Sugar 2g
Fiber 0.5g 2%
Protein 0.5g

Traditional Greek Salad

PREP TIME: 15 mins, TOTAL TIME: 15 mins

INGREDIENTS

- •1 medium red onion
- •4 Medium delicious tomatoes
- •1 English cucumber (hothouse cucumber) to some degree stripped, making a striped example
- •1 green chime pepper cored
- •Greek pitted Kalamata olives a small bunch as you would prefer
- •genuine salt a squeeze
- •4 tablespoon quality additional virgin olive oil I utilized Early Harvest Greek olive oil
- •1-2 tablespoons red wine vinegar
- •Blocks of Greek feta cheddar don't disintegrate the feta; leave it in huge pieces
- •½ tablespoon dried oregano.

PREPARATION

•Slice the red onion down the middle and meagerly cut it into half-moons. (If you have any desire to bring some relief, place the cut onions in an answer of chilled water a tad before adding to the serving of mixed greens.

•Cut the tomatoes into wedges or huge pieces (I cut some into rounds and cut the rest in wedges).

•Slice the to some degree stripped cucumber down the middle length-wise, then, at that point, cut into thick parts (basically ½" in thickness)

•Daintily cut the chime pepper into rings.

•Place all that on an enormous plate of mixed greens dishes. Add a decent, modest bunch of pitted kalamata olives.

•Season daintily with fit salt (simply a squeeze) and a touch of dried oregano.

•Pour the olive oil and red wine vinegar all around the plate of mixed greens. Give everything an exceptionally delicate preparation to blend (don't over blend, this salad isn't intended to be dealt with something over the top).

•Presently add the feta blocks on top and add sprinkle a greater amount of dried oregano.

•Present with dried-up bread.

NUTRITION FACTS Calories: 102.9kcal
Carbohydrates: 4.7g, Protein: 0.7g
Fat: 9.5g
Saturated Fat: 1.3g
Sodium: 2.8mg
Potassium: 135mg
Fiber: 1.1g
Vitamin A: 125.9IU
Vitamin C: 18.7mg
Calcium: 20.9mg
Iron: 0.5mg

Mediterranean Tomato Feta Salad

PREP TIME: 15 mins, COOK TIME: 0 mins, TOTAL TIME: 15 mins

INGREDIENTS

- 6 to 7 medium ready tomatoes, cut into wedges (on-the-plant tomatoes or treasure tomatoes liked)
- 1 medium red onion, divided, then, at that point, daintily cut
- 3 garlic cloves, minced
- 1 cup pressed slashed new parsley leaves, hacked
- 1 cup stuffed hacked new dill, slashed
- 2 ½ teaspoons ground sumac
- However, you would prefer
- As you would prefer
- 1 lemon, juice of
- 2 teaspoon white wine vinegar
- ⅓ cup additional virgin olive oil
- As you would prefer

PREPARATION

•In a huge plate of mixed greens or a blending bowl, add the tomatoes, onions, new spices, and garlic.

•Add sumac, genuine salt, and a liberal sprinkle of newly ground pepper. Add lemon juice, white wine vinegar, and additional virgin olive oil. Throw to join. Taste and change are prepared as you would prefer.

•Move to a serving platter or bowl. Top with enormous bits of value feta cheddar (discretionary). Appreciate!

NUTRITION FACTS

Calories: 128.3kcal
Carbohydrates: 5.1g
Protein: 1.1g
Fat: 10.6g
Saturated Fat: 1.7g
Potassium: 170.8mg
Fiber: 1.3g
Sugar: 1.4g
Vitamin A: 1447IU
Vitamin C: 31.3mg
Calcium: 41.7mg
Iron: 1.4mg

Mediterranean Chickpea Egg Salad

Prep Time: 15 minutes, **Total Time:** 15 minutes

INGREDIENTS

For dressing

- 2 ½ tsp Dijon mustard
- 1 huge lemon, zested and squeezed
- ⅓ cup Private Reserve Greek additional virgin olive oil (or Early Harvest Greek additional virgin olive oil)
- 1 garlic clove, minced
- 1 tsp sumac
- ½ tsp coriander
- ½ tsp cayenne pepper
- Salt and pepper

For Egg Salad

- 2 jars of chickpeas, washed and depleted
- 2 celery ribs, hacked

•2 Persian cucumbers (or ½ seedless English cucumber), diced
•2 to 3 green onions, managed and hacked (both white and green parts)
•½ cup destroyed red cabbage
•2 jalapeno peppers, hacked (discretionary)
•½ cup stuffed cleaved new parsley leaves
•½ cup stuffed cleaved new mint leaves
•5 huge hard bubbled eggs, cut
PREPARATION
•In a little bowl or bricklayer container, combine one of the dressing fixings. Put away for the present.
•In a huge blending bowl, add all the plates of mixed greens fixings except the eggs. Give the dressing a fast whisk and pour over the plate of mixed greens. Blend to join. Add the cut eggs, and blend delicately once more. Taste and change the salt and pepper. Add a sprinkle of more sumac. Put away a couple of moments before effectively permitting flavors to merge. (See recipe notes for getting ready ahead). Appreciate!

NUTRITION FACTS
Calories 339.8
Total Fat 13.7 g
Saturated Fat2.2 g
Polyunsaturated Fat2.3 g
Monounsaturated Fat 7.1 g
Cholesterol 4.2 mg
Sodium 673.3 mg
Potassium 415.8 mg
Total Carbohydrate 44.4 g
Dietary Fiber 8.8 g
Sugars2.1 g
Protein 12.1 g
Vitamin A 25.1 %
Vitamin B-12 0.0 %

Vitamin B-6 42.5 %
Vitamin C 80.2 %
Vitamin D 0.0 %
Vitamin E 0.9 %
Calcium 7.9 %
Copper 16.9 %
Folate 31.7 %
Iron 15.4 %
Magnesium 14.0 %
Manganese 54.8 %
Niacin 2.8 %
Pantothenic Acid 6.2 %
Phosphorus 16.8 %
Riboflavin 5.0 %
Selenium 7.2 %
Thiamin 5.4 %
Zinc 12.6 %

Couscous Salad

Prep Time: 15 mins, **Cook Time:** 10 mins, **Total Time:** 25 minutes

INGREDIENTS

For the Lemon-Dill Vinaigrette

•enormous lemon, juice of

•⅓ cup additional virgin olive oil (I utilized Greek Private Reserve)

•1 tsp dill weed

•1 to 2 garlic cloves, minced

•salt and pepper

For the Pearl Couscous

•2 cups Pearl Couscous

•Confidential Reserve additional virgin olive oil

•Water

•2 cups grape tomatoes, split

- ⅓ cup finely slashed red onions
- ½ English cucumber, finely slashed
- 15 oz can chickpeas, depleted and flushed
- 14 oz can artichoke hearts, generally slashed if necessary
- ½ cup pitted kalamata olives
- 15-20 new basil leaves, generally slashed or torn; something else for decorating
- 3 oz new child mozzarella (or feta cheddar), discretionary

PREPARATION

- To make the lemon-dill vinaigrette, place the vinaigrette fixings in a bowl. Whisk together to join. Put away momentarily.
- In a weighty medium-sized pot, heat two tablespoons of olive oil. Saute the couscous in the olive oil momentarily until brilliant brown. Add 3 cups of bubbling water (or the sum educated on the bundle), and cook as per bundle. At the point when prepared, channel in a colander. Put away in a bowl to cool.
- In an enormous blending bowl, join the leftover fixings short the basil and mozzarella. Then gather the couscous and the basil and blend them into a single unit delicately.
- Presently, give the lemon-dill vinaigrette a fast whisk and add it to the couscous salad. Blend again to consolidate. Test and change salt, if necessary.
- At last, blend in the mozzarella cheddar. Embellish with all the more new basil. Appreciate!

NUTRITION FACTS

Total Fat 13g 17%
Saturated Fat 1.8g
Trans Fat 0g
Total Carbohydrate 57.5g 21%
Dietary Fiber 5.9g 21%

Protein 13.1g 26%
Vitamin A 4%
Vitamin C 24%
Calcium 9%
Iron 10%
Magnesium 12%
Potassium 7%
Zinc 12%
Phosphorus 17%
Thiamin (B1) 13%
Riboflavin (B2) 8%
Niacin (B3) 15%
Vitamin B6 10%
Folic Acid (B9) 19%
Vitamin B12 3%
Vitamin K 15%

Chickpea Salad

Prep Time: 20 mins, **Cook Time:** 10 mins, **Total Time:** 30 minutes

INGREDIENTS

•1 large eggplant, cut lean (about ¼ inch thick)

•Salt

•Oil for broiling, preferably additional virgin olive oil

•1 cup cooked or canned chickpeas spent

•3 tbsp za'atar flavor, disconnected

•3 Roma tomatoes, diced

•½ English cucumber, diced

•1 little red onion, cut into ½ moons

•1 cup cleaved parsley

•1 cup cleaved dill

For the Garlic Vinaigrette:

•1-2 cloves of garlic, hacked

•1 goliath lime, juice out

•⅓ cup early reap additional virgin olive oil

•salt+pepper

PREPARATION

•Plan aubergines (to taste). Place the cut aubergines on a huge plate and sprinkle liberally with salt. Let sit for 30 minutes (the eggplant will "work" its sharpness as it sits.) Now line one more goliath plate or baking sheet with a paper sack covered with a paper towel and set it close to the stove.

•Bubble eggplants (to taste). Wipe the eggplant. Heat 4 to 5 tablespoons extra additional virgin olive oil on the two sides/medium-extreme focus until sparkling, however not smoking. Sear the aubergines in groups in the oil (ensure the dish doesn't spill over). At the point when the aubergine pieces turn gleaming brown on one side, turn and sear on the opposite side. Eliminate the eggplant pieces with an open spatula and coordinate them on a paper towel-lined plate to deplete and cool.

•When cool, gather the eggplants on a serving platter. Sprinkle with 1 tablespoon of za'atar.

•Plan chickpea salad. In a medium blending bowl, consolidate tomatoes, cucumber, chickpeas, red onion, parsley, and dill. Add the overabundance of za'atar and blend tenderly.

•Set up the dressing. In a little bowl, whisk the dressing. Sprinkle 2 tablespoons of the blended serving of mixed greens dressing plate over the burned eggplant; Pour the leftover dressing over the chickpea salad and puree.

•Orchestrate the chickpea salad with the aubergine on the plate.

NUTRITION FACTS

Calories: 368 calories
Sugar: 4 grams
Fat: 22 grams
Carbohydrates: 31 grams
Fiber: 10 grams
Protein: 13 grams

Fig & Goat Cheese Salad

Prep Time: 10 mins, Total Time: 10 mins

INGREDIENTS

•2 cups blended salad greens

•4 dried figs, stemmed and cut

•1-ounce new goat cheddar disintegrated

•1½ tablespoons fragmented almonds, ideally toasted

•2 teaspoons extra-virgin olive oil

•2 teaspoons balsamic vinegar

•½ teaspoon honey

•Spot of salt

•Newly ground pepper to taste

PREPARATION

•Join greens, figs, goat cheddar, and almonds in a medium bowl. Mix oil, vinegar, honey, salt, and pepper.

•Not long before serving, sprinkle the dressing over the plate of mixed greens and throw.

NUTRITION FACTS
Per Serving: 340 calories; protein 10.4g; carbohydrates 31.8g; dietary fiber 7g; sugars 21.8g; fat 21g; saturated fat 5.9g; cholesterol 13mg; vitamin a iu 3288.9IU; vitamin c 18.1mg; folate 138.1mcg; calcium 186.1mg; iron 3.2mg; magnesium 83mg; potassium 676.2mg; sodium 309.5mg; thiamin 0.2mg; added sugar 3g.

Mediterranean Quinoa Salad

Prep Time: 20 mins, **Cook Time:** 2 hrs, **Total Time:** 2 hrs, 20 mins

INGREDIENTS

- ½ cup additional virgin olive oil
- 6 tablespoons red wine vinegar
- 3 tablespoons cleaved new oregano
- 1 ½ teaspoon honey
- 1 ½ teaspoon Dijon mustard
- ¼ teaspoon squashed red peppers
- 3 cups cooked quinoa, cooled (see related recipes)
- 2 cups meagerly cut English cucumber
- 1 ½ cups meagerly cut red onion
- 1 cup grape tomatoes, partitioned
- ½ cup pitted Kalamata olives, partitioned
- 1 (15-ounce) jar of unsalted chickpeas, washed
- 1 cup destroyed feta, separated
- 3 cups child spinach (around 3 ounces)

PREPARATION

•Whisk together the oil, vinegar, oregano, honey, Dijon, and squashed peppers in an enormous bowl. Add quinoa, cucumber, onion, tomatoes, olives, chickpeas, and 1/2 cup feta. Toss cautiously to merge. Cover and refrigerate for 30 minutes.

•Add the spinach and throw delicately until firm. Sprinkle with 1/2 cup abundance feta and serve right away.

NUTRITION FACTS

Per Serving: 472 calories; protein 12.1g; carbohydrates 39.1g; dietary fiber 6.9g; sugars 7.4g; fat 30.1g; saturated fat 7g; cholesterol 6.3mg; vitamin a iu 2268.3IU; vitamin c 16mg; folate 75.9mcg; calcium 209.1mg; iron 3.3mg; magnesium 106.6mg; potassium 393.3mg; sodium 608.8mg; added sugar 1.5g.

White Bean & Veggie Salad

Prep Time: 10 mins, Total Total: 10 mins

INGREDIENTS

•2 cups mixed leaf lettuce

•3/4 cup veggies of your choice, like sliced cucumbers and cherry tomatoes

•⅓ cup canned kidney beans washed and used up

•1/2 avocado, diced

•1 tablespoon red wine vinegar

•2 teaspoons extra virgin olive oil

•1/4 teaspoon real salt

•Newly ground pepper to taste

PREPARATION

•In a medium bowl, toss together greens, greens, beans, and avocado. Drizzle with vinegar and oil and season with salt and pepper. Throw to stabilize and move to a giant slab.

NUTRITION FACTS

Per Serving: 360 calories; protein 10.1g; carbohydrates 29.7g; dietary fiber 13.3g; sugars 2.9g; fat 24.6g;

saturated fat 3.6g; vitamin a in 3221.1IU; vitamin c 30mg; folate 261.9mcg; calcium 140.1mg; iron 4.5mg; magnesium 104mg; potassium 1291.6mg; sodium 321.3mg; thiamin 0.2mg.

Pita Panzanella Salad with Meatballs

Prep Time: 50 mins, Total Time: 50 mins

INGREDIENTS

•1½ pounds 93%-lean ground turkey

•½ cup panko breadcrumbs

•¼ cup ground red onion, in addition to 3/4 cup quartered and daintily cut

•1 huge egg, gently beaten

•1 tablespoon minced new oregano in addition to 2 tsp., or 1 1/2 tsp. dried oregano, separated

•3 teaspoons minced garlic, separated

•2 teaspoons olive oil in addition to 3 Tbsp., separated

•¾ teaspoon salt

•½ teaspoon ground pepper

•3 (6-inch) entire wheat pita bread

•3 tablespoons red wine vinegar

•1 teaspoon honey

•1 teaspoon Dijon mustard

•1 huge English cucumber, cut
•1¾ cups diced plum tomatoes (3-5 tomatoes)
•¾ cup cut pitted Kalamata olives

PREPARATION

•Preheat stove to 425 degrees F. Cover a huge rimmed baking sheet with a cooking shower.

•Combine as one turkey, breadcrumbs, ground onion, egg, and 1 Tbsp. New oregano (or 1 tsp. dried), 2 tsp. Garlic, 2 tsp. oil, salt, and pepper in a huge bowl just until joined. Utilizing a tablespoon, structure the blend into around 42 meatballs, each around 1 inch in width. Organize on the pre-arranged baking sheet. Heat the meatballs until caramelized, and a moment-read thermometer embedded in the focus registers 165 degrees F, 10 to 12 minutes.

•Divide pitas in half evenly into flimsy rounds, then, at that point, attack half-moon shapes. Organize on a baking sheet and prepare until brilliant brown and fresh, 5 to 7 minutes. Let cool, then break the pitas into scaled-down bread garnishes.

•Whisk vinegar, the leftover 3 Tbsp. oil, 2 tsp. new oregano (or 1/2 tsp. dried), 1 tsp. garlic, honey, and mustard in a huge bowl. Add cucumber, tomatoes, olives, and cut onion; throw to consolidate. Mix in the pita bread garnishes. Serve the plate of mixed greens with the meatballs.

NUTRITION FACTS

Per Serving: 380 calories; protein 34g; carbohydrates 30g; dietary fiber 4g; sugars 5g; fat 15g; saturated fat 4g; cholesterol 76mg; potassium 290mg; sodium 698mg.

Creamy Pesto Chicken Salad with Greens

Total Time: 30 mins

INGREDIENTS

- 1 pound boneless, skinless chicken bosom prepared
- ¼ cup pesto
- ¼ cup low-fat mayonnaise
- 3 tablespoons finely hacked red onion
- 2 tablespoons additional virgin olive oil
- 2 tablespoons red wine vinegar
- ¼ teaspoon salt
- ¼ teaspoon ground pepper
- 1 5-ounce heap of blended leaf lettuce (around 8 cups)
- 1 16-ounce grape or cherry tomato, separated

PREPARATION

- Place the chicken in a medium pot and add water to cover 1 inch. Intensity to limit. Cover, lessen the power to low, and delicately sauté until presently not pink in the middle, 10 to 15 minutes. Change to an unblemished cutting board; shred into diminished down pieces when sufficiently cool to deal with.

•In a medium bowl, blend the pesto, mayonnaise, and onion. Add the chicken and throw it onto the cover. Whisk together the oil, vinegar, salt, and pepper in an enormous bowl. Add the vegetables and tomatoes and cover. Split the green piece of blended salad greens between 4 plates and embellishment with the chicken part of blended mixed greens.

NUTRITION FACTS
Per Serving: 324 calories; protein 27.1g; carbohydrates 9.2g; dietary fiber 2.3g; sugars 3.2g; fat 19.7g; saturated fat 4.1g; cholesterol 71.4mg; vitamin a iu 1777.3IU; vitamin c 17.6mg; folate 57.4mcg; calcium 153mg; iron 2.1mg; magnesium 47.5mg; potassium 542.2mg; sodium 453.9mg; thiamin 0.1mg; added sugar 1g.

Quinoa Chickpea Salad with Roasted Red Pepper Hummus Dressing

Prep Time: 10 mins, Total Time: 10 mins

INGREDIENTS

•2 tablespoons hummus, unique or simmered red pepper flavor

•1 tablespoon lemon juice

•1 tablespoon cleaved simmered red pepper

•2 cups blended salad greens

•½ cup cooked quinoa

•½ cup chickpeas washed

•1 tablespoon unsalted sunflower seeds

•1 tablespoon slashed new parsley

•Spot of salt

•Spot of ground pepper

PREPARATION

•Mix hummus, lemon juice, and red peppers in a little dish. Slight with water to wanted consistency for dressing.

•Organize greens, quinoa, and chickpeas in an enormous bowl. Top with sunflower seeds, parsley, salt, and pepper. Present with the dressing.

NUTRITION FACTS
Per Serving: 379 calories; protein 16g; carbohydrates 58.5g; dietary fiber 13.2g; sugars 2.9g; fat 10.5g; saturated fat 1.3g; vitamin a iu 4185.4IU; vitamin c 45.3mg; folate 300.1mcg; calcium 138.7mg; iron 5.8mg; magnesium 155.9mg; potassium 891.7mg; sodium 606.8mg; thiamin 0.3mg.

Cucumber, Tomato & Arugula Salad with Hummus

Prep Time: 10 mins, Total Time: 10 mins

INGREDIENTS

•2 cups arugula
•⅓ cup cherry tomatoes, divided
•⅓ cup sliced cucumber
•1 tablespoon chopped red onion
•1 ½ tablespoon extra-virgin olive oil
•2 teaspoons red wine vinegar
•⅛ teaspoon ground pepper
•1 tablespoon feta cheddar
•1 4-inch whole-wheat pita
•¼ cup hummus

PREPARATION

•In a bowl, mix arugula with tomatoes, cucumber, onion, oil, vinegar, and pepper. Top with feta. Serve with pita and hummus.

NUTRITION FACTS

Per Serving: 422 calories; protein 10.9g; carbohydrates 30.5g; dietary fiber 7.3g; sugars 4.3g; fat 29.9g; saturated fat 5.3g; cholesterol 8.3mg; vitamin a iu 1456.6IU; vitamin c 15mg; folate 119.1mcg; calcium 153.5mg; iron 3.3mg; magnesium 96.9mg; potassium 543.8mg; sodium 485.8mg.

Greek Orzo Salad

Prep Time: 15 minutes, **Cook Time:** 10 minutes, **Total Time:** 25 minutes

INGREDIENTS

•8 ounces orzo pasta (1 ¼ cup dry)

•1 cup canned chickpeas, used up and rinsed

•1/2 lemon, juice, and punch (about 2 tablespoons juice)

•¼ cup chopped shallot or red onion

•1/2 English cucumber (2 cups diced or substitute for a regular striped cucumber)

•2 cooked red peppers from a holder or ½ new red ringer pepper (½ cup diced)

•⅓ cup chopped dill, plus more for garnish

•⅓ cup divided mint

•2 tablespoons white wine vinegar

•3 tablespoons extra virgin olive oil

•½ teaspoon Dijon mustard

•1 teaspoon dried oregano

•½ cup crumbled feta cheddar
•⅓ cup Kalamata olives, split
•Blunt Pepper
PREPARATION
•Set up the orzo according to the group rules. Taste the orzo not long before the natural product to make sure it's "still a little firm" (chewy but with some stiffness in the middle). When it's done, channel it and then wash it under cold water until it reaches room temperature.
•Place the chickpeas in a bowl with lemon zest, lemon juice, and ¼ teaspoon salt.
•Slice the red onion and immediately place it in a bowl of water (this will help eliminate the pungent onion flavor). Dice cucumber. Dice the cooked red peppers. Share the flavors.
•Blend orzo, chickpeas, some lemon juice, red onions, cucumber, bell pepper, dill, mint, white wine vinegar, olive oil, Dijon mustard, oregano, grated feta, dark olives, and some hot peppers. Taste and season with real salt if necessary.
NUTRITION FACTS
Total Fat 8.9g 11%
Saturated Fat 2.4g
Total Carbohydrate 28.4g 10%
Dietary Fiber 3g 11%
Sugars 1.8g
Protein 7.2g 14%
Vitamin A 33.9pg 4%
Vitamin C 13.4mg 15%
Calcium 108.8mg 8%
Iron 2.7mg 15%
Vitamin D 0.1pg 0%
Magnesium 37.7mg 9%
Potassium 218.8mg 5%
Vitamin B6 0.3»g 17%
Vitamin 812 0.2pg 7%

Lentil Salad with Feta

Prep Time: 15 minutes, **Cook Time:** 15 minutes, **Total Time:** 30 minutes

INGREDIENTS

For the lentils

•1-pound dark beluga lentils or French lentils
•1-liter vegetable broth + 2 cups of water
•1 teaspoon legitimate salt
•1 teaspoon dried thyme
•½ teaspoon garlic powder

For the lentil salad

•2 tablespoons red wine vinegar
•2 tablespoons lemon juice + zing of 1 lemon
•1 teaspoon Dijon mustard
•½ teaspoon onion powder
•1 teaspoon dried oregano
•6 tablespoons olive oil
•1 shallot

•1 red pepper
•2 tablespoons chopped new mint or chives (optional)
•½ teaspoon real salt + freshly ground pepper
•1 cup arugula plus more for serving
•1 cup crumbled feta cheddar plus extra for garnish
•½ cup pistachios, plus extra for garnish
•3 radishes to decorate

PREPARATION

•For the lentils: In a large saucepan or deep pan, sauté the lentils with broth, water, salt, thyme, and garlic powder until tender, about 15 to 20 minutes. Channel overflow of liquid.

•Make the dressing: In a large bowl, whisk together the red wine vinegar, lemon juice, lemon zest, Dijon mustard, onion powder, and oregano. Add olive oil, one tablespoon at a time, until velvety and emulsified.

•Cutting the vegetables: Thinly slice the shallot. Slice the peppers, then cut the slices in half to create pieces about 2 inches long. If using the spices, chop them up.

•Combine the mixed vegetable platter into one: place the lentils in the giant bowl with the dressing. Add shallots, pepper, spices, arugula, feta cheddar, and pistachios. Add ½ teaspoon salt and freshly ground pepper and mix everything.

•Serving: Serve with arugula if desired. Garnish with thinly sliced radish and sprinkle with feta and pistachios. Refrigerate any extras for up to 4 days (if you plan to make them for snacking, discard the pistachios). It saves well, and extras taste surprisingly better!

NUTRITION FACTS
Total Fat 15g 19%
Saturated Fat 3.9g
Total Carbohydrate 31.5g 11%
Dietary Fiber 5.6g 20%

Sugars 2.2g
Protein 14.7g 29%
Vitamin A 27.4ug 3%
Vitamin C 3.5mg 4%
Calcium 100.9mg 8%
Iron 3.4mg 19%
Vitamin D 0.1pg 1%
Magnesium 34mg 8%
Potassium 398mg 8%
Vitamin B6 0.4mg 25%
Vitamin B12 0.3pg 11%

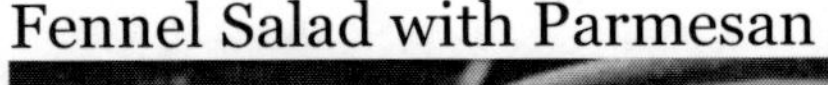

Fennel Salad with Parmesan

Prep Time: 15 minutes, **Cook Time:** 0 minutes, **Total Time:** 15 minutes

INGREDIENTS

•2 heads of fennel (4 to 5 cups cut), notwithstanding fennel fronds

•1 apple

•¼ cup shaved parmesan cheddar (vegan not included)

•2 tablespoons lemon juice, apart from squeezing ½ lemon

•1 tablespoon olive oil

•¼ teaspoon real salt

•Newly ground dark pepper

PREPARATION

•With the sharpness of an immense connoisseur, cut the fennel stalks and save them for frivolity. Then cut off the root end of the fennel. Remove and discard any outer layers of the fennel. Cut the convergence point of the fennel bulb. Lay it on the cut side and make extra pathetic crescent-shaped cuts in line with the root end. (See How to Chop Fennel for more info. You can also use a mandolin to chop up extra small pieces if you have one.)

•Cut the apple carefully. Place the fennel and apple pieces in a medium bowl and add the grated parmesan cheddar (shavings with a vegetable peeler).

•Add lemon juice, lemon punch, olive oil, real salt, and freshly ground weak pepper. Peel and generally tear off the thin parts (the fronds) with your fingers. Add enough for about 2 to 3 tablespoons. Put them in the bowl.

•Using your hands, gently arrange the portion of leafy greens until evenly coated, being careful not to break the apple pieces. Enjoy immediately or refrigerate until ready to serve. Keeps refrigerated for 3 days; Liven up the flavors with a sprinkling of salt and a squeeze of lemon squeezer or punch at each spot.

NUTRITION FACTS

Total Fat 5g 6%, Saturated Fat 1.4g
Total Carbohydrate 10.2g 4%, Dietary Fiber 2.5g 9%
Sugars 6.7g, Protein 2.6g 5%, Vitamin A 33.7µg 4%
Vitamin C 10.3mg 11%
Calcium 87.2mg 7%
Iron 0.4mg 2%
Vitamin D 0.1µg 0%
Magnesium 12.7mg 3%
Potassium 241.5mg 5%
Vitamin B6 0mg 3%
Vitamin B12 0.1µg 3%

Chickpea salad

Prep Time: 10 minutes, **Cook Time:** 0 minutes, **Total Time:** 10 minutes

INGREDIENTS

•400g can of chickpeas, used up and washed
•a small packet of cilantro, usually chopped
•a small packet of parsley, usually chopped
•1 red onion, finely sliced
•2 giant tomatoes, chopped
•2 tbsp olive oil
•2 tbsp harissa
•1 lemon, squeezed

PREPARATION

•Combine each side dish into one and mash them up a bit, so the chickpeas are a bit hard around the edges - this will absorb the dressing. (Can be made a day ahead and kept in the freezer.)

NUTRITION FACTS
Kcal 123
Fat 6g
Saturates 1g
Carbs 12g
Sugars 4g
Fiber 5g
Protein 4g
Salt 0g

DESSERTS RECIPES

Kulich

Prep Time: 20mins, Cook time: 45 mins, Total Time: 1hrs, 5 mins

INGREDIENTS

- •7 Method Steps
- •2 tbsp sweet sherry or squeezed apple
- •75g blended dried natural product (like dried cranberries, blended strips, currants, or sultanas)
- •1/4 cup (60ml) tepid milk
- •1/4 cup (60ml) tepid water
- •3 tsp (1 1/2 sachets/10g) dried yeast
- •1/3 cup (75g) caster sugar
- •3 cups (450g) plain flour
- •2 tsp finely ground lemon skin
- •1/2 tsp salt
- •2 eggs, softly whisked
- •100g margarine, dissolved, cooled
- •1 cup (160g) icing sugar combination

•Pink fluid food shading
•100's and 1000's, to improve
PREPARATION
•Join sherry or squeezed apple and dried natural product in a pot over low intensity. Cook for 1-2 mins or until just warmed through. Put away to cool.
•In the meantime, consolidate the milk, water, yeast, and 1 tsp of sugar in a little bowl, put away for 5 mins or until foamy.
•Join flour, lemon skin, salt, and remaining sugar in a huge bowl. Make a well in the middle. Add yeast combination, egg, and spread and mix to consolidate. Turn onto a gently floured surface and ply for 10 mins or until smooth and versatile. Add the natural product combination and ply for 2-3 mins or until recently consolidated. Place in a daintily lubed bowl and cover with saran wrap. Put away in a warm, without a draft place for 11/2 hours or until the mixture pairs in size.
•Preheat broiler to 180°C. Oil a 15cm (base estimation) round cake skillet and line the base with baking paper. Line the side with 2 baking paper layers, allowing it to broaden 12cm over the edge.
•Turn the batter onto a floured surface and manipulate it until smooth. Shape into a ball. Place in the pre-arranged dish. Freely cover with cling wrap and spot in a warm, sans draft place for 30 mins or until mixture transcends the edge of the skillet.
•Prepare for 35-40 mins or until the portion sounds empty when tapped on top. Put away for 10 mins before moving to a wire rack to cool.
•Filter the icing sugar into a medium bowl. Mix in sufficient water to make a runny glue. Use food shading to color the icing pink. Spread on top of the portion. Sprinkle with 100's and 1000's. Put away to set.

NUTRITION FACTS
Energy 1610 kj (385cal) 19%
Protein 6.5g 13%
Total Fat 10.4g 15%
Saturated 6.2g 26%
Cholesterol 0.1g -
Carbohydrate Total 65.3g 21%
Sugars28.1g 31%
Dietary Fiber 1.8g 6%
Sodium 78.1mg 3%
Calcium 28.6mg 4%
Magnesium 12.9mg 4%
Potassium 86.3mg -
Iron 2.4mg 20%
Zinc 1mg 8%
Phosphorus 81.3mg 8%
Vitamin A 91.2μg 12%
Vitamin C 1.3mg 3%
Niacin B3 3.1mg 31%
Folic Acid B9 158.8 79%
Vitamin B12 0.1μg 5%
Vitamin D 0.2μg 2%
Vitamin K 0.9μg 1%

Granola and yogurt tarts

Prep Time: 20mins, Cook time: 35 mins, Total Time: 55 mins

INGREDIENTS

- 1 1/2 cups (135g) moved oats
- 1/4 cup (20g) destroyed coconut
- 1/4 cup (35g) normal cut almonds, coarsely cleaved
- 1 tbsp flaxseed feast
- 1 tbsp chia seeds
- 1/3 cup (80ml) softened coconut oil
- 1/4 cup (60ml) maple syrup
- 1 tsp vanilla concentrate
- 500g Alpro Plant Based Vanilla yogurt
- Blended new organic product to serve.

PREPARATION

- Preheat broiler to 170°C. Gently oil six 12cm (base estimation) round fluted tart tins with removable bases and line the bases with baking paper. Put the tins on a baking plate.

•Join oats, destroyed coconut, almond, flaxseed feast, and chia seeds in an enormous bowl. Make a well in the Center. Add the coconut oil, maple syrup, vanilla, and 2 tbs water and mix to join. Put away for 5 mins to drench.
•Spoon the oat combination uniformly among the pre-arranged tins and utilize the rear of the spoon to press the blend equally over the base and side of each tin. Prepare for 30-35 mins or until brilliant and fresh. Put away to cool.
•Move the tart cases to a serving platter. Fill every tart case with yogurt. Top with products of the soil right away.

Dessert platter

Prep Time: 20mins, Cook time: 5 mins, Total Time: 25 mins

INGREDIENTS

•Chilled doughnuts to serve

Chocolate-plunged cherries

•50g CADBURY Baking Dark Chocolate, White Chocolate, or Milk Chocolate Melts

•250g new cherries, washed, dried

Baileys plunge

•250g cream cheddar, slashed, at room temperature

•125g (1/2 cup) harsh cream

•1 1/2 tbsp earthy-colored sugar

•60ml (1/4 cup) Baileys Irish Cream alcohol

Chocolate brownie plunge

•200g dim chocolate, finely slashed

•125ml (1/2 cup) pouring cream

•100g locally acquired chocolate brownies, broken into little lumps

•1 tbsp slashed walnuts or pecans

•Softened white chocolate to sprinkle

PREPARATION

•For the chocolate-plunged cherries, line a plate with baking paper. Liquefy the chocolate in a microwave-safe bowl in the microwave, mixing like clockwork until dissolved. Permit to be somewhat cool.
•Holding a cherry by the stem, dunk it into the liquefied chocolate, then, at that point, put it on the pre-arranged plate. Then, rehash with the excess cherries. Move to the cooler for 5 minutes for the chocolate to set.
•For the Baileys plunge, utilize electric mixers to beat cream cheddar until smooth. Add harsh cream, earthy-colored sugar, and alcohol and beat until smooth. Spoon into a serving bowl.
•For the Chocolate brownie plunge, place chocolate and cream in a heatproof bowl over a pan of stewing water (ensure the bowl doesn't contact the water). Mix until smooth.
•Orchestrate the brownie pieces in the foundation of a serving bowl. Sprinkle with a portion of the walnuts or pecans. Spoon chocolate sauce over the top. Shower with dissolved white chocolate and top with staying nuts.

Choc caramel dessert lasagne

Prep Time: 20mins, Cook time: 5 mins, Total Time: 25 mins

INGREDIENTS

•2 x 350g parcels of frozen chocolate cake

•1 cup thick caramel (dulce de leche), in addition to extra, to serve

•1 cup milk

•70g sachet chocolate mousse blend

•300ml container of thickened cream

•1/3 cup chocolate-covered almonds, coarsely slashed.

PREPARATION

•Open up and marginally defrost frozen cakes, utilizing an enormous serrated blade on a level plane and cut each cake down the middle.

•Place the chilled half of 1 cake in a 20cm square baking dish. Utilize 66% of the foundation of 1 cake to cut and fill any holes in the dish to cover the base.

•Spoon caramel over the collected cake and utilize the rear of the spoon to tenderly spread everywhere (the cake may not be completely covered).

•Consolidate the milk and mousse blend in a bowl and set up the combination following the bundle bearings. Spread over the caramel layer and smooth the surface. Place in the refrigerator for 1 hour or until set.
•Place the excess chilled cake half, chilled side up, on top of the mousse layer, utilizing 66% of the excess cake base to cut and fill holes. (Save the offcuts for a treat!)
•Utilize electric blenders to whisk the cream in a bowl until firm pinnacles structure. Spread over the top of the cake. Cover with cling wrap and spot in the refrigerator for 6 hours or short-term to set.
•To serve, sprinkle with hacked chocolate almonds and shower with additional caramel.

NUTRITION FACTS
Energy 2014 kj (481cal) 23%
Protein 5.8g 12%
Total Fat 24.7g 35%
Saturated 14.0g 58%
Carbohydrate Total 59.2g 19%
Sugars36.0g 40%
Dietary Fiber 3.4g 11%
Sodium 288mg 13%
Calcium 41.8mg 5%
Magnesium 3.9mg 1%
Potassium 181.3mg -
Iron 5.9mg 49%
Phosphorus 32.5mg 3%
Vitamin A 66.2μg 9%
Vitamin B12 0.2μg 10%
Vitamin D 0.4μg 4%
Vitamin K 0.1μg 0%

Chocolate and cheese dessert platter

Prep Time: 40mins, Cook Time: 15 mins, Total Time: 55 mins

- •Lindt Fruit Sensation chocolates, to serve, to serve
- •Lindt Excellence 70% Cocoa chocolate
- •Milk and dim Lindt Lindor balls to serve
- •Debris triple cream brie, to serve

Halva and choc dates

- •150g halva (find at chosen grocery stores)
- •75g new ricotta
- •24 new Medjool dates
- •100g Lindt Dessert 70% Cocoa cooking chocolate, softened

Exquisite baked good meshes

- •2 sheets of great quality frozen spread puff cake, recently defrosted
- •1 egg, daintily beaten
- •1 tsp cayenne pepper
- •40g (1/2 cup) finely ground parmesan
- •2 tsp fennel seeds
- •1 tsp ocean salt pieces

PREPARATION

•For the Halva and choc dates: Place the halva and ricotta in a food processor. Process until smooth, then, at that point, move to a funneling pack fitted with a star spout.

•Line a plate with baking paper. Utilize a little paring blade to chop down the focal point of each date, trying not to cut as far as possible 40g (1⁄2 cup) finely ground parmesan 2 tsp fennel seeds 1 tsp ocean salt pieces 1 Preheat broiler to 220°C/200°C fan constrained. Oil 2 baking plates and line with baking paper. 2 Cut 1 baked good sheet into 1cm-thick strips. Working with 3 strips all at once, press the tops together and cautiously mesh the strips. Move the mesh to the arranged plate. Rehash with residual cake strips, then the leftover baked goods sheet. 3 Brush the meshes with egg. Sprinkle around 50% of the interlaces with the cayenne pepper and parmesan. Sprinkle the excess interlaces with the fennel seeds and salt. Heat for 12-15 minutes or until brilliant and fresh. Put away to cool, then serve. Present with • Lindt Fruit Sensation chocolates • berries • Manchego • Lindt Excellence 70% Cocoa chocolate • milk and dull Lindt Lindor balls • debris triple cream brie • fig and walnut wafers • pistachio sheep's cheddar • classic cheddar • blue cheddar • salted caramel and almond dim chocolate crisps • honey • cabernet glue • muscatels through. Eliminate the seed. Pipe the halva blend into the dates until filled and move to an arranged plate.

•Sprinkle over the liquefied chocolate. Place in the cooler for 30 minutes or until the chocolate has set.

•For the Savory baked good meshes: Preheat broiler to 220C/200C fan constrained, oil 2 baking plates and line with baking paper.

•Cut 1 good baking sheet into 1cm-thick strips. Working with 3 strips all at once, press the tops together and cautiously twist the strips. Move the twist to the arranged plate. Rehash with outstanding baked goods strips, then the excess cake sheet.

•Brush the plaits with egg. Sprinkle a portion of the meshes with the cayenne pepper and parmesan. Sprinkle the excess interlaces with the fennel seeds and salt. Heat for 12-15 minutes or until brilliant and fresh. Put away to cool, then, at that point, serve.

Turkish lemon dessert cakes

Prep Time: 20mins, Cook Time: 25 mins, Total Time: 45 mins

INGREDIENTS

- •125g unsalted margarine, at room temperature, in addition to extra for brushing
- •215g (1 cup) caster sugar
- •1 tbsp finely ground lemon skin
- •2 eggs
- •130g (2/3 cup) semolina
- •200g (1 1/3 cups) self-raising flour, filtered, in addition to extra for tidying
- •125ml (1/2 cup) milk

Lemon syrup

- •215g (1 cup) caster sugar
- •125ml (1/2 cup) stressed lemon juice
- •1 lemon, meagerly cut

Ricotta Cream

- •250g smooth ricotta
- •1 tbsp caster sugar

PREPARATION

•Preheat broiler to 180C/160C fan-constrained. Brush twelve 160ml (2/3 cup) Texas biscuit skillets with margarine and gentle dust with flour.

•Utilize electric blenders to beat the spread, sugar, and skin until pale and smooth. Add eggs, each, in turn, beating great after every option. Mix in the semolina, flour, and milk.

•Spoon combination equally among the biscuit container. Heat for 25 minutes or until a stick embedded into the middle tells the truth.

•In the meantime, make lemon syrup. Place the sugar, juice, and 125ml (1/2 cup) cold water in a pot over low intensity. Cook, mixing, for 5 minutes or until the sugar has disintegrated. Increment intensity to high and bring to the bubble. Bubble, without blending, for 5 to 7 minutes or until the combination thickens. Remove from heat. Add lemon cuts. Put away until required.

•For the ricotta cream, place the ricotta and sugar in a little bowl until joined.

•Move lemon cuts to a plate. Spoon around 50% of the syrup over the cakes and represent 10 minutes.

•Serve the cakes finished off with ricotta cream and lemon cuts, and shower with the leftover syrup.

NUTRITION FACTS

Energy 3109 kj (743cal) 36%
Protein 12.2g 24%
Total Fat 24.2g 35%
Saturated 14.4g 60%
Cholesterol 0.1g -
Carbohydrate Total 121.5g 39%
Sugars75.2g 84%
Dietary Fiber 2.1g 7%
Sodium 474.7mg 21%
Calcium 253.9mg 32%

Magnesium	31.2mg	10%
Potassium	267.6mg	-
Iron	2.2mg	18%
Zinc	1mg	8%
Phosphorus	353.4mg	35%
Vitamin A	240.2µg	32%
Vitamin C	13.4mg	34%
Niacin B3	2.8mg	28%
Folic Acid B9	130.2	65%
Vitamin B12	0.6µg	30%
Vitamin D	0.5µg	5%
Vitamin E	1mg	10%
Vitamin K	1.9µg	2%

Lemon dessert lasagne

Prep Time: 4 hrs, 30mins, **Total Time:** 4 hrs, 30 mins

INGREDIENTS

•2 3/4 cups milk
•16 Dutch speculaas treats (see notes)
•1kg new ricotta (see notes)
•1 1/2 tbsp finely ground lemon skin
•2 tbsp lemon juice
•2/3 cup caster sugar
•100g bundle vanilla enhanced dessert blend
•1/2 cup lemon spread, relaxed (see notes)
•2 tbsp bubbling water
•1 tbsp gelatine powder
•300ml thickened cream
•1 tsp. vanilla concentrate
•The lemon cuts to brighten
•Little new mint leaves to adorn

PREPARATION

•Eliminate milk from the refrigerator. Represent 30 minutes to permit to come to room temperature. Orchestrate rolls, in a solitary layer, over the foundation of a 4cm-profound, 20cm x 28cm (base) baking dish, managing rolls to fit if important.

•Place ricotta, lemon skin, lemon juice, and 1/2 cup sugar in a food processor. Process until smooth and consolidated. Equitably spread ricotta blend over bread rolls. Refrigerate until required.

•Make vanilla sweet, utilizing milk and following parcel headings. Race in the lemon spread. Place bubbling water in a little bowl. Sprinkle over gelatine. Mix until the gelatine breaks down. Whisk the gelatine into the lemon blend. Refrigerate for 15 minutes or until the blend thickens somewhat. Tenderly pour the lemon blend over the ricotta combination. Refrigerate for 4 hours or until set.

•Utilizing an electric blender, beat cream, vanilla, and remaining sugar until just-firm pinnacles structure. Spread the cream over the lemon layer. Finish with lemon cuts and mint leaves. Serve.

NUTRITION FACTS

Energy 2127 Ki (508cal) 24%
Protein 12.1g 24%
Total Fat 31.0g 44%
Saturated 18.3g 76%
Cholesterol 0.1g -
Carbohydrate Total 44.8g 14%
Sugars 32.0g 36%
Dietary Fiber 0.4g 1%
Sodium 362.5mg 16%
Calcium 316.4mg 40%
Magnesium 29.4mg 9%
Potassium 374.4mg -
Zinc 1mg 8%
Phosphorus 305.4mg 31%
Vitamin A 570.3μg 76%, Vitamin C 5.9mg 15%
Folic Acid B9 1.8 1%, Vitamin B12 1.2μg 60%
Vitamin D 0.8μg 8%, Vitamin K 0.8μg 1%

French strawberry dessert cake

Prep Time: 25 mins, Cook Time: 1hrs,5 mins, Total Time: 30 mins

INGREDIENTS

•125g spread at room temperature

•2 tsp vanilla concentrate

•270g (1 1/4 cups) caster sugar

•2 eggs

•1/4 tsp salt

•225g (1 1/2 cups) self-raising flour, in addition to 1 tbsp extra

•170g (2/3 cup) sharp cream

•375g new strawberries, hulled

PREPARATION

•Preheat stove to 180C/160C fan-constrained, oil and line base and side of a 23cm (base estimation) round springform container with baking paper.

•Utilize electric mixers to beat the margarine, vanilla, and 1 cup sugar in a huge bowl until pale and velvety. Add eggs, each, in turn, beating great after every option. Add salt and a portion of the flour and beat until recently consolidated. Add a portion of the sharp cream and beat until recently consolidated. Rehash with residual flour and harsh cream.

•Split 125g of the strawberries and put them away. Coarsely cleave the remaining strawberries. Throw cleaved strawberries with additional flour to cover. Crease into the cake combination until recently consolidated. Spoon the blend into arranged skillet and smooth the surface.

•Sprinkle the top with 1 ½ tablespoon of the leftover sugar. Heat for 35 to 40 minutes or until a slender covering has framed on the top. Orchestrate divided strawberries, cut-side down, on the highest point of the cake, squeezing somewhat into the covering. Sprinkle with outstanding sugar. Heat for 20 to 25 minutes or until a stick in the Center confesses everything. Serve the cake warm or at room temperature.

NUTRITION FACTS
Energy 1400 Ki (335cal) 16%
Protein 4.1g 8%
Total Fat 14.6g 21%
Saturated 8.4g 35%
Cholesterol 0.1g -
Carbohydrate Total 47.4g 15%
Sugars28.9g 32%
Dietary Fiber 1.3g 4%
Sodium 311.8mg 14%
Calcium 107.3mg 13%
Magnesium 12.1mg 4%
Potassium 121.2mg -
Iron 1.4mg 12%
Phosphorus 175.9mg 18%
Vitamin A 132.1µg 18%, Vitamin C 21.3mg 53%
Niacin B3 1.5mg 15% , Folic Acid B9 83.2 42%
Vitamin B12 0.1µg 5%, Vitamin D 0.2µg 2%
Vitamin E 1mg 10%, Vitamin K 2µg 3%

Choc mint dessert lasagne

Prep Time: 20 mins, **Cook Time:** 2hrs, 30 mins, **Total Time:** 2 hrs, 50 mins

INGREDIENTS

•350g pkt Sara Lee frozen chocolate cake

•250g pkg cream cheddar, slashed, at room temperature

•80g (1/2 cup) icing sugar combination

•1 1/2 tsp peppermint quintessence

•Green fluid food shading to color

•600ml thickened cream

•Spearmint leaves, to serve, in addition to extra, cut, to enrich

•Mint Aero chocolate, coarsely slashed, to serve

•Darrell Lea Minty Crunchy Chocolate Balls, coarsely slashed, to serve

PREPARATION

•Utilize an enormous serrated blade to manage the icing from the cake. Save. Slice the cake down the middle on a level plane. Place the two cake parts in the foundation of a 16 x 24cm rectangular baking dish.

Coarsely cleave the saved icing. Disperse cleaved icing over the cake.

•Utilize electric blenders to beat the cream cheddar, icing sugar, peppermint quintessence, and 10-12 drops of food shading in a bowl until smooth.

•In a spotless bowl, use electric blenders to beat half of the cream until firm pinnacles are formed. Utilize a huge metal spoon to overlap 33% of the whipped cream into the cream cheddar blend until recently consolidated. Rehash with the leftover whipped cream until the blend is all around joined.

•Spread the cream-cheddar combination over the cake. Cover and spot in the cooler for 2 hours or until chilled and somewhat firm.

•Utilize electric blenders to beat the excess cream in a bowl until delicate pinnacles structure. Spread over the mint layer. Place in the ice chest for 30 minutes or until the cream is firm.

•Not long before serving, sprinkle with the hacked Mint Aero, chocolate balls, and spearmint leaves.

Lemon dream dessert

Prep Time: 8 hrs, 50 mins, **Total Time:** 2 hrs, 50 mins

INGREDIENTS

•400g pkt plain stomach-related bread rolls, broken into pieces

•175g salted margarine, liquefied

•125g salted margarine, at room temperature

•55g (1/4 cup) crude caster sugar

•250g cream cheddar, relaxed

•150g (1 cup) delicate icing sugar

•300ml can of thickened cream, whipped to firm pinnacles

•3/4 cup locally acquired lemon curd

•1 tsp vanilla concentrate

PREPARATION

•Oil a 26 x 20cm cut dish. Line with baking paper.

•Place rolls in the food processor and cycle until the blend looks like coarse morsels. Add softened margarine and sugar and cycle until joined. Move 66% of the blend to the pre-arranged container. Utilize a

level-lined glass to press the blend uniformly over the base. Place in the cooler to chill for 30 minutes.
•Utilize a stand blender with the oar connection to beat the cream cheddar, relaxed spread, icing sugar, and vanilla until pale and rich.
•Overlap the cream cheddar and lemon curd through the whipped cream.
•Spread cream blend over the rolling base and smooth the surface. Sprinkle over leftover roll morsel. Place in the refrigerator to chill for 4 hours or short term.

NUTRITION FACTS
Energy 3021 Ki (722cal) 35%
Protein 4.4g 9%
Total Fat 50.8g 73%
Saturated 30.2g 126%
Cholesterol 0.1g -
Carbohydrate Total 62.4g 20%
Sugars 34.6g 38%
Dietary Fiber 1.2g 4%
Sodium 408.3mg 18%
Calcium 31.7mg 4%
Magnesium 2.9mg 1%
Potassium 121.3mg -
Phosphorus 34mg 3%
Vitamin A 308.2µg 41%
Folic Acid B9 3.2 2%
Vitamin B12 0.1µg 5%
Vitamin E 1mg 10%
Vitamin K 2.6µg 3%

Peach dessert cake

Prep Time: 20 mins, **Cook Time:** 1hrs, 15 mins, **Total Time:** 1 hrs, 35 mins

INGREDIENTS

•825g can peach cuts in juice

•125g spread, cleaved, at room temperature

•215g (1 cup) caster sugar

•2 tsp vanilla concentrate

•2 eggs

•375g smooth ricotta

•190g (1 1/4 cups) self-rising flour

•75g (3/4 cup) almond feast

•60ml (1/4 cup) milk

•Cream, whipped to firm tops, to serve

PREPARATION

•Preheat broiler to 170C/150C fan-constrained. Oil a 6cm-profound, 22cm round cake dish. Line the base and side with 2 layers of baking paper. Channel the peaches, saving 60ml (¼ cup) of the juice. Finely hack an adequate number of peaches to fill a 1/2 cup measure.

•Utilize electric blenders to beat the spread, sugar, and vanilla until pale and rich. Add the eggs, 1 all at once, beating until recently joined. Add the ricotta and beat until smooth.

•Consolidate the flour, almond feast, and milk with the margarine blend. Overlay in the slashed peaches. Spoon the blend into the pre-arranged skillet and smooth the surface. Orchestrate remaining peaches over the hitter.

•Prepare for 1 hour 15 minutes or until a stick embedded into the Center tells the truth. Put away in the prospect hour to cool somewhat before moving to a wire rack to cool.

•Spoon over held squeeze and serve warm or cold with whipped cream.

NUTRITION FACTS

Energy	1666 Ki (398cal)	19%
Protein	8.4g	17%
Total Fat	19.3g	28%
Saturated	9.6g	40%
Cholesterol	0.1g	-
Carbohydrate Total	49.8g	16%
Sugars	30.3g	34%
Dietary Fiber	2.5g	8%
Sodium	286.1mg	12%
Calcium	186.6mg	23%
Magnesium	18.9mg	6%
Potassium	292.4mg	-
Iron	1.6mg	13%
Zinc	1mg	8%
Phosphorus	214.5mg	21%
Vitamin A	251.8µg	34%
Vitamin C	3mg	8%
Niacin B3	1.7mg	17%
Folic Acid B9	65.3	33%
Vitamin B12	0.4µg	20%
Vitamin D	0.2µg	2%
Vitamin E	1mg	10%
Vitamin K	2.6µg	3%

Salted caramel dream dessert

Prep Time: 20 mins, Total Time: 20 mins

INGREDIENTS

•400g Arnott's Granita bread rolls, coarsely slashed

•175g margarine, softened, in addition to 125g extra, hacked, at room temperature

•250g cream cheddar, at room temperature, slashed

•150g (1 cup) icing sugar combination

•1 tsp. vanilla concentrate

•300ml thickened cream, whipped to firm pinnacles

•170g (1/2 cup) dulce de leche

•3 tsp. ocean salt drops

PREPARATION

•Oil a 5cm-profound, 20cm x 26cm simmering skillet and line it with baking paper, permitting the paper to overhang the long sides

•Place bread rolls into a food processor and interact until coarse pieces. Add dissolved margarine and interact until consolidated.

•Move 66% of the blend to the pre-arranged dish. Utilize a level-lined glass to squeeze the blend equally over the base. Place in the cooler for 30 minutes to chill. Move the remaining morsel blend to a bowl. Cover and put away at room temperature.

•Utilize electric mixers to beat cream cheddar, additional spread, and icing sugar and vanilla in a huge bowl until pale and velvety.

•Utilize a spatula to overlay the cream into the cream cheddar blend until recently consolidated. Crease whipped cream into a cream cheddar combination. Spoon half over the rolling base. Top with dulce de leche and twirl tenderly. Sprinkle with salt. Top with an outstanding cream-cheddar combination.

•Sprinkle over excess roll morsels. Place in the cooler for 4 hours or up to expedite to set. Move to a serving board. Cut into 16 parts of serve.

Lemon ricotta dessert cake

Prep Time: 20 mins, **Cook Time:** 45 mins, **Total Time:** 1 hrs, 5 mins

INGREDIENTS

•125g margarine, at room temperature, cleaved

•155g (3/4 cup) caster sugar

•1 lemon, skin finely ground

•250g new ricotta (see note)

•3 eggs

•150g (1 cup) self-raising flour

•60ml (1/4 cup) new lemon juice

•100g (1/4 cup) lemon curd, in addition to extra to serve

•Unadulterated icing sugar to tidy

•Vanilla frozen yogurt, to serve

PREPARATION

•Preheat broiler to 170C/150C fan-constrained. Oil and line the foundation of a 20cm spring structure cake container with baking paper.

•Utilize electric blenders to beat the spread, sugar, and lemon skin until pale and velvety. Add the ricotta and beat until recently consolidated. Add the eggs, each, in turn, beating great after every option.

•Utilize an enormous metal spoon to crease the flour into the combination. Mix in the lemon juice. Move the combination to the pre-arranged skillet and dab with lemon curd. Utilize a level-bladed blade to whirl the lemon curd into the player. Delicately tap the container on the seat to settle the hitter. Prepare for 45 minutes or until the cake springs back when softly contacted (see note).

•Cool the cake in the prospect minutes, then, at that point, discharge the side of the skillet. Cut the cake into wedges, serve warm, dust with icing sugar, shower with additional curd, and finish with frozen yogurt.

NUTRITION FACTS

Energy 1569 Ki (375cal) 18%
Protein 6.7g 13%
Total Fat 18.5g 26%
Saturated 10.9g 45%
Cholesterol 0.1g -
Total carbohydrates 46.3 g 15%
Sugar 27.7g 31%
Fiber 0.8g 3%
Sodium 296.2mg 13%
Calcium 148.1mg 19%
Magnesium 12.8mg 4%
Potassium 135.7 mg
Iron 1.2mg 10%
Zinc 1mg 8%
Phosphorus 199.9 mg 20%
Vitamin A 183.7 µg 24%
Vitamin C 5.2mg 13%
Niacin B3 1.2mg 12%
Folic acid B9 67.8 34%
Vitamin B12 0.4µg 20%
Vitamin D 0.3µg 3%
Vitamin E1mg 10%
Vitamin K 1.4µg 2%

Healthy dessert mug cake

Prep Time: 5 mins, Cook Time: 1 min, Total Time: 6 mins

INGREDIENTS

•1 new date, pitted, finely hacked

•1 egg

•60ml (1/4 cup) unsweetened apple puree

•2 1/2 tbsp oat grain

•2 tsp cocoa powder, in addition to extra, to clean

•1/4 tsp ground cinnamon

PREPARATION

•Place the date in a medium-estimated heatproof bowl, add one teaspoon of bubbling water and crush with a fork.

•Add the egg, apple, oat grain, cocoa powder, and cinnamon and mix until smooth and very much joined.

•Spoon blend into a 160ml (2/3 cup) limit microwave-safe mug or ramekin. Microwave on HIGH for 1 1/2 minutes or until the cake begins to leave away from the sides and the top is simply firm. Serve tidied with additional cocoa.

NUTRITION FACTS
Energy 976 Ki (233cal) 11%
Protein 10.4g 21%
Total Fat 6.6g 9%
Saturated 1.9g 8%
Carbohydrate Total 29.5g 10%
Sugars16.8g 19%
Dietary Fiber 7.4g 25%
Sodium 9.2mg 0%

Mini dessert calzones

Prep Time: 10 mins, Cook Time: 20 mins, Total Time: 30 mins

INGREDIENTS

- 250g new pizza batter
- 1 tablespoon Wonka Nerds rainbow
- 12 new raspberries
- 40g popping treats chocolate
- Icing sugar to serve.

PREPARATION

- Preheat stove to 200°C/180°C fan constrained. Partition pizza batters into four equivalent segments. Line a baking plate with baking paper. On a daintily floured surface, carry out the mixture segments into circles around 10-12cm in width. Dissipate a teaspoon of Nerds over each circle and tenderly press into the batter.
- Put 3 raspberries on each circle. Split the chocolate between circles. Brush the batter edges with a touch of water and crease into equal parts. Squeeze and curve the edges to seal.
- Put on the pre-arranged plate. Prepare for 15-20 minutes or until brilliant brown and fresh. Dust with icing sugar. Put away for 10 minutes to cool marginally. Serve.

Banoffee dessert cake

Prep Time: 20 mins, **Cook Time:** 1 hrs, **Total Time:** 1 hrs, 20 mins

INGREDIENTS

•4 enormous ready bananas
•125g margarine, mellowed
•2/3 cup earthy-colored sugar
•2 eggs
•1/2 tsp bicarbonate of pop
•1 1/2 cups self-raising flour
•1/2 cup milk
•1 cup thickened cream
•1 cup harsh cream
•1 tbsp icing sugar
•1/4 cup slashed cooked hazelnuts
•Dim chocolate twists to serve
•Tacky Caramel Sauce
•60g margarine
•1/2 cup earthy-colored sugar
•1/2 cup thickened cream

PREPARATION

•Preheat broiler to 180C/160C fan-constrained. Oil a 6cm-profound, 20cm round cake skillet. Line the base and side with baking paper.
•Pound 2 bananas. Utilizing an electric blender, beat margarine and earthy-colored sugar until light and soft. Beat in eggs, each in turn. Beat in crushed banana. Filter bicarbonate of pop and a portion of the flour over the banana blend. Add a portion of the milk. Overlay until recently consolidated. Rehash with outstanding flour and milk.
•Spread cake combination into skillet. Heat for 1 hour or until a stick embedded into focus confesses all. Stand cake in prospect minutes. Move to a wire rack to cool.
•In the meantime, make Sticky Caramel Sauce. Liquefy margarine and earthy-colored sugar in an enormous skillet over medium-high intensity. Cook for 2 minutes or until liquefied and smooth. Add cream. Mix to consolidate. Bring to a stew. Diminish intensity to medium. Stew for 2 to 3 minutes or until sauce is marginally thickened. Put away for 15 minutes to cool.
•Utilizing an electric blender, beat cream, acrid cream, and icing sugar until just-firm pinnacles structure. Cut the cake evenly into 3 layers. Put 1 cake layer on a serving plate. Spread with 1/3 of the cream blend. Top with the second layer, then around 50% of the leftover cream blend. Sandwich with outstanding layer. Dab with the residual cream blend. Cut leftover bananas into adjusts. Orchestrate on top. Shower with caramel sauce. Sprinkle with hazelnuts and chocolate. Serve right away.

NUTRITION FACTS

Energy	2119 Ki (506cal) 24%
Protein	5.1g 10%
Total Fat	35.2g 50%

Saturated 20.3g 85%
Cholesterol 0.1g -
Carbohydrate Total 44.8g 14%
Sugars25.3g 28%
Dietary Fiber1.9g 6%
Sodium 257.7mg 11%
Calcium 128.5mg 16%
Magnesium 26.2mg 8%
Potassium 292.5mg
Iron 1.4mg 12%
Phosphorus 181.1mg 18%
Vitamin A 166.3µg 22%
Vitamin C 4.2mg 11%
Niacin B3 1.5mg 15%
Folic Acid B9 74.1 37%
Vitamin B12 0.2µg 10%
Vitamin D 0.3µg 3%
Vitamin E 1mg 10%
Vitamin K 1.7µg 2%

Fairy bread dessert lasagne

Prep Time: 6 hrs, 45 mins, **Total Time:** 6 hrs, 45 mins

INGREDIENTS

•450g pkt Madeira cake, closes made due
•85g Airplane Original Strawberry jam valuable stones
•2 x 250g pkts cream cheddar, cut at room temperature
•85g Airplane Original Berry Blue jam valuable stones
•395g can work on thick milk
•1 tbsp vanilla concentrate
•2 1/2 tsp. gelatine powder
•30g (1/4 cup) splendid sprinkles, notwithstanding 2 tbs extra to decorate
•85g Airplane Original Lemon jam jewels
•300g bought vanilla custard
•85g Airplane Original Raspberry jam valuable stones
•185ml (3/4 cup) thickened cream, whipped

PREPARATION

•Cut cake lengthways into 5 even cuts. Coordinate cake pieces over the groundwork of an 8cm-significant, 22cm (base assessment) square baking dish, figuring out how to fit.

•Place valuable strawberry jam stones in a heatproof bowl. Add 125ml (1/2 cup) gurgling water and use a fork to race until valuable stones deteriorate. Process a part of the cream cheddar in a food processor until smooth. Gradually pour in the warm strawberry dilemma mix. Process until smooth and united. Move the cream cheddar mix to a bowl. Place in the cooler for 30 minutes or until thickens and somewhat set (expecting that blend is too wet and slight, it will acclimatize into a cake layer). Spoon over the cake and use the back of a spoon to smooth the surface. Place in the cooler for 10 minutes to set.

•Wash the food processor bowl and dry it. Place blue jam jewels in a heatproof bowl. Add 125ml (1/2 cup) percolating water and use a fork for rushing until the jewels separate. Process remaining cream cheddar in the food processor until smooth. Constantly pour in the warm blue predicament mix. Process until smooth and solidified. Working quickly, pour the blue jam cream cheddar mix over the back of a huge metal spoon over the strawberry jam layer. Smooth the surface and return to the cooler for 10 minutes to set.

•The place worked on combining milk in a bowl. Blend in vanilla. Pour 160ml (2/3 cup) gurgling water into a little heatproof holder. Sprinkle over the gelatine and race with a fork until the gelatine separates. Set aside to cool, possibly.

•Add gelatine mix to solidified milk mix and competition to join. Place in the fridge for 30 minutes or until thickened. Blend in sprinkles. Pour the united milk mix over the back of a tremendous metal spoon over the blue jam layer. Smooth the surface. Place in the cooler for 20 minutes to set.

•Place yellow jam jewels in a heatproof bowl. Add 125ml (1/2 cup) gurgling water and use a fork for rushing until valuable stones separate. Rush in custard. Pour the yellow jam mixture over the back of a colossal metal spoon over the thick milk layer. Smooth the surface. Place in the cooler for 20 minutes to set.

•Meanwhile, place valuable raspberry jam stones in a heatproof holder. Add 250ml (1 cup) percolating water. Blend until valuable stones have crumbled. Blend in 125ml (1/2 cup) cold water. Set aside for 1 hour to cool to room temperature. Carefully pour jam over the cut. Place in the cooler for something like 4 hours or until set.

•Top raspberry jam with whipped cream, light up with extra sprinkles.

NUTRITION FACTS
Energy 1776 Ki (424cal) 20%
Protein 10.0g 20%
Total Fat 21.7g 31%
Saturated 13.3g 55%
Carbohydrate Total 47.7g 15%
Sugars40.4g 45%
Dietary Fiber 0.3g 1%
Sodium 293.9mg 13%
Calcium 126.7mg 16%
Magnesium 9.5mg 3%
Potassium 134.5mg
Phosphorus 96.1mg 10%
Vitamin A 144.6μg 19%
Vitamin C 17.6mg 44%
Folic Acid B9 5.7 3%
Vitamin B12 0.2μg 10%
Vitamin K 0.8μg 1%

Double choc dessert lasagne

Prep Time: 2 hrs, 25 mins, **Cook Time:** 2 mins, **Total Time:** 2 hrs, 27 mins

INGREDIENTS

•600ml tub of thickened cream

•500g new ricotta

•60g (1/3 cup) unadulterated icing sugar, filtered

•2 tsp. vanilla bean glue

•1 tbsp marsala

•2 tbsp chocolate hazelnut spread

•12 (around 200g) McVitie's Milk Chocolate Digestive Biscuits

•12 (around 200g) McVitie's Dark Chocolate Digestive Biscuits

•250g milk chocolate.

PREPARATION

•Pour 1/2 of the cream into a huge bowl, using electric mixers to beat until delicate pinnacles are formed.

•Place the ricotta, icing sugar, and vanilla bean glue in an enormous bowl. Utilize electric blenders to beat until smooth and very much consolidated (see note). Move 1/2 the ricotta blend into a little bowl. Add the

Marsala to the enormous bowl of ricotta. Beat until very much consolidated. Add the chocolate hazelnut spread to the little bowl of ricotta. Beat until very much joined.

•Overlay 1/2 of the whipped cream into the plain ricotta blend and the excess 1/2 into the chocolate ricotta combination. Clean the blenders and whip 160ml (2/3 cup) of the excess cream until delicate pinnacles structure.

•Orchestrate 9 dull chocolate bread rolls, chocolate-side down over the foundation of a square 20cm (base estimation) 1.5L (6 cups) limit dish, managing the bread rolls to fit and to top off the vast majority of the holes. Spread the plain ricotta blend equally on top. Top with 9 milk chocolate rolls, chocolate-side down. Spread the chocolate ricotta blend equally on top. Top with the whipped cream and spread uniformly. Place in the refrigerator for 2 hours or short term.

•Cut 50g of the milk chocolate into coarse shards. Cleave the excess chocolate and spot it in a little microwave confirmation bowl with the leftover cream. Heat in the microwave on HIGH for 30 seconds. Mix and rehash until the combination is smooth and all-around consolidated.

•Break half of the excess milk and dim chocolate rolls into coarse pieces. Cleave up the rest. Spoon a portion of the chocolate sauce over the whipped cream and top with the roll and chocolate shards. Present with the excess chocolate sauce as an afterthought.

NUTRITION FACTS

Energy	2515 Ki (601cal)	29%
Protein	8.9g	18%
Total Fat	39.2g	56%
Saturated	23.9g	100%
Carbohydrate Total	53.3g	17%

Sugars33.8g 38%
Dietary Fiber 3.1g 10%
Sodium 239.5mg 10%
Calcium 164.8mg 21%
Magnesium 28.8mg 9%
Potassium 230.1mg
Iron 1mg 8%
Zinc 1mg 8%
Phosphorus 140.5mg 14%
Vitamin A 78.2µg 10%
Folic Acid B9 3.4 2%
Vitamin B12 0.6µg 30%
Vitamin E 1mg 10%
Vitamin K 1.8µg 2%

Cheat's mango cheesecake dessert cups

Prep Time: 5 mins, Total Time: 5 mins
INGREDIENTS

•250g cream cheddar, at room temperature
•1 cup thickened cream
•125ml twofold cream
•1/4 cup caster sugar
•1 lemon, skin finely ground
•1 tbsp lemon juice
•1 little mango, stripped, pitifully cut
•Excitement normal item pound, to serve
•Mint leaves to serve
•Consumable blooms to serve.

PREPARATION

•Beat cream cheddar in a bowl until smooth. Add thickened cream, twofold cream, sugar, and lemon skin. Beat for 2-3 minutes, until thick and rich. Blend through lemon juice until joined.

•Yet, some cream cheddar mixed in the groundwork of four 250ml glasses. Top with cut mango. Continue to layer and wrap up with mango cuts. Top with energy regular item squash, mint leaves, and consumable blooms, if you like.

NUTRITION FACTS
Energy 3075 Ki (735cal) 35%
Protein 5.2g 10%
Total Fat 67.9g 97%
Saturated 41.3g 172%
Cholesterol 0.1g
Carbohydrate Total 25.6g 8%
Sugars22.9g 25%
Dietary Fiber 0.8g 3%
Sodium 220.9mg 10%
Calcium 67.3mg 8%
Magnesium 10.3mg 3%
Potassium 160.9mg
Phosphorus 73.7mg 7%
Vitamin A 574.7µg 77%
Vitamin C 19.8mg 50%
Folic Acid B9 23.2 12%
Vitamin B12 0.1µg 5%
Vitamin E 1mg 10%
Vitamin K 2.8µg 3%

5-minute passion fruit cream dessert

Prep Time: 5 mins, Total Time: 5 mins
INGREDIENTS
•8 Anzac or Granita bread rolls, squashed
•1 cup enthusiasm organic product curd
•185ml (3/4 cup) thickened cream
•8 purchased small-scale meringues
PREPARATION
•Split bread roll between the foundations of four 250ml (1 cup) serving glasses, top with the enthusiasm of organic product curd, smoothing the top.
•Use electric blenders to whisk the cream in a bowl until delicate pinnacles structure, then spoon over the curd layer.
•Disintegrate the meringues over each glass and serve right away.

NUTRITION FACTS

Energy	2344 Ki (560cal)	27%
Protein	4.6g	9%
Total Fat	33.1g	47%
Saturated	20.7g	86%
Carbohydrate Total	61.4g	20%

Sugars51.4g 57%
Dietary Fiber 1.0g 3%
Sodium 140.5mg 6%
Iron 1mg 8%
Vitamin C 2.4mg 6%

APPETIZERS AND SNACKS

PREP TIME: 15 mins, TOTAL TIME: 15 mins

INGREDIENTS

- 1/4 cup extra virgin olive oil
- 1 lemon juice (~2 tablespoons)
- 1 cup new dill, washed and huge stems dispensed with
- 1 clove of garlic, hacked
- 4 green onions (scallions), severed
- 2 cups feta
- 3/4 cup cream cheddar

PREPARATION

- Eliminate feta and cream cheddar from the cooler around thirty minutes before making. You can loosen up in case you can't manage this step. It will all end up perfect!
- Add olive oil, lemon juice, dill, garlic, and green onion to a food processor. Cut until minced.
- Add feta and cream cheddar. Process until all trimmings are solidified, and cheeses are mixed.

NUTRITION FACTS

Calories: 158kcal

Carbohydrates: 2g
Protein: 5g
Fat: 15g
Saturated Fat: 7g
Polyunsaturated Fat: 1g
Monounsaturated Fat: 6g
Cholesterol: 38mg
Sodium: 328mg
Potassium: 79mg
Fiber: 1g
Sugar: 2g
Vitamin A: 638IU
Vitamin C: 5mg
Calcium: 149mg
Iron: 1mg

Lebanese Hummus

PREP TIME: 15 mins, TOTAL TIME: 15 mins

INGREDIENTS

•2-15 ounces jars of chickpeas, depleted and flushed
•2 cloves garlic, squashed
•1/4 cup tahini glue
•1/3 cup newly crushed lemon juice
•1/4 cup additional virgin olive oil
•1/4 tsp paprika
•1/2 tsp salt
•3 tbsp cold water
•pine nuts for decorating

PREPARATION

•Start by cleaving the garlic in the food processor.
•Add the other fixings and mix in the food processor until wanted consistency.
•Mix with cold water for a smoother consistency.

NUTRITION FACTS
Calories: 152kcal
Carbohydrates: 5g
Protein: 2g

Fat: 15g
Saturated Fat: 2g
Polyunsaturated Fat: 3g
Monounsaturated Fat: 9g
Sodium: 224mg
Potassium: 78mg
Fiber: 1g
Sugar: 1g
Vitamin A: 15IU
Vitamin C: 6mg
Calcium: 20mg
Iron: 1mg

Muhammara (Roasted Red Pepper and Walnut Dip)

PREP TIME: 10 mins, COOK TIME: 20 mins, TOTAL TIME: 30 mins

INGREDIENTS

- 2 stewed peppers
- 1 cup walnuts
- 2 cloves of garlic
- 1 tsp pomegranate syrup
- 1/2 lemon juice
- 1 tsp cumin
- Smash 1 cleaved red pepper
- 1 tsp salt
- 1/4 cup additional virgin olive oil
- 1/4 cup breadcrumbs

PREPARATION

- Cook ringer peppers on a sheet container at 400 degrees each moment by cutting them down the middle and deseeding. Pivot. You can barbecue your pecans simultaneously by putting the pecans on a baking sheet and cooking them for very nearly 10 minutes (be mindful so as not to eat them).

•Add red peppers and pecans to a blender with arranged fixings and puree endlessly smooth.
•Decorate with a shower of olive oil, a sprinkle of pomegranate molasses, and a spot of squashed red or Aleppo pepper.

NUTRITION FACTS
Calories: 696kcal
Carbohydrates: 22g
Protein: 11g
Fat: 66g
Saturated Fat: 8g
Polyunsaturated Fat: 31g
Monounsaturated Fat: 25g
Sodium: 1773mg
Potassium: 378mg
Fiber: 5g
Sugar: 3g
Vitamin A: 232IU
Vitamin C: 22mg
Calcium: 114mg
Iron: 4mg
Pesto Genovese

PREP TIME: 10 mins, TOTAL TIME: 10 mins

INGREDIENTS

•3.5 ounces Genovese basil leaves (sweet basil)

•1 cup Parmesan cheddar

•1/4 cup Pecorino Sardo cheddar

•1/3 cup pine nuts

•1 clove garlic

•1/2 tsp coarse sea salt

•1/2 cup extra virgin olive oil (notwithstanding 1 tbsp to add on top)

PREPARATION

•Gently wash basil leaves under cold water and channel them until they are incredibly dry.

•In a food processor, blend Parmesan cheddar, Pecorino Sardo, pine nuts, and garlic.

•Add basil leaves and salt.

•Step by step, continue to blend until you show up at a smooth consistency, sprinkling the olive oil on top of various trimmings during the connection. Be careful not to over-blend the sauce, or the bleeding edges will start to cook the basil.

•Finally, move the pesto into a holder and cover it with more olive oil to avoid oxidation.

NUTRITION FACTS
Calories: 222kcal
Carbohydrates: 2g
Protein: 7g
Fat: 22g
Saturated Fat: 5g
Polyunsaturated Fat: 3g
Monounsaturated Fat: 12g
Cholesterol: 12mg
Sodium: 384mg
Potassium: 86mg
Fiber: 1g
Sugar: 1g
Vitamin A: 767IU
Vitamin C: 2mg
Calcium: 205mg
Iron: 1mg

Loaded Tzatziki Yogurt Sauce with Fresh Dill, Garlic, and Cucumber

PREP TIME: 20 mins, TOTAL TIME: 20 mins

INGREDIENTS

•1 cucumber, peeled
•1/2 tsp sea salt
•1 cup new dill, stems removed
•2 cups Greek yogurt
•1/4 cup additional virgin olive oil
•6 garlic cloves, pressed through a garlic press or finely chopped

PREPARATION

•Mash the cucumber in a colander set over a bowl. Sprinkle salt on the ground cucumber. Let this sit for about 15 minutes while you plan the rest of the tzatziki (water will come out of the cucumber).
•Chop the dill, then add Greek yogurt, olive oil, and crushed garlic to a bowl. Mix well.
•Extract the juice from the cucumber and then add it to the tzatziki. Salt, to taste. They can serve immediately,

but the seasons merge in the long run. I generally like digging in the fridge for 60 minutes.

NUTRITION FACTS
Calories: 100kcal
Carbohydrates: 4g
Protein: 6g
Fat: 7g
Saturated Fat: 1g
Polyunsaturated Fat: 1g
Monounsaturated Fat: 5g
Trans Fat: 1g
Cholesterol: 3mg
Sodium: 168mg
Potassium: 174mg
Fiber: 1g
Sugar: 2g
Vitamin A: 483IU
Vitamin C: 7mg
Calcium: 77mg
Iron: 1mg

Greek Fava

PREP TIME: 10 mins, COOK TIME: 45 mins, TOTAL TIME: 55 mins

INGREDIENTS

•1/2 pound dried yellow split peas (1/2 pound, dried)
•1 medium earthy-colored onion, slashed
•1 little clove of garlic, squashed
•1/2 lemon juice
•1 tsp olive oil
•salt and dark pepper, to taste
•paprika and olive oil to decorate

PREPARATION

•Pick over the split peas to eliminate any stained ones, and flush. Place them in an enormous pot with the onions and enough water to cover a couple of creeps over the beans.

•Bring to the bubble, then lessen the intensity and stew for 30 to 45 minutes, adding more water if necessary, until the split peas are thick and soft. If there is still some water staying toward the end, channel it off before moving the peas to a bowl.

•Beat in the garlic, lemon squeeze, and oil until thick and all around mixed. Pass on to cool, then add salt and pepper to taste and trim with paprika. Shower olive oil on top whenever wanted.

NUTRITION FACTS
Calories: 215kcal
Carbohydrates: 37g
Protein: 14g
Fat: 2g
Saturated Fat: 1g
Polyunsaturated Fat: 1g
Monounsaturated Fat: 1g
Sodium: 10mg
Potassium: 603mg
Fiber: 15g
Sugar: 6g
Vitamin A: 85IU
Vitamin C: 5mg
Calcium: 39mg
Iron: 3mg

Cacik

PREP TIME: 10 mins, TOTAL TIME: 10 mins

INGREDIENTS

- 1 cup plain greek yogurt
- 1/3 cup cold water
- 1 medium cucumber
- 2 garlic cloves, minced
- 3 twigs of new dill
- 2 branches of new mint leaves
- 1 tsp additional virgin olive oil
- salt
- 1/2 tsp dried mint
- 1/4 tsp red pepper chips
- For Serving
- additional virgin olive oil for sprinkling
- dried mint
- red pepper chips
- new mint leaf

PREPARATION

- Whisk the plain yogurt with half of the virus water in a huge bowl, continue whisking and adding the water steadily, and put away.
- Cut the cucumbers into little dice. Finely hack the new dill and the mint leaves and then, at that point, put them away.
- Mince the garlic with a sprinkle of salt, add it to the yogurt bowl and whisk it.
- Add the dried mint and red pepper chips to the bowl and whisk it. Continue rushing while at the same time adding the olive oil.
- Add the diced cucumber, hacked dill, and new mint to the bowl and blend it.
- Shower olive oil and sprinkle the dried mint and red pepper chips on top before serving.

NUTRITION FACTS
Calories: 103kcal
Carbohydrates: 8g
Protein: 11g
Fat: 3g
Saturated Fat: 1g
Polyunsaturated Fat: 1g
Monounsaturated Fat: 2g
Trans Fat: 1g
Cholesterol: 5mg
Sodium: 47mg
Potassium: 372mg
Fiber: 1g
Sugar: 5g
Vitamin A: 265IU
Vitamin C: 6mg
Calcium: 144mg
Iron: 1mg

Baba Ganoush (Lebanese Eggplant Dip)

PREP TIME: 10 mins, COOK TIME: 50 mins, TOTAL TIME: 1 hr

INGREDIENTS

•1 medium eggplant, washed
•1/4 cup tahini
•1 clove of garlic, crushed
•1/2 tsp cumin
•1/2 tsp smoked paprika
•1/2 lemon juice
•1/8 cup new parsley
•salt and pepper, to taste
•2 tbsp extra virgin olive oil

PREPARATION

•Set up the eggplant at 425 F for 50 minutes, and let it cool.
•Once cooled, take off the skin with your brain and let the inside tissue cool for 5 minutes.
•Add the tissue close by different trimmings to a food processor, Mix until smooth.

NUTRITION FACTS
Calories: 184kcal
Carbohydrates: 11g
Protein: 4g
Fat: 15g
Saturated Fat: 2g
Polyunsaturated Fat: 4g
Monounsaturated Fat: 8g
Sodium: 9mg
Potassium: 359mg
Fiber: 4g
Sugar: 4g
Vitamin A: 321IU
Vitamin C: 7mg
Calcium: 39mg
Iron: 1mg

Ful Medames

PREP TIME: 10 mins, COOK TIME: 10 mins, TOTAL TIME: 20 mins

INGREDIENTS

- 15 ounces 1 can fava beans
- 1/2 tsp cumin
- 3 tbsp tahini
- 1 lemon juice
- 1 small bunch of new conferences slashed
- 1/4 red onion, diced
- 1 tomato, diced
- additional virgin olive oil for showering

PREPARATION

- Put the fava beans with the fluid in a little pot of high intensity.
- Heat to boiling, add cumin, salt, and pepper, and lower to medium intensity. Cook for 10 minutes, mixing frequently.
- Eliminate heat. Squash beans with a fork to want consistency.
- Whisk together tahini and lemon juice, add to fava beans. Blend well.

•Move the beans to a serving bowl. Top generously with new hacked parsley, diced tomato, diced onion, and a shower of additional virgin olive oil.

NUTRITION FACTS
Calories: 307kcal
Carbohydrates: 36g
Protein: 16g
Fat: 13g
Saturated Fat: 2g
Polyunsaturated Fat: 5g
Monounsaturated Fat: 5g
Sodium: 977mg
Potassium: 819mg
Fiber: 10g
Sugar: 3g
Vitamin A: 725IU
Vitamin C: 23mg
Calcium: 105mg
Iron: 4mg

Quiche Lorraine

PREP TIME: 20 mins, **COOK TIME:** 45 mins, **TOTAL TIME:** 1 hr 5 mins

INGREDIENTS

•2 cups of regular flour

•4 tbsp spread, room temperature

•3/4 cup cold water

•1 tsp salt

•3 eggs

•1/2 cup cream

•3 tbsp sharp cream

•1/2 cup destroyed Swiss cheddar

•3/4 cup cubed ham

•Salt and pepper

PREPARATION

•Preheat the stove to 390°F.

•Begin with the batter. In a major bowl, blend the regular flour in with salt. Add the margarine and begin to ply (you can likewise utilize a robot or Kitchenaid blender, it's simpler) with your hands. Then, pour the virus water and keep working for a couple of moments. When the mixture is homogeneous and somewhat flexible, it's prepared.

•Add some flour to your work surface and roll the batter utilizing a moving pin. Roll until the mixture can be placed on your pie plate and it isn't excessively thick. You will most likely have an overabundance of the mixture; with a blade, cut the overabundance of batter around the edges of the pie plate. Prick the mixture with a fork in a few places, so it inhales during cooking.
•For the egg combination, in a major bowl, break the eggs, add the cream, harsh cream, and salt and pepper. Whisk. Add the cubed ham and the destroyed cheddar, and blend in with a spatula. Fill the mixture and spot it in the broiler for 45 minutes or until the top is cooked and the egg is set.
•Present with salad.

NUTRITION FACTS
Calories: 337kcal
Carbohydrates: 34g
Protein: 13g
Fat: 17g
Saturated Fat: 9g
Polyunsaturated Fat: 1g
Monounsaturated Fat: 4g
Trans Fat: 1g
Cholesterol: 128mg
Sodium: 704mg
Potassium: 119mg
Fiber: 1g
Sugar: 1g
Vitamin A: 536IU
Vitamin C: 1mg
Calcium: 121mg
Iron: 2mg

Grilled Flatbread with Burrata Cheese

PREP TIME: 15 min, COOK TIME: 20 min, TOTAL TIME: 35 min

INGREDIENTS

Tomato Skewers

•8 oz cherry tomatoes

•olive oil

•genuine salt

•newly ground pepper

•sticks utilized for barbecuing

Flatbread

•1 lb new pizza batter

•flour for cleaning

•3/4 cup olive oil

•8 oz burrata cheddar, depleted in a colander

•8 oz parmesan cheddar, ground

•2 tbsp new basil, hacked

PREPARATION

•Partition the tomatoes equally and penetrate them with the sticks. Pour a limited quantity of olive oil over each stick, and sprinkle with salt and pepper.

•Turn the barbecue on. Over low intensity, lay tomato Skewers at the focal point of the barbecue for 5-10 minutes pivoting ½ way through.
•While tomatoes are on the barbecue, get ready flatbread mixture. Begin by cutting the pound of batter into 4 equivalent parts. Utilizing flour, fold each part of the mixture into ¼ inch thickness. Utilizing a cake brush, cover one side of the mixture with a liberal measure of olive oil.
•Take tomatoes off the barbecue and put batter oil side down on the barbecue. Cautiously cover the opposite side of the batter with oil. At the point when huge air pockets begin framing the top side of the mixture, flip the batter utilizing a metal spatula. After flipping the batter, sprinkle parmesan cheddar equally over the four flatbreads. Cautiously remove burrata cheddar from the colander, and pull little pieces off, setting them uniformly over the four barbecued flatbreads. Finally, cover the barbecue top for a couple of mins to allow the cheddar to dissolve.
•Take flatbread off the barbecue and sprinkle it with basil. Present with tomato sticks.

NUTRITION FACTS
CALORIES 722
PROTEIN 23 g
CARBOHYDRATES 34 g
TOTAL FAT 57 g
DIETARY FIBER 3 g
CHOLESTEROL 54 mg
SODIUM 832 mg
TOTAL SUGARS 1 g

Avocado Toast

Prep Time: 15 minutes, **Total Time:** 15 minutes

INGREDIENTS

•2 avocados

•2 tsp lemon juice

•salt and pepper to taste

•4 cups of toasted bread

•½ cup feta cheddar

•1 cup of cherry tomatoes segregated

•¼ cup basil

•balsamic vinegar

PREPARATION

•Chop the avocado down the middle and put the tissue in a little bowl. Add lemon pound, salt, and pepper. Then, with a fork, squash the decorations together.

•Spread the mix over the toast.

•Top with feta cheddar, tomatoes, and basil.

•Season some way you would like with salt and pepper.

•Pour a little stream of balsamic vinaigrette on top.

NUTRITION FACTS
Calories: 294kcal
Carbohydrates: 25g
Protein: 8g
Fat: 20g
Saturated Fat: 5g
Polyunsaturated Fat: 2g
Monounsaturated Fat: 11g
Trans Fat: 1g
Cholesterol: 17mg
Sodium: 366mg
Potassium: 638mg
Fiber: 8g
Sugar: 4g
Vitamin A: 488IU
Vitamin C: 20mg
Calcium: 150mg
Iron: 2mg

Fruicuterie Board (Aka the Fruit Charcuterie Board)

PREP TIME: 20 MIN, COOK TIME: 0 MIN, TOTAL TIME: 20 MIN

INGREDIENTS

•4 ounces blue cheddar, similar to Danish Blue

•4 ounces developed goat cheddar, for instance, Cypress Grove Midnight Moon

•4 ounces Brie, similar to President Brie

•4 ounces fragile triple crème cheddar, as Fromagerie Germain

•4 ounces Cotswold cheddar

•3 kiwis, stripped and thickly cut

•3 splendid kiwis, stripped and thickly cut

•2 mangoes, stripped and diced

•4 little bunches of grapes

•4 little lots of cherries

•8 figs, quartered

•2 peaches, thickly cut

•2 white peaches, thickly cut

•3 apricots, thickly cut

•3 plums, thickly cut

•1 cup cubed watermelon

•1 cup cubed melon

•1 cup isolated strawberries

- 1 cup blackberries
- 1 cup raspberries
- 1 cup splendid raspberries

PREPARATION

- Put the cheeses on a tremendous platter and let them sit at room temperature for 20 to 30 minutes until mellowed. Put together the normal item in packs around the cheddar.

NUTRITION FACTS
234 calories
11g fat
27g carbs
10g protein
21g sugars

air fryer roasted pumpkin seeds

Prep time: 5 MINUTES **cook time:** 10 MINUTES **total time:** 15 MINUTES

INGREDIENTS

•pumpkin

•1/4 cup olive oil

•1 tbsp ocean salt

PREPARATION

•Split the pumpkin

•remove all seeds

•Wash seeds and eliminate all mash

•Preheat the air fryer to 400 degrees

•Brush seeds with olive oil and ocean salt

•Prepare for 5 minutes in a single layer

•Blend and cook for a further 2-3 minutes until shiny brown.

NUTRITION FACTS
CALORIES: 53
TOTAL FAT: 5g
SATURATED FAT: 1g
TRANS FAT: 0g
UNSATURATED FAT: 5g
CHOLESTEROL: 0mg
SODIUM: 698mg
CARBOHYDRATES: 1g
FIBER: 0g
SUGAR: 1g
PROTEIN: 0g

Tuna Protein Box

Prep Time: 10 mins, Cook Time: 10 mins, Total Time: 20 mins

INGREDIENTS

- 4 whole eggs
- 4 carrots, peeled and split
- 2-3 sticks of celery, chopped
- 1 cup of grapes
- 1 cup blueberries
- 8 ounces diced cheddar

Fish salad

- 5-ounce container of fish used up
- 2 tablespoons mayonnaise
- 2 tbsp celery, finely chopped
- salt and pepper to taste

PREPARATION

- Boil and chill hard-boiled eggs (I used my Instant Pot). You can leave them with the skin or peel them off after they've cooled completely.

•Mix the fish salad side dishes and divide them among the compartments.
•Divide any remaining fasteners between the compartments.
•Store in the fridge for up to 4 days.
•Appreciate the cold.

NUTRITION FACTS
Serving: 1 Snackbox Calories: 414kcal Carbohydrates: 20g Protein: 27g Fat: 25g Saturated Fat: 13g Cholesterol: 237mg Sodium: 616mg Potassium: 537mg Fiber: 3g Sugars: 13g Vitamin A: 11170IU, vitamin C: 9 mg, calcium: 471 mg, iron: 2.2 mg

Rainbow Heirloom Tomato Bruschetta

PREP TIME: 15 MIN, COOK TIME: 0 MIN, TOTAL TIME: 15 MIN

INGREDIENTS

•1 serving, meagerly cut and toasted
•3 garlic cloves, broken
•16 ounces ricotta cheddar entire milk
•Certified salt and newly ground dark pepper
•¼ cup basil pesto
•2 tablespoons of olive oil
•2 tablespoons balsamic vinegar
•2 tablespoons cleaved dill branches
•1 red tomato, finely cleaved
•1 yellow tomato, cleaved and finely slashed
•1 green tomato, cleaved and finely slashed
•1 16 oz treasure cherry tomatoes, cut
•Youthful basil leaves to serve

PREPARATION

•Rub the external layer of each cut piece with the garlic cloves. Season the ricotta with salt and pepper and spread over the part cuts.

•Consolidate pesto, olive oil, balsamic vinegar, and dill in a medium bowl. Add the tomatoes and throw tenderly to cover.
•Chipping away at combination blocks, planning divided tomatoes; Season with salt and pepper; cover with basil leaves.

NUTRITION FACTS
284 calories
15g fat
27g carbs
12g protein
5g sugars

APPLE, BEET, CARROT & KALE SALAD

Prep Time: 15 min Total Time: 15 minutes

INGREDIENTS

- •1 large apple (green or red - I used Fuji), pitted and julienned
- •2 beets, peeled and julienned
- •1 1/2 cups (173g) julienned carrots
- •3 - 4 wavy kale leaves, focus vein, eliminated and cut
- •1/3 cup (56g) cranberries (preferably natural)
- •nuggets or sunflower seeds to decorate Orange Sauce
- •4 tablespoons of squeezed orange
- •1 tablespoon of apple cider vinegar
- •2 teaspoons dijon mustard
- •2 pieces of onion powder
- •mineral salt stain
- •various toils of new dark pepper

PREPARATION

•**Sauce:** In a small bowl, combine the squeezed orange, apple juice vinegar, dijon, onion powder, salt, and pepper. Put away.

•**Salad:** Place the pre-arranged apple, beets, carrots, kale, and cranberries in a large bowl, pour in the dressing and prepare to coat.

•**Serve:** Place portions on individual plates and sprinkle with nuggets or sunflower seeds.

NUTRITION FACTS
Calories 205
Total Fat 3.8g 5%
Saturated Fat 0.6g
Cholesterol 0mg 0%
Sodium 234.8mg 10%
Total Carbohydrates 42.5g 15%
Dietary fiber 7.6g 27%
Sugars 30.4g
Protein 4.7g 9%
Vitamin A 60%
Vitamin C 31%
Calcium 5%
Iron 10%
Vitamin D 0%
Magnesium 18%
Potassium 15%
Zinc 10%
Phosphorus 13%
Thiamine (B1) 12%
Riboflavin (B2) 9%
Niacin (B3) 10%
Vitamin B6 13%
Folic acid (B9) 33%
Vitamin E 8%
Vitamin K 61%

{Ajvar} Roasted Pepper and Eggplant Spread Recipe

PREP TIME: 30 mins, COOK TIME: 20 mins TOTAL TIME: 50 mins

INGREDIENTS

•2 pounds yellow, red, or orange peppers (around 5 to 6)
•1 little eggplant (around 12 ounces)
•3 tablespoons secluded additional virgin olive oil
•3 cloves of garlic are normally minced
•1 ounce of new chives
•1 tablespoon newly crushed lemon juice
•1 tablespoon of red wine vinegar
•1 teaspoon crude sugar
•1/4 teaspoon squashed red pepper chips
•Genuine salt and newly ground dark pepper

PREPARATION

•Barbecue the Eggplant and Peppers: Heat the oven to 450°F and organize the racks in the top third. Part each pepper, eliminating the stems and seeds. Place the peppers, cut side down, on a baking sheet covered with aluminum foil.

•Slice the eggplant down the middle the long way and sprinkle with around 1 tablespoon of olive oil and somewhat salt, and spot it, cut side down, on the baking sheet. Cook the peppers and eggplant until brilliant and smoky, and the eggplant self-destructs when you press, around 30 minutes.

•Eggplant and Pepper Removal: Remove the eggplant and let it cool marginally. Dispose of the peppers, place them in a bowl and cover with cling wrap until somewhat cooled, something like 5 minutes. Utilize a spoon or spoon of frozen yogurt to eliminate the eggplant puree from the skin and dispose of the skin.

•Place the eggplant in a food processor with 1 tablespoon of olive oil and garlic. Beat the eggplant a couple of times with the goal that it is, by and large, separated.

•Make the Ajvar Dip: When the peppers are adequately cool to deal with, eliminate them (saving any juices that develop), dispose of the strip, and add the peppers and 2 to 3 tablespoons of bean stew fluid to the food processor. Add chives and heartbeat 5 to a few times to slash coarsely. Blend lemon juice, vinegar, red pepper drops, and sugar.

•Taste and add more sugar; if it turns into a harsh knot, add salt and newly ground dark pepper as desired. Serve hot or at room temperature as a spread or sauce.

BAKED POPCORN CHICKEN

Prep time: 45 MINUTES, **Cook time:** 25 MINUTES, **Total time:** 1 HOUR 10 MINUTES

INGREDIENTS

•1 1/2 pounds boneless, skinless chicken thighs, cut into 1-inch pieces

•2 cups low-fat buttermilk

•3 garlic cloves, crushed

•1 teaspoon dried basil

•1 teaspoon dried oregano

•1/2 teaspoon dried thyme

•1/4 teaspoon cayenne pepper, optional

•Authentic salt and ground black pepper to taste

•3 cups Onion Kettle Brand® Whipped Cream and French Fries

•1/4 cup unsalted margarine, condensed

•2 tablespoons chopped fresh parsley leaves

PREPARATION

•Preheat the chicken to 400 degrees F. Cover a cooling rack with a nonstick showerhead and place it on a baking sheet.

•In a large bowl, combine the chicken, buttermilk, garlic, basil, oregano, thyme, cayenne pepper, salt, and pepper to taste; marinate for about 30 minutes. Channel well.

•Working in meetings, dig the chicken into the crushed fries, pressing down to coat. Place on a coordinated baking sheet; sprinkle with spread.

•Place on the grill and cook, turning the pieces in half, until they are new and cooked through, about 20 to 25 minutes.

•Serve immediately, garnished with parsley to taste.

NUTRITION FACTS

Total Fat 3g
Sodium 269.9mg 12%
Potassium 129.9mg 3%
10g of carbohydrates
9g net carbs
Sugar 1g
Fiber 1g 5%
11g of protein
Vitamins and minerals
Vitamin A IU 0IU
Vitamin B6 0.5mg 39%
Vitamin C 0mg 0%
Calcium 20.2mg 3%
Iron 1.1mg 14%
Phosphorus 199.9mg 20%
Thiamine 1.7mg 113%
Niacin 10mg 50%

Hummus Wraps

Prep Time: 10 minutes, **Total Time:** 10 minutes

INGREDIENTS

•1 medium entire grain tortilla (no added sugar or added substances)

•¼ cup of organized hummus

•1 cup dino kale (or 1 huge leaf, cleaned and scoured for a superior surface.)

•¼ cup hacked tomato

•¼ cup cut yellow onion

•½ medium avocado

PREPARATION

•Put the tortilla on a level surface and spread the hummus over the tortilla.

•Get over different trimmings.

•Roll up like a burrito and secure the two finishes with toothpicks, slice down the middle and dispose of the toothpicks before serving.

NUTRITION FACTS
Calories: 142kcal | Carbs: 17g | Protein: 6g | Fat: 6g | Sodium: 334mg | Potassium: 414mg | Fiber: 4g | Sugar: 3g | Vitamin A: 2170IU | Vitamin C: 33.7mg | Calcium: 74mg | Iron: 2.4mg.

COWBOY CAVIAR

PREP TIME: 10 minutes, **COOK TIME:** 1 hour, **TOTAL TIME:** 1 hour 10 minutes

INGREDIENTS

•1 can of dark beans depleted and washed

•1 can of corn depleted and washed or 1.5 cups of new corn

•3 Roma tomatoes diced

•2 diced avocados

•1/4 cup red onion diced

•1/4 cup cilantro hacked finely

•Juice of 1 lime

•1/2 tsp salt

•1/2 cup Italian dressing

PREPARATION

•Place beans, corn, tomatoes, avocado, onion, and cilantro into a huge blending bowl.

•Press lime juice over the avocados, so they don't brown as fast. Sprinkle in salt and pour in Italian dressing. Mix until very much joined.
•Cover and chill in the cooler for an hour to marinate seasons together. This is best served that very day. The avocado could begin to brown the next day, yet at the same time tastes perfect!

NUTRITION FACTS
Calories: 120kcal (6%)Carbohydrates: 11g (4%)Protein: 2g (4%)Fat: 7g (11%)Saturated Fat: 1g (5%)Sodium: 326mg (14%)Potassium: 312mg (9%)Fiber: 4g (16%)Sugar: 1g (1%)Vitamin A: 200IU (4%)Vitamin C: 6.8mg (8%)Calcium: 15mg (2%)Iron: 0.8mg (4%)

EASY CREAMY PROSCIUTTO CRACKER APPETIZER

PREP TIME: 10 minutes, **COOK TIME:** 1 minute, **TOTAL TIME:** 11 minutes

INGREDIENTS

- •7 oz whipped cream cheddar
- •1 tbsp minced garlic
- •1 1/2 tsp olive oil
- •3 ounces cut Prosciutto
- •40 saltines I utilized ritz
- •Salt and pepper to taste
- •finely cleaved parsley for garnish
- •Honey for sprinkling

PREPARATION

- •In a little bowl, blend cream cheddar, garlic, olive oil, salt, and pepper. Put away.
- •Cut prosciutto into little square shapes.
- •Spread a little combination onto every wafer until every saltine is meagerly covered.
- •Roll every prosciutto up and put it on top of the saltines.
- •Shower a limited quantity of honey over each and sprinkle with parsley.

NUTRITION FACTS
Calories: 42kcal (2%) Carbohydrates: 2g (1%) Fat: 3g (5%) Saturated Fat: 1g (5%) Cholesterol: 6mg (2%) Sodium: 56mg (2%) Potassium: 14mgVitamin A: 65IU (1%) Vitamin C: 0.1mgCalcium: 10mg (1%) Iron: 0.2mg (1%)

Ham & Cheese Apple Wraps | MOMables

Prep Time: 5 minutes, **Total Time:** 5 minutes

INGREDIENTS

•1 little Granny Smith or Pink Lady apple, cut into 8 wedges

•8 hams (cut into slim cuts)

•8 Colby Jack or cheddar, daintily cut

PREPARATION

•Put a ham cut on a level surface and overlay it into equal parts. Place a cut of cheddar in the ham cut. Put the apple cut on the edge of the ham cut and begin wrapping the apple with the ham and cheddar cuts.

NUTRITION FACTS

Calories: 306Sugar: 7.1gSodium: 1455.6mgFat: 18Saturated Fat: 8.6gCarbohydrates: 11.6gFiber: 2gProtein: 25.6gCholesterol: 80mg

CROCKPOT HONEY GARLIC LITTLE SMOKIES SAUSAGES

PREP TIME: 5 minutes, **COOK TIME:** 3 hours, **TOTAL TIME:** 3 hours 5 minutes

INGREDIENTS

•1/4 cup earthy-colored sugar
•1/3 cup of honey
•1/2 cup of ketchup
•2 tablespoons of soy sauce
•3-4 minced garlic cloves
•28 oz. Lil smokies or any weenies mixed drink

PREPARATION

•Join earthy-colored sugar, honey, ketchup, soy sauce, and garlic in a medium bowl.
•Mix, so they are equitably covered. Cook on HIGH for 2-3 hours or on LOW for 4 hours, blending frequently.
•These Crockpot Honey Garlic Little Smokies will be the hit of your next date!

NUTRITION FACTS
Calories: 72kcal (4%) Carbohydrates: 18g (6%) Sodium: 312mg (13%) Potassium: 62mg (2%) Sugar: 17g (19%) Vitamin A: 60IU (1%) Vitamin C: 0.7mg (1%) Calcium: 8mg (1%) Iron: 0.2mg (1%)

Grilled Pineapple

Prep time: 5 minutes, cook time: 6 minutes, marinate time: 30 minutes, total time: 41 minutes

INGREDIENTS

•1 new pineapple

•2 tablespoons of olive oil

•2 spoons of brown sugar

•¼ teaspoon of powdered ginger

•¼ teaspoon of salt

PREPARATION

•Preheat the grill to medium-high.

•Peel the pineapple and cut it into ½" circles.

•Mix the oil, ground sugar, and ginger in a small bowl. Add to pineapple, mix well to coat, and marinate for about 30 minutes or up to 24 hours.

•Remove the pineapple from the marinade and sprinkle with salt.

•Grill the pineapple for 3-4 minutes on each side or until the sugar caramelizes into a sandy variety.

NUTRITION FACTS
Calories: 132 | Carbohydrates: 24g | Protein: 1g | Fat: 5g | Saturated Fat: 1g | Polyunsaturated Fat: 1g | Monounsaturated Fat: 3g | Sodium: 100mg | Potassium: 171mg | Fiber: 2g | Sugar: 19g | Vitamin A: 88IU | Vitamin C: 72mg | Calcium: 23mg | Iron: 1mg

Frito Corn Salad

Prep time: 10 minutes, **cook time:** 0 minutes, **total time:** 10 minutes

INGREDIENTS

•3 cups new corn on the cob or two 12-14 ounce pots of corn, exhausted

•½ red ringer pepper, cut into ¼-inch cubes

•½ green pepper, diced ¼ inch

•½ red onion, diced ¼ inch

•4 ounces depleted and cut canned jalapenos, or 4 ounces depleted soft green chiles

•⅔ cup mayonnaise

•2 teaspoons of powdered beans

•1 ½ cup shredded cheddar

•5 ounces of French fries

PREPARATION

•Combine all ingredients, except French fries, in a large bowl and mix well.

•Not long before serving, stir in the Fritters.
•Season with salt and pepper to taste.

NUTRITION FACTS
Calories: 155 | Carbohydrates: 10g | Protein: 4g | Fat: 10g | Saturated Fat: 3g | Cholesterol: 16mg | Sodium: 251mg | Potassium: 89mg | Fiber: 1g | Sugar: 1g | Vitamin A: 525IU | Vitamin C: 21.9mg | Calcium: 124mg | Iron: 0.4mg

Cheesy Stuffed Biscuits

Prep time: 10 minutes, **cook time:** 10 minutes, **total time:** 20 minutes

INGREDIENTS

•3 ounces store ham diced

•½ cup cheddar destroyed

•1 tablespoon margarine softened

•½ teaspoon Dijon discretionary

•1 can refrigerated bread rolls 16 ounces

•1 teaspoon sesame seeds

PREPARATION

•Preheat broiler to 375°F. Oil a biscuit tin.

•In a little bowl, join diced ham and cheddar. In a different little bowl, combine one liquefied margarine and Dijon if utilized.

•Delicately cut bread roll open, like a sandwich bun, preventing ¼-inch from the end.

•Open the bread roll and spot 1 tablespoon of ham and cheddar combination in the batter.

•Close the roll and seal the edges by squeezing it as far as possible, rehash with residual bread rolls.
•Place bread rolls in the biscuit skillet, brush with the Dijon/margarine combination, and sprinkle with sesame seeds.
•Heat for 10 to 12 minutes or caramelize, try not to overheat.
•Cool in pan for 5 minutes.

NUTRITION FACTS
Calories: 224 | Carbohydrates: 23g | Protein: 6g | Fat: 12g | Saturated Fat: 3g | Polyunsaturated Fat: 3g | Monounsaturated Fat: 5g | Trans Fat: 1g | Cholesterol: 14mg | Sodium: 585mg | Potassium: 134mg | Fiber: 1g | Sugar: 2g | Vitamin A: 93IU | Vitamin C: 1mg | Calcium: 66mg | Iron: 2mg

Crispy Coconut Shrimp

Prep time: 15 minutes, **cook time:** 15 minutes, **total time:** 30 minutes

INGREDIENTS

•1 pound colossal shrimp stripped and deveined

•2 eggs beaten

•½ cup cornstarch

•½ teaspoon salt

•⅛ teaspoon cayenne pepper

•1 cup worked on a chipped coconut

•1 cup panko bread pieces

•cooking shower

PREPARATION

•Preheat grill to 425°F.

•Join cornstarch, salt, and cayenne pepper in a little bowl. Place beaten egg in an alternate bowl.

•Place coconut in a food processor and heartbeat to make a fairly better surface (or hack with an edge). You don't require it too fine; just isolate a dab. Mix in with bread pieces.

•Dig shrimp in cornstarch blend and shake to dispose of any wealth of cornstarch. Plunge in egg, and dunk into the coconut mix, crushing to stick. Shower with a cooking sprinkle.

•Put shrimp in a material-lined holder and plan for 8 minutes. Flip shrimp and intensity an additional 5-10 minutes or until cooked. Cook 1 second at whatever point is needed.

•Serve warm with sweet bean stew plunge.

NUTRITION FACTS

Calories: 329 | Carbohydrates: 38g | Protein: 21g | Fat: 10g | Saturated Fat: 7g | Polyunsaturated Fat: 1g | Monounsaturated Fat: 1g | Trans Fat: 1g | Cholesterol: 225mg | Sodium: 1136mg | Potassium: 266mg | Fiber: 3g | Sugar: 9g | Vitamin A: 349IU | Vitamin C: 1mg | Calcium: 104mg | Iron: 2mg

Cheesy Garlic Monkey Bread

Prep time: 15 minutes, **cook time:** 30 minutes, **rest time:** 10 minutes, **total time:** 55 minutes

INGREDIENTS

•Garlic spread

•1 stick salted Challenge spread softened, ½ cup

•2 cloves garlic finely minced, or 1 teaspoon garlic powder

•1 tablespoon new parsley finely slashed

•Messy monkey bread

•1 can roll mixture 16 ounces

•1 teaspoon new chives finely slashed, discretionary

•½ cup cheddar finely destroyed

•¼ cup mozzarella cheddar destroyed

•2 tablespoons parmesan cheddar ground

PREPARATION

Garlic spread

•Consolidate the garlic margarine fixings in a little bowl and blend well.

Monkey bread get together

•Preheat the broiler to 350°F, liberally oil a 9×9 or 2-quart baking dish.

•Cut every roll into four pieces.

•Pour ¼ cup of the garlic spread from a higher place (hold the rest for brushing) and blend in with chives in a huge bowl.

•Add the bread rolls and throw well. Add cheeses and blend to join.

•Place in the pre-arranged container and top with any excess cheddar and margarine blend from the bowl.

•Heat for 25 minutes or until brilliant brown. Rest 10 minutes before serving. Brush with held garlic margarine and serve warm.

NUTRITION FACTS

Calories: 715 | Carbohydrates: 57g | Protein: 13g | Fat: 49g | Saturated Fat: 21g | Polyunsaturated Fat: 8g | Monounsaturated Fat: 16g | Trans Fat: 1g | Cholesterol: 83mg | Sodium: 1447mg | Potassium: 296mg | Fiber: 2g | Sugar: 4g | Vitamin A: 1012IU | Vitamin C: 2mg | Calcium: 233mg | Iron: 4mg

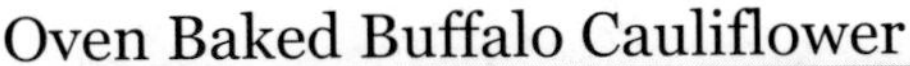

Oven Baked Buffalo Cauliflower

Prep time: 15 minutes, **cook time:** 30 minutes, **total time:** 45 minutes

INGREDIENTS

•1 head of cauliflower washed and dried

•1 cup milk

•1 cup flour

•1 tablespoon olive oil

•1 teaspoon garlic powder

•pepper to taste

•⅔cup Panko bread scraps

•⅔cup hot sauce

PREPARATION

•Preheat stove to 450°F.

•Cut cauliflower into scaled-down pieces and dispose of the center.

•Consolidate milk, flour, oil, garlic powder, and pepper in a huge bowl. Place player and cauliflower in an enormous zippered sack and tenderly throw until cauliflower is covered.

•Empty cauliflower into a huge sifter, allowing any overabundance hitter to trickle off. You simply need a light covering of the hitter. Sprinkle with Panko breadcrumbs and delicately throw.

•Put on a foil-lined skillet and heat for 15 minutes. Eliminate from the broiler and delicately throw with hot sauce. You need the cauliflower covered but not doused.

•Put the cauliflower back on the skillet and prepare for an extra 5-10 minutes or until the cauliflower is delicate and fresh.

•Present with farm or blue cheddar dressing.

NUTRITION FACTS

Calories: 123 | Carbohydrates: 20g | Protein: 4g | Fat: 2g | Cholesterol: 1mg | Sodium: 684mg | Potassium: 290mg | Fiber: 2g | Sugar: 3g | Vitamin A: 60IU | Vitamin C: 34.7mg | Calcium: 64mg | Iron: 1.3mg

Conclusion

At this point, the Mediterranean weight-reduction plan is not best associated with a couple of capability ingesting propensities; likewise, a social rendition incorporates how dinners are chosen, delivered, handled, and dispersed. The Mediterranean dietary example is offered now as of now not best as a social rendition but as a healthy and charming earth form. UNESCO's standing of the Mediterranean weight-reduction plan as an Intangible Cultural Heritage of Humanity addresses the strong permeability and prominence of the Mediterranean weight-reduction plan worldwide. This, along with higher and additional clinical confirmation addressing its favors and adequacy on life span, top of the line of ways of life, and disease avoidance, has taken this nourishing example to an old second unprecedented. This is an invaluable situation that could enable the Mediterranean weight-reduction plan across the world, further developing global wellness signs and bringing down ecological impacts through the method of assembling and transporting dinner assets. To this end, the Mediterranean weight-reduction plan must be noticeable for what it is: a really and exceptionally healthy, economical, and ecologically supportable dinners variant, notwithstanding a verifiable social verifiable past that presents recognizable proof and has a place. From the coronary heart to the earth through the road of culture, the Mediterranean weight-reduction plan is a socially verifiable past that shows up from now on.

Made in United States
North Haven, CT
23 January 2023